FROM FOLLY TO FORTUNE
The Firing of James Richardson Forman

Collusion and Corruption
in Nova Scotia Railway
Politics: 1854-58

For my sister Jane
and our mutual friend "Sidney".

Book designed and typeset in Adobe Garamond Pro,
ITC Garamond, and Myriad MM by
DCAD Enterprises, Montreal.
Graphic grid designed by Primeau & Barey, Montreal.
Printed and bound in Canada by AGMV Marquis.
Distributed by LitDistCo.

Copyright © Jay Underwood, 2007.

Legal Deposit, *Bibliothèque et Archives nationales
du Québec* and the National Library of Canada,
3rd trimester, 2007.

Library and Archives Canada Cataloguing in Publication

Underwood, Jay, 1958-
From folly to fortune: the firing of James Richardson
Forman: collusion and corruption in Nova Scotia railway
politics, 1854-58 / Jay Underwood.

Includes bibliographical references and index.
ISBN 978-1-897190-24-1 (bound).
– ISBN 978-1-897190-23-4 (pbk.)

1. Forman, James R. (James Richardson), 1822-1900.
2. Railroads–Political aspects–Nova Scotia–History–19th
century. 3. Railroads–Nova Scotia–Design
and construction–History–19th century.
4. Political corruption–Nova Scotia–History
–19th century. 5. Executives–Dismissal of
Nova Scotia–History–19th century.
6. Libel and slander–Nova Scotia–History –19th century.
I. Title.

TF203.U54 2007   385.09716'09034
C2006-906114-9

For our publishing activities, Railfare❄DC Books
gratefully acknowledges the financial support of
the Canada Council for the Arts, of SODEC, and of
the Government of Canada through the Book
Publishing Industry Development Program (BPIDP).

Canada Council   Conseil des Arts
for the Arts   du Canada

*Société
de développement
des entreprises
culturelles*

Québec ✚✚

No part of this publication may be reproduced or stored
in a retrieval system or transmitted in any form or by any
means, electronic, mechanical, recording, or otherwise,
without written permission of the publisher,
Railfare❄DC Books

In the case of photocopying or other reprographic
copying, a license must be obtained from Access
Copyright, Canadian Copyright Licensing Agency,
1 Yonge Street, Suite 800, Toronto, Ontario M5E 1E5.
info@accesscopyright.ca

Railfare❄DC Books

Ontario office:
1880 Valley Farm Road, Unit #TP-27
Pickering, Ontario L1V 6B3

Business office and mailing address:
Box 666, St. Laurent Station,
Montreal, Quebec H4L 4V9
railfare@videotron.ca
www.railfare.net

CONTENTS

IV   ACKNOWLEDGEMENTS

1   INTRODUCTION

      CHAPTER 1
7   Into the Fire

      CHAPTER 2
23   A Riotous Affair

      CHAPTER 3
37   Unexpected Developments

      CHAPTER 4
57   Laurie's Report

      CHAPTER 5
79   Defensive Measures

      CHAPTER 6
109   Exoneration Delayed

      CHAPTER 7
127   Scottish Success

157   EPILOGUE

169   AFTERWORD

177   END NOTES

187   INDEX

Front Cover: A modern-day steam train carries tourists across Scotland's Glenfinnan Viaduct, at the half-way point of the West Highland Railway line (see map page 130). After his return to Scotland, the viaduct was engineered by James Richardson Forman and his son Charles. The line stands as a substitute for the opportunity to build Canada's first national railway, denied to James Richardson Forman by the venality of Nova Scotia politics 150 years ago.
(Courtesy VisitScotland,
Scottish Viewpoint Picture Library - 13610).

ACKNOWLEDGEMENTS

ONCE again I am convinced that no one person can write a single book, and the efforts of a great many people from around the world have been invested in this work. I must first thank those closest to home, Roslyn Morrison and Karen King of the Elmsdale branch of the Colchester-East Hants Regional Library, for their unfailing efforts to locate books through the inter-library loan service, and to my son Andrew for running the errands I could not do myself.

Illustrating this work proved to be quite difficult, because although it was the largest public work of its kind undertaken in Nova Scotia for almost five years, and there were certainly professional photographers in business in the city of Halifax at the time, no photographs of the works under way, or the workers, appear to be extant. Many of the people whose names follow assisted by finding or suggesting photographs that would be appropriate.

The staff of the Nova Scotia Archives and Records Management Service in Halifax, especially Gary Shutlak, has always been ready to help, even with my more complex requests for obscure information. Philip Hartling and Anjali Vohra also assisted by finding the photographs for me.

Ron Day of Ratho, Edinburgh has been a great source of assistance and inspiration, as has Andrew Forman of Skipton, Yorkshire, scion of the Forman family who supplied with me with genealogical data not readily available in Nova Scotia. Brian Forman provided a rare photograph of Charles deNeuville Forman, and additional items of information that helped piece together a puzzle created by two elusive men. Similarly Liz Rowe, of Perth, Australia, used her contacts in Scotland to unearth information on James Forman that I could never otherwise have acquired. Also from the extended Forman family, Sarah Stille of Denbighshire, Wales, provided information and access to photographs.

Other genealogical information was supplied by Jim Hill and Douglas Sinnis, by way of the internet and the genealogy forums open to anyone with a query about family roots, even if it's not their own family. Also helping from Nova Scotia were Bill McAllister and Dave Blanchard, scouting out suitable locations for photographs on what is now the Windsor & Hantsport Railway's line. Similarly Dorthy Selig helped me unravel the sometimes incongruous references made by Laurie to various trouble spots on the railway, especially the "third lake."

Assistance also came from Michel Gallant, manager of protocol and secretariat service for the Supreme Court of Canada.

Kate Davies and Carol Morgan of the Institution of Civil Engineers, London, supplied invaluable reference material on both James Richardson Forman, and Charles DeNeuville Forman. Carol Reese of the American Society of Civil Engineers provided the image of James Laurie. Also deserving of thanks are: A. Morrison, reading room, Edinburgh Central Library, Jill Ten Cate, corporate archivist CIBC archives, Heather MacKay of Glasgow University archives, Professor Hugh Sutherland of Glasgow, Enda Ryan of Glasgow city council library and archives, and Ian Wolfe, associate archivist, Scotiabank Group in Toronto, and Peter Brewer of the Rannoch station tea room.

Ewan Crawford, webmaster of RailScot (http://www.railscot.co.uk/) generously provided the map showing the Forman railways compared with the total Scottish system.

It was a task far more complicated than the simple map I created showing the lines in Nova Scotia, and serves as a graphic example of the importance of the contribution the son of Nova Scotia made to old Scotland.

Louise Harris, locations manager for Scottish Screen in Glasgow provided the picture of Rannoch station. Also assisting from Scotland were Maud Devine and Chris Hood of East Renfrewshire Council, providing the photographs of Busby Viaduct, and Judith Tewson and Fiona Stewart of the Scottish Viewpoint Picture Library agency, for the photographs from Glenfinnan and Maillaig.

I am deeply indebted to Dr. John McGregor of Glasgow and the Open University in Scotland, for sharing his expert knowledge of the West Highland Railway, and for reviewing Chapter Seven to ensure my details on Forman's Scottish railway lines were accurate. His latest book, *The West Highland Railway: Plans, Politics and People* examines the political complexities faced by the Formans in the development of that line.

Alison Watkins, personal assistant to Hon. Sir William McAlpine, provided the photograph of Robert ("Concrete" Bob) McAlpine. Ronnie Scott, author of *Death by Design*, a veritable catalogue of the monuments in Glasgow's Necropolis, kindly sought out and photographed James Richardson Forman's final resting place. Finding a photograph of James Richardson Forman was a particularly difficult task, since none are extant in the collection of the Nova Scotia Archives. Ron Day located an article from a book published by the East Kilbride Libraries, and in turn, John McLeish, assistant librarian with the South Lanarkshire Central Library conjured up the portrait used here.

My many colleagues in the Nova Scotia Railway Heritage Society must also be thanked. Again my publishers are to be thanked for agreeing to publish something that places a Father of Confederation in an unfavourable light, but Charles Tupper's reputation as a vindictive and mean-spirited political animal is well preserved in the newspapers of his day – James Richardson Forman's place in history may be that he was one of Tupper's few victims who was not in the political arena, and survived the future prime minister's wrath.

Lastly, I must thank Herb MacDonald of Dartmouth, Nova Scotia for his incisive direction. Herb may not realize it, but he has taught me a great deal about the writing of history.

Having made all the foregoing acknowledgments, I must point out that any errors in this work are mine alone.

Jay Underwood
May 2007

ABOUT THE AUTHOR

JAY Underwood's fourth book of Nova Scotia railway history, *From Folly to Fortune,* follows on the recent success of *Built For War: Canada's Intercolonial Railway* (Railfare DC Books, October 2005.) A graduate of the journalism program of Holland College of Applied Arts and Technology in Charlottetown, Prince Edward Island, Underwood began his career in newspapers as a nightshift proof reader and obituary writer with the *Charlottetown Guardian-Patriot*. He then moved to the New Glasgow, Nova Scotia *Evening News,* as a reporter-photographer, and to the Truro, Nova Scotia *Daily News* as city editor. Briefly serving as city editor at the Timmins, Ontario *Daily Press,* he returned to Nova Scotia as editor and publisher of the *Springhill-Parrsboro Record,* and the *Enfield Weekly* Press, before joining the staff of the *Halifax Daily News* as senior copy editor and a member of the editorial board.

Disabled by complications of diabetes that took most of his sight in 1999, Underwood focused on his love of history and railways, producing *Ketchum's Folly* in 1995, and *Full Steam Ahead: The Life and Locomotives of Alexander Mitchell* in 1996. Both of these books were published by Lancelot Press.

Now in his third term as president of the Nova Scotia Railway Heritage Society, Underwood and his colleagues were successful in preventing the historic 1905 vice-regal railway car "Alexandra" from being scrapped, and the car is now being relocated to a museum site at Tatamagouche, Nova Scotia for restoration and public display. The society is planning to celebrate the 150th anniversary of the opening of main line railway operations in Nova Scotia in 2008, which will include the railway built by James Richardson Forman.

Jay Underwood is a frequent contributor to *Canadian Rail,* the journal of the Canadian Railroad Historical Association. He lives in Elmsdale Nova Scotia with his wife Kathy and son Derek.

Left: Author Jay Underwood.

INTRODUCTION

In *Ketchum's Folly*, I attempted to show how some nineteenth century engineers were tempted to undertake great works as monuments to their ability, just as rich men were wont to erect follies – decorative buildings – as monuments to their wealth. This does not appear to be the case with James Richardson Forman, who never got the recognition he deserved for his work as a railway engineer in Nova Scotia, his native land, or in Scotland, his adopted home after he was spurned.

In the March 1999 edition of the Institution of Civil Engineers' newsletter, Jim Shipway relates a story that may give some insight into the essence of Forman, through the actions of his son, Charles Forman:

"'Amid the eternal hills, man's work alas, is mortal.'
In the mid-1950s, more than forty years ago, a letter appeared in the correspondence columns of *The Scotsman* newspaper. It commented on a previous article, which had told of the difficulties of railway construction and maintenance in remote areas. The letter was from the retired deputy Chief Engineer of the LNER, a Mr. J G MacGregor. In his letter he spoke of the humility of the civil engineer in the midst of his demanding work, and quoted an inscription in Latin on the pilaster of a high viaduct which, when translated, read: 'Amid the eternal hills, man's work alas, is mortal.' I later got to know Mr. MacGregor quite well, and when he died in 1963, aged eighty-four, I wrote his obituary for *The Scotsman*.

Over the years I often thought of this Latin inscription and wondered where it was. Mr. MacGregor had told me in passing, but somehow it failed to register with me and I could not remember. I had an idea it was on a railway viaduct, but where? I made inquiry of various people including Mary Murphy, ICE Archivist, Mike Chrimes, ICE Head Librarian, Professor Roland Paxton, Chairman of the Panel for Historical Engineering Works (PHEW), Professor Jack Simmons, doyen of railway historians, and many others. None knew of the quotation or the viaduct. I also contacted the chief bridge inspector of the West Highland Railway and other railway staff, but the reply was always the same – 'Never heard of it.' An eminent historian went even further and said there was no such bridge. Fortunately, this discouraging remark did not prove fatal.

I then began a search of likely bridges, particularly on the West Highland Line. Many of them were certainly amid the eternal hills, and remote, and took a lot of getting close to. I had to visit them mostly in winter when the leaves were off the trees and I could view the piers and abutments with binoculars. I actually discovered a bridge on the former Newcastle to Carlisle line with a Latin inscription, but it referred to local worthies.

The central library in Edinburgh held back numbers of *The Scotsman*, and I began looking for Mr MacGregor's original letter to see whether it held a clue. I looked through three years or more of microfilmed newspaper, guessing the likely year, but could not find it.

By now you may be asking yourself, 'Why all this fuss over a supposed Latin quote on a viaduct?' I can't explain it. It was one of those things which nagged at me down the years, and was made worse by the fact that so many well-informed people knew nothing of it.

The mystery persisted until two years ago, 1997, when one day at home I received a crackly incoherent message on a mobile telephone. It was from the bridge inspector on the West Highland Line – yes, on an abutment pilaster of a viaduct high in the hills above the Gareloch, he had discovered Latin words. Badly weathered and almost indecipherable, they appeared to read *Laruntur Anni Mortalia Facta Peribunt*. Imaginatively translated, they fitted Mr. MacGregor's translation. My quest was over.

Who put the inscription there? The viaduct is the first major bridge on the West Highland Railway between Craigendoran on the Clyde and Fort William, and was constructed in 1893. The likely author is Charles de Neuville Forman (1852-1901) of Formans & McCall, the engineers for that section of the West Highland line. The firm was responsible for more railway building in the West of Scotland than any other, and the WHR was their greatest work. The bridge and the inscription make a fitting commemoration of Charles Forman and his firm, and indeed to all who participated in the construction of the line."[1]

Whatever translation one chooses for the inscription, the younger Forman may well have written a fitting epitaph for his father, whose work is ignored, overlooked, misunderstood, and simply anonymous to most Nova Scotians. Like Shipway, I suffered from a nagging feeling: that something had to be put right about James Richardson Forman's record. I began checking his history as I planned to induct him into my Nova Scotia Railway Hall of Fame web site: www.nsrwayhalloffame.com. The feeling increased every time I ran across references to Forman – mostly in the newspapers of the day, or the *Journal of the Proceedings of the Legislative Assembly*. Some things did not add up to answer the questions: Why was he dismissed from the Nova Scotia Railway? Did he deserve the opprobrium meted out to him? Why, since the railway was the largest public works program of its kind in the province at the time, was Forman's name allowed to be forgotten, almost unrecorded?

There are few railway enthusiasts in Scotland who need an introduction to the achievements of James and Charles Forman. Many, if not most, Nova Scotia railway enthusiasts barely know of these men. This book is an attempt to right that condition, and fill in a piece of Nova Scotia history that has been missing for almost one hundred fifty years. For those who thought they knew the story, it was one of a man who found himself overwhelmed by the task, even though it involved the construction of less than one hundred fifty miles of railway through some fairly easy terrain. In fact, the saga shows that Forman was a thoroughly "mortal" man, seeking no monument to himself. He took on a Herculean task and was thwarted by a thoroughly human foible – the penchant of other men to impose their will on the process and seek a scapegoat when that process fails.

In that sense what began as a "local" history takes on national significance, because the man who contributed the most to Forman's ouster went on to become the provincial premier, later becoming the federal minister of railways and canals when the Canadian Pacific Railway was under construction, and eventually a prime minister – Charles Tupper. It can be argued that Tupper took what he learned from his experience with

Forman and applied it to the national railway, and such is the force of Tupper's character that even this history began to become all about him. It is a fascinating story, involving intrigue, conspiracy theories, and character assassination, ambitious engineers and conniving politicians, rioting gangs of brawling navvies and deep-seated religious hatreds.

Forman left Nova Scotia under a cloud of failure, but given his accomplishments in the years after he left the Nova Scotia Railway, who is to say what might have awaited him, had he remained in his native land? In his 1967 history of Canadian National Railways, G.R. Stevens noted that the redoubtable Scot, Sandford Fleming, was chosen as Chief Engineer for the Intercolonial Railway, the line that built the nation of Canada, because it was "manifestly impossible for the Maritimes to find a representative of the calibre of Fleming." [2]

The claim is untrue. The Maritime provinces could have offered the names of George Wightman, Alexander Luders Light, or Collingwood Schreiber, all of whom were known as capable railway engineers. [3] James R. Forman could easily have been on that list. Less than ten years after Forman's dismissal, Nova Scotia was in search of such an engineer to represent its interests in the construction of the Intercolonial. Upon his return to Scotland after being dismissed from the Nova Scotia Railway, James Forman proved he was easily the equal of Fleming. Had it not been for the petty vindictiveness of Nova Scotia politics, the honour claimed by Fleming might well have fallen to Forman and his son Charles.

This is merely harmless speculation, however, for Charles Tupper had succeeded to the premiership of the province by the time the search for an engineer for the Intercolonial Railway had begun, and it would have been unlikely that he would invite Forman to take the lead, or that Forman would have accepted the challenge from the man who had done so much to undermine his reputation. It seems the province with a history of losing its brightest minds to the lure of greater things in other lands – notably the United States – succeeded in this instance in driving one away with the force of its own venality. Forman's story also has an international significance, if, as I attempt to prove in Chapter Three, the Gourley Shanty riot that was a catalyst to his removal, was the act of a nascent "Molly Maguire" movement initiated miles from its supposed source in the coal fields of Pennsylvania.

An admirer once said of Sir Christopher Wren, the architect credited with the works that give the City of London its great character, "if you seek his monument, look around you." The same can be said of James and Charles Forman. James Forman's monument in Nova Scotia is a line that is still in operation over an unremarkable landscape, offering blue-collar vistas to passengers on Via Rail's *Ocean*, North America's oldest continuously scheduled passenger train. In Scotland the monuments to both Formans, father and son, include everything from mundane industrial branch lines to the spectacular West Highland Railway, which invites thousands of tourists every year to envelop themselves in the romance and majesty of glens and mountains that are aristocratic in comparison. Some of these lines, especially the West Highland line, and Glasgow's underground railway, are well worth the visit by Nova Scotians seeking to re-live the experience of Nova Scotia's unfortunate son abroad.

There is, however, a startling contrast in the way the old and new world disseminate their heritage, one that puts the myth to the old concept of Scots' thrift. One of the unique features of this book is that it will make James Richardson Forman's image available to Nova Scotia readers for the first time since he left his native land. This is largely thanks to the generosity of the East Lanarkshire Council library system in Scotland, which found the photograph and provided the copy at negligible cost. This book also marks the first time William Baillie Smellie's image has been made public to Nova Scotia readers (and perhaps to Scottish readers as well).

Jay Underwood,
Elmsdale, Nova Scotia,
May, 2007

Below: An Intercolonial express train, bound for Truro, Nova Scotia, crosses the bridge over the Sackville River at Bedford, Nova Scotia, in this 1900s-era postcard published by Valentine & Co. The bridge was the first of three iron spans used by James Richardson Forman on the mainline of the Nova Scotia Railway. See page 80.
(Jay Underwood collection)

INTRODUCTION

Below: A rare detail from the map of the 1848 survey by Major William Robinson, Royal Engineers, for the Intercolonial Railway from Halifax to Amherst. James Richardson Forman followed Robinson's route from Halifax to Truro almost exactly.
(Jay Underwood collection)

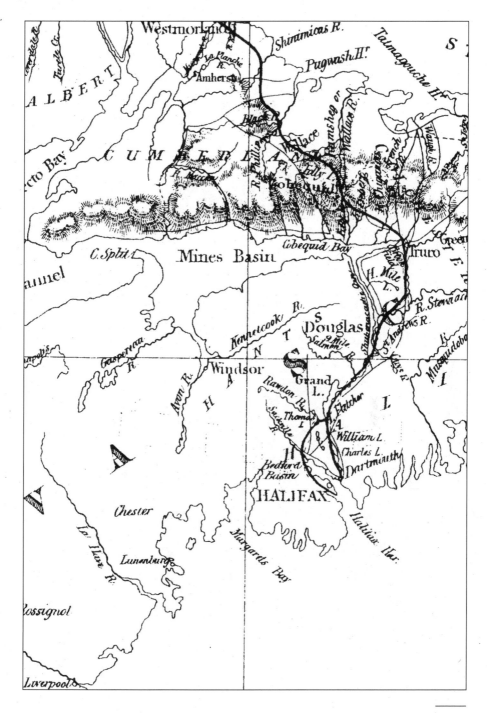

JAMES RICHARDSON FORMAN (ABOVE)
James Richardson Forman, victim of Nova Scotia's venal politics, was the first casualty of the battle between Joseph Howe and Charles Tupper. This photo was taken in Scotland when he was at the peak of his profession.
(Courtesy South Lanarkshire Central Library)

CHAPTER 1

Into the Fire

It is an injustice of history that the Roman Empire is remembered for its feats of advanced engineering prowess, earning reputations for the emperors who ordered them, but only obscurity for the engineers who designed and executed the great works. For Nova Scotia's Joseph Howe, the provincially built Nova Scotia Railway was to be a public work of Roman magnitude, a great highway of commerce and immigration – in a fashion never before undertaken in any corner of the British Empire – and which would further enhance his reputation as Nova Scotia's greatest politician.

For James Richardson Forman, a lesser fate awaited. Born in 1822, in Halifax, Nova Scotia, at a time when the colony was obliged to import much of its engineering ingenuity from the Mother country, Forman would join a phalanx of colonials who applied themselves to the development of society, but he would take a different course from the likes of George Wightman and William Fairbanks, who distinguished themselves by their construction of roads and canals. Wightman had assisted Major William Robinson in the 1846 survey for the inter-colonial railway which promised to unite the British North American possessions, leading the parties cutting the path for the proposed Whitehaven route from Canso to the New Brunswick border, and the Halifax-Windsor route that would later prove to be part of Forman's undoing. Fairbanks was the driving force behind the Shubenacadie canal.

Given his railroad experience elsewhere, his knowledge of the land between Halifax and Windsor in particular, and his Nova Scotia roots, one might have expected Wightman to be Howe's first choice for the Chief Engineer's position. Howe was effusive in his praise for the man who authored a two-volume treatise on the construction of highways. During a speech in the House of Assembly on the prospect of a Windsor railway, Howe said: "My calculations are based upon the report of Mr. George Wightman, who, rough in his manner though he be, self-taught though he be, is a Nova Scotian of whom we may be justly proud."[1] Wightman's lack of formal education may have counted against him in the selection process, or perhaps Forman was the result of a political compromise in order to gain support for Howe's railway bill.

Forman's antecedents had arrived in Nova Scotia from the Coldstream area of Berwickshire in 1780, devout Protestants with an aristocratic lineage. One of Forman's ancestors was Sir John Forman, who in 1513 was standard-bearer to Scotland's King James IV at Flodden Field, where the Scottish monarch lost his life in the battle against Henry VIII of England. The Forman family tree shows Forman's grandfather, James Pringle Forman, marrying Mary Gardner in Halifax in 1791. He was a man of means, and a principal in a prominent Halifax business with George Grassie:

"Forman, Grassie and Company... was a large wholesale wine company. And James Forman Senior had been one of a group which was formed in 1801 with the aim of founding a public bank and which was said to have raised £50,000 for this unrealized project in a single day. Like Enos Collins, John Lawton, and many other prominent Haligonians, he had been involved in the disposal of cargoes taken by privateers."[2]

The James Pringle Formans had five girls and six boys, one of whom was James Richardson Forman's father, James Forman Senior, born in Halifax in 1795. He married Margaret Ann Richardson in 1821. James Forman Senior succeeded in his father's goal of establishing a public bank, and was named the cashier for the Bank of Nova Scotia in 1832. In that position he would undoubtedly have come into contact with Joseph Howe. J. Murray Beck makes note of Howe's association with the bank:

"The year 1832 was the first in which Joseph Howe put on the general trappings of a reformer. Some believe that his part in the winning of responsible government has been exaggerated. Yet more than in any other province, the accomplishment was that of one man. Blanchard and the Scribblers had forced him to peer into the motive forces of Nova Scotia society, and the more deeply he peered, the less he liked what he saw. Between 1832 and 1834, two matters in particular – the interrelated bank and currency issues and the civil list and quit rent questions – let him see the weaknesses of the council and assembly in their utter nakedness as he reported the debates. In 1832 he was hoping, as an entrepreneur and borrower, to have the Bank of Nova Scotia incorporated by legislative charter so as to provide competition to the Halifax Banking Company, which had 'flourished like the green bay tree.' It appalled him to find that a self-serving council, which included five directors of that company, had inserted highly stringent precautions with the result that the new bank started up with 'more safeguards against disaster than any bank of its time in British North America.' Over the next two years he became more outraged as the difficulty of coping with a serious recession worsened because of an inundation of paper money resulting from the manipulations of bankers, councilors, and assembly-men. The experience taught him that 'even in idyllic Nova Scotia the machinations of individuals in their own interest took the same form and manifested the same subtlety as in more complex societies, and that the assemblymen themselves became part and parcel of the process.'"[3]

Phyllis Blakely and Diane Barker note:

"The incorporation was granted on 30 March (1832), and William Lawson became the bank's first president; on 24 May the bank appointed James Forman as its first cashier – a position equivalent to general manager. After a period at the Bank of New Brunswick in Saint John, where he studied the accounting system, Forman took up his new duties. When Forman's friend, Mather Byles Almon, succeeded Lawson in March 1837, the cashier was placed in a position of great trust, which he maintained throughout Almon's 30-year presidency. During these years Forman was active in the community as a member of the Nova Scotia Literary and Scientific Society, treasurer of the Halifax Mechanics' Institute, a trustee for the Provincial Building Society, and president of the North British Society of Halifax."[4]

Schull and Gibson note that while he was among the original petitioners for the bank, Forman did not own any shares in it. More will be said of the scandal he faced in his twilight years, later in this history.

James Richardson Forman also came from a family with political connections. His uncle John (1798-1832) was born in Halifax and practiced law in Shelburne, where he was the Member of the Legislature from 1828 until his death. He took his seat in the fourteenth assembly on November 20th 1830. C. Bruce Fergusson's *Directory of MLAs of Nova Scotia* lists his death as being "in or near Yarmouth, August 23rd 1832."[5] A clerk of the peace from 1828-1832, John Forman was also a judge of the probate court. He missed serving alongside Joseph Howe by a matter of years. Howe was first elected as an MLA for Halifax County in 1836, but was well known in political circles prior to his election as the editor and legislature reporter of the *NovaScotian*. At that point Howe was known to be a Conservative; his election would mark the turnaround in his thinking to the Reform platform.

James Richardson Forman had a brother Robert and two sisters, Mary and Louise. Louise appears to have married well, to Commander (later Admiral Sir) William King-Hall, and she died at Admiralty House in Devonport, England in 1875. This union would prove advantageous for the new brother-in-law, James Richardson Forman, for William King-Hall would become another acquaintance of Joseph Howe.

Louise's grandson George St. George Grogan, went on to become a First World War hero with the Worcestershire Regiment:

"On 27 May 1918 at the River Aisne, France, Brigadier General Grogan was in command of the remnants of the infantry of a division and attached troops. His utter disregard for personal safety, combined with sound practical ability, helped to stay the onward thrust of the enemy. He rode up and down the front line encouraging his troops under artillery, trench mortar, rifle and machine-gun fire, and when one horse was shot under him, he continued encouraging his men on foot until another horse was brought. As a result of his actions, the line held."[6]

There must have been a close family connection between the Formans and Grogans, because James Richardson Forman's daughter Ida Georgina (born 1857 at Halifax) married a Colonel Edward G. Grogan. Ida was one of three of Forman's children born in Halifax after his return to manage the railway construction. Robert was born in 1854, and Florence was born in 1856. Such family credentials clearly placed the Formans in the elite ranks of Halifax society for three generations. It was in this milieu that James Forman (he was called "the younger" at that time) worked with Joseph Howe as a co-incorporator of the Halifax Mechanics' Institute in 1850. He was also associated with Alexander Keith – a Halifax mayor and brewer – as a trustee of the Masonic Hall in the city (the act was passed March 28th 1850). Keith was provincial grand master for the province, and Forman was deputy provincial grand master.

James Richardson Forman's early education came at Horton Academy, in what is now Wolfville, at a school that is now famed for its divinity curriculum. Founded by Baptists in 1828, the school is better known today as Acadia Divinity College, part of Acadia University, a name it took in 1841. His attendance at the academy would set the scene for a showdown later in his career.

Patricia Lotz suggests it was his father's friendship with Royal Engineers stationed at Halifax that led young James to pursue a career in civil engineering, but at the same time he was at Horton academy, he was surrounded by some of the leading proponents of railway construction. Indeed, Lotz suggests there had been "none of the interest in railways" in Nova Scotia that Forman would find in Great Britain in the wake of the first railway mania. This is not accurate, since, while there was no construction actively underway, the newspapers were alive with talk of railways from Halifax to Windsor, thence to Saint John and Portland, Maine.

Judge Thomas Chandler Haliburton, the Windsor-based writer of the Sam Slick stories, made frequent mention of the railway proposal in his highly popular novels, first published in installments in the September 23rd 1835 edition of the *NovaScotian*. In doing so, Haliburton successfully took the talk of railway construction out of the boardrooms of British capitalists and caucus chambers of Halifax politicians, and into the parlance of "ordinary" people.

"In spite of stormy weather and almost impassable roads, over 150 inhabitants consisting of members of the Legislative Assembly, clergy, magistrates, and the more weighty and influential freeholders of Windsor and its vicinity gathered in Windsor on Saturday, 4 December 1845, to discuss transportation in general and, in particular, a railway between Halifax and Windsor."[7]

Four years earlier, in 1841, according to his obituary in the Minutes of Proceedings of the Institution of Civil Engineers, James Richardson Forman had been apprenticed to the firm of Neil Robson of Glasgow. Nineteen years old seems like a late start, for boys were usually taken into apprenticeships at thirteen to fifteen years – an age that today would be considered tender – as this advertisement from the Glasgow Herald of February 2nd 1818 indicates:

"AN APPRENTICE WANTED, to engage for seven years. A young man, not less than 14, nor more than 16 years of age, who has discovered a decided taste for Drawing and Mathematics, and whose parents or guardians reside in Glasgow. No premium required. Particulars will be learnt at No.7, Great Hamilton Street, up one stair."[8]

Robson would be a capable teacher. He was one of the many surveyors who went into business in the early 1800s, as the city of Glasgow underwent its tremendous industrial growth.

"In 1800, the *Glasgow Directory* listed only two surveyors – Charles Abercrombie and Thomas Richardson. Twenty years later, this number had risen to six, with Henry Creighton, a civil engineer, Peter Fleming, William Kyle, David Smith and John Warden joining Richardson. By 1841, the composition of the profession had become far less clear. Nine land surveyors were listed – namely, Robert Climie, Robert Harvie, Thomas Kyle, William Low, Archibald McAslan, Andrew McFarlane, George Martin, Neil Robson and David Smith. However, several are described also as civil engineers in addition to five others solely listed as such. Neil Robson is known to have advertised his further ability to execute 'surveys and plans of coal and other mining operations.'"[9]

For James Richardson Forman, this profession was one that would prove expensive for his father to provide, but lucrative in which to practice:

"As a consequence of the demand, civil engineers could choose apprentices on a far more selective basis, requesting on occasion premiums of 100 guineas for a five-year training. The contemporary press regularly contained notices seeking young men for drawing offices or engagements for surveyors of various specialisation. Depending on their experience, they could earn in the region of £75 per annum by the late 1830s. For a premium of fifty guineas, an experienced surveyor would provide an opening for two apprentices...."[10]

Robson was a leader in the field. Born in Galloway (south west Scotland) in 1807, he became a member of the prestigious Institution of Civil Engineers in 1845, and was a founding member of the Institution of Engineers and Shipbuilders in Scotland in 1857. Like many leading men in the technological revolution of the era, he became a member of the Philosophical Society of Glasgow in December of 1848. The firm of Robson & McCall combined Robson's surveying prowess with the engineering expertise of Thomas McCall, and the firm soon joined in the "railway mania" that swept Great Britain, taking Forman with them. Forman's obituary in the Institution's *Minutes* notes:

"... he was appointed in 1845 Resident Engineer on the Wilsontown, Morningside & Coltness Railway, then in course of construction, in connection with which serious difficulties had arisen between the Company and contractor. After successfully completing and equipping that railway, Mr. Forman remained as manager until 1851...."[11]

(In a short biographical article published in September of 1997, A.J.C. Clark claims Robert Hazelton Robson, Neil Robson's son, was Forman's mentor.)

So began James Richardson Forman's career as a railway builder. The Morningside line – one of several feeding the Glasgow-Edinburgh area – opened on June 5th 1845 from Morningside to Longridge, with stations at Morningside, Daviesdykes, Blackhall, Headlesscross, Crofthead, and Longridge. The railway soon ran into predictable difficulties. In March of 1848 the station at Daviesdykes closed, followed in December of 1852 by the stations at Blackhall, Headlesscross, Crofthead, and Longridge. It was not until October of 1864 that some vitality would be restored, with the line re-opened to passengers at Blackhall and Crofthead, and new stations at Bents and Whitburn. The station at Bents still stands.

In its own way, the Morningside line had something in common with Nova Scotia's railway. Critics of Howe's plan to build a government funded and operated line insisted it could not make a profit on the eastern branch between Halifax and Truro, because the population in between was too sparse, and there was no market at the Truro terminus to provide sufficient freight or passenger traffic to the city. Only the Halifax-Windsor route offered any promise, Windsor being the second largest town in the colony at the time, and the home of the vocal chorus of merchants who had begun their lobby for a railway in the 1830s.

On November 22nd 1846, Forman married Isobel (or Isabella) Hill (she died in 1896) when she came to visit friends in Glasgow. He had been a childhood friend. She was the daughter of Charles John Hill and Ann Symons, her father having been a senior manager of the Halifax shipyards, and a colleague of James Forman Senior. Together James and Isobel raised a family of four sons and five daughters.

By the time of the closings on the Wilsontown & Morningside line, however, Forman's reputation had earned him a position as manager of the General Terminus

& Glasgow Harbour Railway (1851). Chartered in 1846, and completed in December of 1848, this railway was presented to Forman as a *fait accompli*, and offered no particular challenge to an engineer. It may have been for that reason that Forman was so ready to accept Howe's offer to oversee the construction of the Nova Scotia Railway.

In August of 1858, when he felt obliged to defend his professional credentials from the attacks of a partisan newspaper editor, Forman described his career in the following terms:

> "I stated before the Committee that my employment as an engineer extended over a period of eighteen years, and that during my whole stay in Scotland I was not a day out of work – that I had laid out not tens but hundreds of miles of works, and I had acted as Chief Engineer on two railways. I further stated that the importance of the General Terminus Railway at Glasgow was not to be determined by its length, as it was a shipping place for a large portion of the Railway traffic brought to the Clyde, and consisted principally of Depot works and machinery, and that the length of this line, irrespective of its branches and sidings, might be two or three miles.
>
> Before entering upon the duties of my present office, for the information and satisfaction of the Commissioners, I explained the nature and extent of my experience as including Railway Harbour and Water Works, the laying out and executing these works with their general management...."

Left: Nova Scotia's foremost political son, Joseph Howe's relentless enthusiasm and drive could take its toll on friend and foe alike.
(Jay Underwood collection)

Left: Father of James Richardson Forman and chief cashier of the Bank of Nova Scotia, James Forman Senior was active in Nova Scotia's social circles and a leader of the anti-Catholic lobby. (Courtesy Brian Forman)

Below: The Forman home in Halifax, now 5680 Inglis Street. (Andrew Underwood)

"For your information, however, you will please understand that I served a regular apprenticeship with an Engineer in Glasgow, of considerable eminence, and at a time which might emphatically be termed the Railway period of Britain, when I laid out and constructed many extensive and important works, and before the expiry of my apprenticeship my services were solicited by several companies.

The year subsequent to my apprenticeship I laid out fifty miles of Railways, to a great extent unassisted, and I successfully carried them through Parliament, and each year afterwards I was engaged in laying out and extending new roads, and I have been employed as Consulting Engineer on several important works in Scotland. The above is only a part of my experience. I would further add, that the present Chief Engineer of the Great Western Railway of Canada – an important line and well known in this community – was a pupil at the same office in Glasgow as myself, only he was several years my junior.

As regards my position when I left Scotland, I can assure the Editor of the *Colonist* that it was of such nature that no other province except Nova Scotia, and it only because it was my native country, could have induced me to leave it, even though the emoluments were double what I am now receiving." [12]

This last comment is a rather self-serving statement, for whether Forman came to Howe's attention through his father or any other avenues, it was Forman himself who initiated the idea of him working on the Nova Scotia railway scheme. Quick to take up the excitement that was growing in Nova Scotia over the prospect of an inter-colonial railway, he sent a letter to the Executive Council of Nova Scotia, dated March 5th 1849, seeking work on the Nova Scotia portion of that project:

"Understanding the proposed railway through the North American provinces is likely to be made, I take the liberty of soliciting the appointment of engineer on the portion of the line through Nova Scotia.

I have been engaged for several years in laying out lines of railway and in superintending the routing of traffic after they are completed, including the general management of locomotives, carriages etc." [13]

He also received an endorsement through Howe's relationship with the brother-in-law, William King-Hall. In a letter to Howe, King-Hall suggests, "If there is a railway, give Forman his chance with others. Let every one stand or fall by their merits, and that is all he wishes. But because a man is away from his country, informing himself, he wants a friend to see he is not forgotten." [14]

Lotz errs in suggesting there is no record of the executive council's answer to Forman's letter. Howe, a member of the council, had obviously done some research on Forman, as his letter of November 12th 1852, written from a Glasgow hotel indicates:

"Sir:
As it is probable that the government of Nova Scotia will require an engineer to either superintend the construction of our railways, should those be undertaken as government works, or to check the estimates and test the work done, should they be made by contract.

I would be glad to know whether and upon what terms your services could be secured. Though not formally empowered to make any definite agreement, should you be at liberty to make such an offer as appears to be fair, I may assure you that I shall, from the information which I have gathered here, be prepared to recommend to the Lieutenant Governor to give you the appointment.

I have, etc.

JOSEPH HOWE" [15]

This letter indicates the two had never met, but that Howe was prepared to act on the advice of James Forman Senior, or William King-Hall. Forman's response wasn't immediate. His reply – also written in Glasgow – was dated November 24th:

"Dear Sir:

In reply to your favour of the 11th inst., I beg to state that I am willing to undertake either of the situations you refer to, and would name £500 stg. [sterling] per annum as fair remuneration for my services. If these terms are such as you can recommend, I will refuse any opening that may in the meantime offer in this country.

I am, etc.

J.R. FORMAN" [16]

It appears Forman was considering leaving his job at the General Terminal Railway, and anticipating other offers. He asked a modest sum, as time would later show, but Howe didn't give him any time. In a second letter, also dated November 12th, he prevailed upon Forman to provide an estimate of the project's cost, sight unseen:

"Certain propositions are now before the government of Nova Scotia, based upon the assumption that our railroads, viz., a trunk line from the harbour of Halifax, with branch lines to Pictou and Annapolis, can be made for £4000 per mile. As this price is much lower than any which has hitherto been named, I shall be much obliged if you will furnish me with your opinion as to whether that sum can cover all the indispensable outlays of a permanent and durable railway. Should you decide that it can, will you be kind enough to furnish me in detail with the elements of the calculation.

Will you also, even at some cost and trouble, endeavor to furnish me with the names of parties who would be prepared to supply the necessary plant, rails, and rolling stock, at the prices you name in your estimate, taking payment in cash or in provincial bonds." [17]

Forman had no reluctance to accede to Howe's presumption on his time. By his second letter dated November 24th, he provided the estimate Howe sought, with a caveat:

"Of course not having seen a section of the line, I was obliged to form an opinion of the quantity of cutting, and amount of bridging, etc., from general information. I am, however, confident that the rate will be found ample when applied to the whole distance.

I do not think that the present rate high price of iron can be long maintained.

I am obtaining offers for rails, rolling stock, etc.; these will, so soon completed, be forwarded, when I report more fully." [18]

Forman estimated the cost per mile for a single line would be £3,699 14s 8d. He estimated the cost of the physical plant (the locomotives, passenger, and freight cars) at £91,800, and allowing five per cent for offsets, his total cost per mile became £4,206, just slightly above the figure quoted by Howe.

By letter of November 29th, Forman provided written offers for the price of locomotives, carriages, wheels and axles, wagon bodies and mountings, rails, and chairs, from five suppliers with whom he had done business in the construction of the General Terminal and the Wilsontown & Morningside railways. Again, he issued a warning:

> "The whole, with the exception of Messrs. Gray & Waddell's offers for wagons, are within this estimate. The increase on the wagons arises from their being larger than originally intended, and of a rather more expensive construction. The estimate, however, allows of a sufficient margin to cover the excess, as well as to deliver the whole material at a seaport in Nova Scotia. All the parties have been employed on similar works by me, and have given satisfaction.
>
> Several of the parties have agreed to take part payment, say half in provincial bonds, had I been prepared to make any definite proposal.
>
> The iron market is at present firm, and makers of bars are unwilling to bind themselves to an offer unless accepted at once.
>
> I enclose statement, shewing cost of plant and rolling stock, made out in terms of above offers, as compared with estimate.
>
> I cannot obtain proper offers for the rest of the works, without [seeing] a section of the line." [19]

Whether he knew it or not at the time, Forman's inquiries on Howe's behalf did a great deal to boost the image of the province's proposal with investors and suppliers in England. Howe had made several trips to Great Britain in the years prior to his letter to Forman, all in an attempt to persuade the colonial minister at the time to provide imperial funding for the railway. He was met with polite consideration, but each time had been firmly rebuffed. It was his success with the investment bank of Baring Brothers – which agreed to sell £100,000 in provincial bonds to finance the railway – that took it from the realm of a wild-eyed provincial possibility into political reality.

Howe's enduring enthusiasm for the railway was bolstered by Forman's estimates. Enthusiasm was one of Howe's greatest qualities. He was a force unto himself, as J. Murray Beck has noted:

> "Coupled with the attractiveness of his oratory was the great humanity of the man. The sophisticated families of Halifax, who in this context must be equated with the tories, naturally frowned upon a *bon vivant* who was reputed to be a frequent associate of ne'er-do-wells in boisterous carousals. By the eighteen fifties the newspapers opposing him periodically referred to the coarseness of his language and the vulgarity of his stories or language....
>
> Yet ordinary Nova Scotians cared not a whit that he offended the susceptibilities of the high and mighty of Halifax. Many of them could fondly recall incidents associated with 'Joe' Howe." [20]

This was not to suggest Howe was without flaws that could make him difficult to deal with:

"Howe's 'restless agitating uncertainty' made him appear also as extremely egotistical. While his critics exaggerated this trait, he undoubtedly elaborated his accomplishments in a manner calculated to irritate and annoy. Sometimes, when he accompanied this extolling of his own virtues with a fawning, ingratiating attitude towards those who might render him favours, he could be downright obnoxious."[21]

Above all, Beck acknowledges Howe as a pragmatic man, one well aware of the importance of symbolism. In that respect it is understandable why he should choose a man of Nova Scotian birth to give life to the railway that would elevate his colony from – in his grand scheme – provincial backwater to an industrial titan in British North America. In one sense the character of Joseph Howe would be one of Forman's greatest trials, as would those of other political leaders in the province with whom contact was unavoidable.

The Empire had never seen anything like the Nova Scotia Railway before. Prior to its birth, railways outside the "Mother Country" had always been built by mercantile interests founded on private investment, serving definite markets, and controlled by capitalists in London. Under Howe, the Nova Scotia Railway was designed to avoid being built by capitalists. The British firm of Peto, Jackson, Brassey, & Betts had offered to undertake the construction of the line as it was designed to extend from Truro to the New Brunswick border, but Howe had been adamantly opposed to their involvement. The terms attached to the award of the contract were so onerous, and their subsequent involvement in the construction of a railway in the Crimea to support the war against Russia so great, that Jackson pointedly withdrew from any bidding.

With two members of parliament at its head (Peto and Jackson), the Brassey firm (as it was more familiarly known) was the largest railway contracting company in Britain, and had contracts worldwide, including Canada (the Grand Trunk) and New Brunswick (the European & North American). Thomas Brassey, the principal partner, was the de facto general of an army of as many as ten thousand navvies, surveyors and engineers, and the firm's operations were directed from its headquarters at Birkenhead, known as the Canada Works.

Likewise, the firm of James Sykes & Co. of Sheffield, which had built successful railways in Ireland, withdrew from the contract to build the line from Halifax and Windsor to Annapolis Royal and Digby, and the US firm of Burnett, Serrell & Co. of New York withdrew from the bidding for the contract in the Annapolis Valley.

Howe had made his philosophy clear. Speaking in the Legislature on March 25th 1850, in support of the resolution to spend public money on a railway between Windsor and Halifax, he said:

"We may be told that the railroads are not matters in which government should interfere. I differ entirely with those who entertain such an opinion, and I do not hesitate to propound it as one of the guiding principles of policy which shall run through the whole course of my after life, that I shall, while in any government, press them to take the initiative in such works as this. It is the first duty of a government to take the front rank in every noble enterprise; to be in advance of the social, political and industrial energies, which they have undertaken to lead. There are things they should not touch or attempt to control; but the great highways – the channels of intercommunication between large and wealthy sections of the country – should claim their special consideration; and when

I am told that we should hand over, for all time to come, this great Western Railway to a private Company, I have to such an assignment a serious objection... this Railroad, which will be the Queen's highway to the Western Counties in all time to come, should be the property of the Province and not of a private association."[22]

He also declared that the public men involved in such a "noble enterprise" should be held to a higher standard:

"I hope to see the time in this province when the question asked of every public man at the Hustings, will be – not 'to what party do you belong?' but – 'what great public improvement do you mean to advocate? To what great public measure tending to advance the general welfare of the people, are you pledged?' The people will hereafter require public measures of public men; and, next to the care of their liberties and political interests, they will look for the development of their resources and the advancement of their condition. Men acting on the public stage should move forward in advance of the times, and not trust too much to the position which they have acquired by past services."[23]

It was clear Howe expected public employees to endorse this philosophy, which – while magnificent in its principle – was lacking in practicability.

The railway had no definite market or natural resources to be exploited. (There were some plaster deposits at Windsor, and coal, if the line was ever extended to Pictou County northeast of Truro.) The "industrious poor" people of Nova Scotia were being encouraged to become investors through the development of a savings bank. In addition, the legislation creating the board of commissioners established a principle that no more than £200,000 was to be spent in any one fiscal year, in order to avoid some of the spectacular financial scandals that had marked other railway schemes elsewhere in the British Empire and the United States. Any unspent funds from one year, however, could be carried into the next.

This self-imposed frugality was a compromise intended to assuage opposition from members of the Legislature who were concerned that Howe's plan would put the colony deeper in debt than it had been at any time in its history. It was also to contribute to Forman's problem with the construction of the railway as it fell behind schedule. Forman also had to answer to a bi-partisan board of very partisan commissioners, initially led by Howe, all of which was enshrined in legislation authorized by an act of the Legislature March 31st 1854. The legislation passed by a narrow margin:

"Howe proceeded confidently, knowing that his old political enemy and the new Tory member for Windsor, L.M. Wilkins, Jr., had declared that he would sacrifice his party to get on with the railroad. Even so, he carried his bills by only one in the council and three in the assembly. Because of the defection of Bourneuf and Comeau, two Acadian Liberals from western Nova Scotia, he could not have done without the votes of Wilkins and three other Tories from Hants at the terminus of the line to Windsor. Nova Scotia could at last enter the railway age."[24]

The narrow majority would set the tone for a bitter legislature, a hornet's nest just waiting to be stirred. James Richardson Forman would step into the nest just as soon as he stepped off the boat in Halifax, with his wife and three youngsters in tow – Margaret

Anne (born 1848), James (born 1849) and an infant, Charles (born in Glasgow August 10th 1852) about whom more will be said later.

Forman's acceptance of the Executive Council appointment had come with a proviso, outlined in a letter to Howe, from Glasgow in May of 1853:

"... I understand my position to be Consulting Engineer, i.e. to consult with the Government as to the course to be pursued in carrying on their views in reference to the Railway schemes proposed by them, reporting on the general nature of the works in relation thereto and in attending to the Company's complying with the conditions laid down by the Government.

In reference to details, that is, making measurements, surveys, plans etc., if these are made under the charge of the Government they will be paid for as detailed and as not included under the Consulting Engineering. Of course this would require the organising, charge and responsibilties connected with a working staff.

I take it for granted that any works carried on by Government and requiring the assistance of an Engineer will be entrusted to me." [25]

Forman arrived in Nova Scotia in the summer of that year, and he could not have been pleased by his reception. On March 4th 1854, Howe introduced his railway bill to the Legislature, and if he had not ignored Forman's proviso outright, it had been sacrificed in the give-and-take often required to get a bill passed through the house. The act stipulated:

"The Governor in Council shall appoint a Chief Engineer to hold office during pleasure, who under the instruction he may receive from the Commissioners, shall have the general superintendence of the works to be constructed under the Act, and whose duty it shall be to measure the work done, and for which payment shall be claimed to report upon the lines to be selected, the permanence of the works to be designed or executed – the strength of the rails – the sufficiency of plant and rolling stock – and the faithful fulfillment of the contracts which be entered into." [26]

This was not the consulting position Forman had envisioned for himself, and certainly not the salary. He had anticipated £500 for what would have been a position requiring less of his time, and was instead to receive £750 for what was now a full-time position. It was also not the position originally intended by the resolution of the house, passed a full year earlier (March 31st 1853) that stated, on Howe's motion:

"That His Excellency the Lieutenant Governor be respectfully requested to employ a competent person as *Consulting Engineer,* to aid the executive government in the location of lines of railway, for which provision has been made by acts passed during the present session, and to discharge such other duties in relation thereto as in the discretion of the Governor in Council may be for the interests of the public service, and this house will make provision for the payment of such engineer." [27] [Italics added for emphasis]

Having cast his lot in Nova Scotia, and brought his family from Scotland, Forman may well have felt he had no choice but to accept the job as it was now presented to him. This included some non-railway work, such as the inspection of several ports

Left: Sir John Gaspard LeMarchant, Lieutenant Governor of Nova Scotia and a career soldier with an interest in civil engineering projects, donated the land that became the Richmond terminus of the Nova Scotia Railway.
(Nova Scotia Archives & Records Management Service / Craig Collection)

Below: Birch Cove Halifax *ca.* 1904. The fill needed to carry the railway around the shores of Bedford Basin almost doubled Forman's original estimate of the cost of construction. This postcard shows the area had not changed in the first fifty years of the railway. This area of Halifax was home to premier James W. Johnston when he could not be at Annapolis Royal.
(Jay Underwood collection)

in Cape Breton, and – on the personal request of Lieutenant Governor LeMarchant – an inspection of the masonry of the Halifax Citadel. In this regard it seems the government made a shrewd move, for had Forman been the Consulting Engineer for the railway alone, he might have expected considerably more than the extra £250 offered for the consulting work on the Cape Breton harbours! The small variation in the wording of the act and the resolution appears to have set the stage for a lingering misunderstanding between Forman and the railway commissioners over the nature of his employment.

He was set immediately to the great task of the railway. Speed appears to have been essential to Howe:

"It proceeded so rapidly that before the year was out it had awarded contracts for building almost seventeen miles from the terminus at Richmond to the head of Bedford Basin. Howe reported the Lieutenant Governor Sir Gaspard le Marchant [sic] as being so amazed that he 'swears that I would undertake the building of a Line of Battle Ship, and lay the keel in 24 hours.'" [28]

The actual agenda was not that fast; the petition to the Lieutenant Governor presented August 25th 1852 called for the construction of thirty miles of railway in each of the years between 1853 and 1862:

"Total 300 miles. Thereby connecting New Brunswick, the Pictou coal mines, and our fertile western counties with Halifax. The direction of the roads to depend upon the action of the legislature, and on the progress which may be made in the neighboring provinces in the construction of inter-colonial lines." [29]

If the longest journey begins with the smallest step, the Nova Scotia Railway's first step began within days of the enabling legislation being proclaimed. Advertisements appeared in the Halifax newspapers seeking a thousand men with wheelbarrows, mules, carts, and shovels, to apply to Messrs. Cameron, Turnbull, and Fraser, the lead contractors on the first seventeen miles of the line from Richmond to the head of the Bedford basin.

CHAPTER 2

A Riotous Affair

James Richardson Forman might have later benefitted from some positive publicity generated early in the railway's construction phase. Some engineers, especially the flamboyant Sandford Fleming, would become masters of the gala event of a sod turning or "Golden Spike" ceremony. The Nova Scotia Railway offered no such opportunity for its Chief Engineer, and it may be that he was not naturally inclined to avail himself of the occasion. In fact, the railway's June 13th 1854 opening was an almost secretive event, given only slight coverage by the press, including the pro-Howe, pro-railway *NovaScotian*. Its coverage in the June 19th edition devoted much of the space to a defence of the project as a public work rather than a private concern, and observed:

"The first sod on the railway track was turned amid the quiet stillness of a summer's morning on Tuesday at the Governor's Farm. Early as was the hour – 6 o'clock – the Lieutenant Governor, the members of the Railway Board, and a number of citizens were on the spot to witness the unostentatious and business-like beginning of an undertaking so momentous in its consequences to the people of the country. About a hundred persons were actively engaged during the day, discoursing eloquent music with 'the shovel and the hod.'"[1]

Perhaps the frugal Howe and his commissioners preferred not to add champagne, canapés, bunting, and bands to the expense sheet, but the day surely deserved some memorable speech from LeMarchant, Howe, and the man who was delegated to give life to the dream. Forman appears to have been a man of few words; his only pronouncements on the state of the works were limited to his official reports to the Legislature. His one public statement in 1858 would be remarkable, and has been largely ignored. Reporting to the House of Assembly in February of 1855, Howe noted three sections of the line leading out of Halifax from its terminus at Governor's Farm in Richmond were under construction, but already it was apparent Forman's rough estimates offered in 1852 were awry:

"The works extend over a distance of 10 miles and 31 chains, admitted to be the most difficult which the board have to encounter. The cost of these sections, for grading and permanent way, as accurately determined, will be £7840 per mile...."[2]

These overruns, which became a continual occurrence, would provide Howe's political opponents with a great deal of ammunition. Howe staunchly defended his engineer's estimates:

"When it is considered that rock and hard gravel had to be removed on almost every portion of these contracts – that heavy embankments had to be formed across coves and arms of the basin, and that the price of labour has, throughout the summer, been one-third higher than at any period for 20 years, the cost per mile will not appear extravagant. Before the approaching summer closes, we hope that our operations, on both lines, will have reached beyond the rocky region which extends from the southern shores of the province, and over which any railways running out of the capital must be constructed. When once the river beds and fertile lands of the interior have been reached, we confidently anticipate a very material reduction in the cost."[3]

Still, these cost overruns delayed the progress of the line. When the £200,000 benchmark was reached, the contractors' work was usually deferred. Forman's task continued unabated:

"The Chief Engineer is now engaged in locating a section of the eastern road, which will carry the works in that direction to the Grand Lake. He is also concluding such preliminary surveys as will enable him to place under contract ten miles of the western road. The board confidently anticipate that these two sections, in addition to the three already in progress, will be completed within this year, while they shall labor very zealously to locate and place under contract other portions of the lines between Halifax and Windsor, and Halifax, and Truro."[4]

The slow speed of the work bothered Howe, who offered further explanation, one that might be considered an apology:

"The board regret that they have not been able, during the short period that has elapsed since they were commissioned, to accomplish more. They met for the first time on the 5th of April (1854). They had an engineering staff to organize, and contractors and skilled workmen to discover. No member of the board had any practical knowledge of railway making. By the 4th of May the first contract for grading was advertised, and on the 13th of June the ground was broken. In less than nine months three sections have been placed under contract – eighty miles of country beyond surveyed – rails and rolling stock have been imported, and a depot sufficient for the present, has been formed."[5]

He went on to outline the progress expected for the coming year: "Twenty miles more will be under contract before the 1st May. The commissioners see no reason to doubt the completion of the line to Windsor, with a corresponding extension into the heart of the eastern counties by the close of 1856."[6] It would be left to Forman to see that this political agenda was met, for within the board there were skeptics. The other members of the first board were Jonathan McCully (who would come to prominence later in the story of the line), William Pryor Jr., P.M. Cunningham, J.H. Anderson, and Thomas Tobin. They were well paid for their effort. Howe received £700 per year as chairman of the board, while the five commissioners were originally to have divided £600 between them. This stipend proved unsatisfactory and by March of 1855 they had succeeded in adding a cost overrun of their own making to the budget:

"And the Lieutenant Governor having been informed that the five commissioners of railways had declined receiving the compensation so awarded to them, as, in their opinion inadequate and insufficient; and a question, as to increased compensation to these last, being under consideration of the board, it is therefore ordered by the Lieutenant Governor in council, subject to the revision and confirmation of the legislature, that the order of the board first above referred to, so far as it respects compensation to the said five commissioners, be rescinded, and that the sum of one thousand pounds currency, be assigned as the full amount of annual salary or compensation to those five commissioners, from the date of their appointments, to be distributed and apportioned amongst them, relatively to their respective services, in such proportions as the board may decide."[7]

This retroactive pay hike would immediately add £800 to the budget, with a further £400 added in ensuing years. In that same year (1855) the commissioners appear to have decided to cast frugality aside, and make amends for the stingy atmosphere that accompanied the sod turning:

"On the 8th June 1855, amid general rejoicing, the Nova Scotia Railway was opened to the public from Richmond to Sackville. A regular bus service was inaugurated, running between Richmond and Province House, Halifax, and the Great Western Stagecoach Company announced that hereafter its terminus would be Sackville. Two trains a day were run.

To celebrate the opening of the railway an elaborate banquet was given at 9 Mile House (Davy's) at which were present the Lieutenant Governor, the Railway Commissioners, and other dignitaries. It was a very successful affair, as is attested by various items appearing in the railway accounts: "£24 for champagne, £10 for wines, £2 for floral decorations."[8]

Sown within the body of the railway board's first report, however, were the seeds that would come to bedevil Forman. Howe's timetable was enthusiastic beyond reason. He had attempted to lay a foundation for rapid advancement before being obliged to cross the Atlantic one more time shortly after his report was issued, to shore up the funding from Barings. The interior of the province proved no less difficult than the rocky shores of the Bedford Basin; the surveys on the Windsor branch and out to the Grand Lake would reveal new challenges, and the cost of labour would develop into a riotous furor that would claim Forman as a political victim.

Forman's first report to the House of Assembly was not made until January 20th 1856, and he described progress far in advance of Howe's earlier assessment. He also indicated that his job entailed far more than Howe had led him to expect in 1852:

"In the office work, the labour of which has necessarily been very great, I have been aided by my pupils, who have also made themselves extremely useful in the field, and it is due to these young gentlemen to say, that it is to a considerable extent owing to their exertions that so much has been accomplished during the year, and it is gratifying to be able to testify to their constant diligence in the office business, notwithstanding they receive no pecuniary remuneration for these services."[9]

Clearly the frugal board of commissioners had found a way to maximize its human resources without adding to the stress on the public purse. It was a policy that would come back to haunt the line. At the same time, reports filed in the legislature show that Forman was also being given tasks associated with the construction and maintenance of wharves, and the St. Peter's Canal (although that work was managed by Capt. P.J.S. Barry of the Corps of Royal Engineers).

In the meantime a nightmare would develop that summer, incidents ignited by the movement for higher wages on the navvy gangs, adding to further cost overruns that could not have been foreseen. A political scandal, fueled by Howe, would emerge from the melee. Historians have been content to dismiss the Gourley shanty riots as nothing more than a brawl between rival navvy gangs that did little more than excite the province for a torrid summer. Beck, in *Joe Howe: Voice of Nova Scotia*, briefly states the salient points of the incident:

"… on May 26th 1856, a clash involving the Irish occurred on the Windsor railway. For some time workers from the eastern counties, Presbyterian in religion, had been taunting the Irish navvies for their belief in the Real Presence of Christ in the Sacrament of the Eucharist; in return the Irish inflicted a merciless beating upon the Protestant workers on the Windsor railway who lived in Gourley's Shanty." [10]

He elaborates that the Catholics: "… assailed fifteen to twenty Presbyterians from the Eastern counties with pickaxe handles." [11] Few historians attach much significance to the events of the day, other than to note they were tied to Howe's attempts to recruit volunteers to fight in the Crimean War. His ensuing anti-Catholic tirade led directly to the defeat of William Young's government – even though Howe was not a member of the government at the time:

"Although [Howe] was no longer a member of the House or the government, he was still considered by the public to be the leader of the Liberals….
Until then, the Liberals had been receiving support from most religious groups. Howe's letter apparently went too far. When the government faced a motion of non-confidence, it was deserted by several Catholic members and others who represented mainly Catholic counties." [12]

Howe had imported many of the Irish navvies to build his railway, following a colonial philosophy outlined in 1847 by George Pemberton, then the Canadian representative on the board of the St. Andrews & Quebec Railway in London. Testifying before Lord Monteagle's committee on immigration in the House of Lords, Pemberton was quoted as saying:

"The natives of Ireland are found to be the best adapted for works requiring great strength. All laborious undertakings in Canada and the United States are carried through by Irish labourers; and they are better adapted for settlers, when without other means, than any other class." [13]

The competition for railway labourers was stiff, and had been for several years prior to the commencement of Howe's railway. The British government's emigration office made numerous references to this situation in its report *Emigration. Papers Relative to Emigration to The British Provinces in North America* (British Parliamentary Papers 1854). The arrivals of navvy gangs were of great public interest, as noted at the Grosse Isle immigration centre at Quebec:

"Arrivals 21st June to 2nd July: 5383 emigrants have landed here since the 21st June; they have arrived in good health; nearly two-thirds are native Irish, a large portion of whom were proceeding to friends and relations in the United States. 60 full passengers by the *Amazon*, from Cork, had engaged their passage in that city direct for Boston and New York, having been able to come this route (owing to the opening of the railway communication between Montreal and these cities), for less money than proceeding direct by sea.

Labourers and mechanics, such as masons, bricklayers, and carpenters, are much inquired for. 5,000 men are now wanted on the Toronto and Sarnia Railroads, wages one dollar per day. Agents are here from Chicago and Cincinnati wishing to engage several thousand men, wages 6s. 3d. per day; and as an inducement, they offer a passage to Chicago, to be repaid out of their first wages."[14]

Howe had gone to the United States to find his workforce, offering them the promise of a chance to join the fight in the Crimea as soon as ships and weapons could be supplied. This was an illegal act, since the US was officially neutral in the Crimean conflict, and one for which Howe would be reprimanded and reviled. His labourers came at a premium.

The first news of the Gourley Shanty riot broke in the May 27th edition of the *Morning Chronicle* and was duly echoed in the June 2nd edition of the weekly *NovaScotian*:

"The City has been distracted by rumours of a sort of faction fight upon the Railway on Monday last, in which it was at first supposed that several lives had been lost.

Yesterday the Hon. Jonathan McCully, the High Sheriff, Messrs. Jennings, Cochran and Shiels, County Magistrates, went up the Windsor Road and spent the day in taking examinations and conducting inquiries into the facts. They returned to town last evening.

We rejoice to learn that no lives have been lost, although several men have been so beaten and bruised that their lives are yet in danger.

It appears that from 80 to 100 men, drawn from Contracts 1 and 2 of the Windsor Branch, suddenly appeared, by evident preconcert, about one o'clock in the day and surrounding two or three Shanties in which were about 30 men and seven or eight women and children. They smashed the windows with stones, drove out the inmates, struck them down with axe-handles and bludgeons as they attempted to escape. A few resolute fellows fought their way through – a few others fled to the woods. The women and children were not beaten, but of course were dreadfully terrified. The ruthless scoundrels did not cease from outrage until there was scarcely a man left who was not felled to the ground, trampled and left for dead.

The Magistrates were, we understand, unable to discover any motive, religious or mercenary, for this outrage. It was no strike for wages but a cold blooded brutal assault by a body of lawless men, without even the excuse of a love of fighting, for those who do love it, love to fight fair, and in this war the proportion stood three to one.

We trust that such a lesson will be read to these people, and such an example made of them as will give to peaceful men, earning their wages on our public works, the full protection of law and order."[15]

From that point onward, the details of the events came not from reporting of the riot itself, but from the subsequent comments of Howe and his antagonist, William

Condon, the president of the local Charitable Irish Society, who locked horns in a public debate that took place at the Halifax Temperance Hall. Howe had attended the meeting to introduce ambassador John F. Crampton to the crowd, as the British diplomat returned home to face the music for his role in Howe's US recruiting mission. Howe and Condon had previously clashed over the Irishman's telegrams to Boston and New York newspapers, warning his countrymen to resist the railway commissioner's attempts to have them join the fight for the British cause in Crimea.

Condon did not deny the incidents took place, but he objected strenuously to Howe's public pronouncement of the guilt of the Irishmen involved in the fracas at Gourley's Shanty, and the perfidy of the society in stepping forward to offer them legal and moral support. Condon claimed, with some justification, that it was up to the courts to decide the issue of guilt, and that Howe had no place introducing the incident at that meeting, since charges had yet to be laid, and some of those in attendance might find themselves empanelled on the jury. Howe shot back in his now famous letter in the June 17th edition of the *Morning Chronicle*, offering more details that have been overlooked by historians. According to Howe:

"Some months ago, an Irishman named Whalen, who was discharged from the girder shop at Sackville for drunkenness and neglect, struck the Superintendent, took to the road, and, armed with a pair of pistols, for about ten days set law and order at defiance. An affidavit was made, a writ was issued, but no Constable could be got willing or able to arrest him. While at large Whalen walked into a cutting on Creelman and Tupper's Contract, felled to the ground with one of his pistol barrels a respectable ganger from Stewiacke, with whom he had never exchanged a word, and jumped upon his body. After this outrage the perpetrator of it paraded about the works, for days together, displaying his pistols and threatening further assaults. A resolute special Constable was at length procured, who went out and arrested Whalen. A rescue was attempted, by his countrymen, which would have succeeded but for the interference of the Contractor. The man was imprisoned, but got clear because the persons assaulted had not been notified or did not appear against him." [16]

Reports of the day in both the *NovaScotian* and *Morning Chronicle* indicate the "riot" was in fact a series of incidents that occurred between Sackville and the end of the track at the Nine Mile River in Elmsdale, Hants County. In his infamous letter in the *Morning Chronicle*, Howe went on to document other "outrages" that preceded the attack on Gourley's Shanty:

"Near to Shultz's there have been several crimes, which, not being reached by law, encouraged the belief that law could not reach offences on the railroad. One man was stabbed in the knee and disabled for months. Another had his ear bitten clean off. These may have been the results of drunken brawls. Of a very different character was the outrage committed by a party of Irishmen, who, some short time ago, went to the house of a person named Brown, from one of our agricultural settlements, and tore his whisker off his cheek, taking skin and part of the flesh with it.

But there was no law for poor Brown. The crime went unpunished, and the idea spread, that there was no law on the Railroad, and that the 'violent and disorderly' might do as they liked.

So rife had this opinion become, that before Messrs. Sutherland & Co. had got fairly under weigh their works were disturbed, and after a fruitless appeal to a magistrate, they armed, in self defence."[17]

This narrative brought Howe to what he believed was the crux of the problem, something that runs contrary to assertions about Irish navvies being willing to work for lower wages (as they had in England), and becoming the target of Scottish and English rivals: "So matters stood, when a party of Irishmen near Windsor, demanded 6s. 3d. per day, and struck because they could not get it. Of course if they could drive all the Pictou, Colchester, and Cape Breton men off the line, they could get what they pleased...."[18]

His report of June 17th in the *Morning Chronicle* continued with an account of another incident at Elmsdale on June 2nd 1856, quoting from the affidavit of Thomas Rowland of Shubenacadie, the superintendent of the sixty men on the works there:

"… that a very large proportion of his laborers are Irishmen, who receive, on an average, 5s per day, are regularly paid, well treated, and have nothing to complain of. That an unlicensed Grog Shop, kept by one Adams, has been opened near one of his Cuttings, where the Nine Mile River Road crosses the Shubenacadie River at Elmsdale, and at which the workmen get liquor, and which is a nuisance to the neighborhood. That on Monday last, the 2nd of June, the men on the works went to this Grog Shop, having got liquor… became turbulent and excited. That he had placed Archibald McLellan, a Scotchman, to superintend the work in his absence, in whose skill and integrity he had confidence. That about eleven o'clock… Deponent met John Lovett and Patrick Fitzgerald, on the Road, armed with sticks, who flourished them over Deponent's head, and threatened to take Deponent's life if he put any men on the works but Irishmen. That if Deponent brought any men from Canada they should not work here, that they, the Irishmen, would kill them if they did. That the men then went upon the works, and knocked down an Englishman, named Lynch, who they maltreated and drove off the line, and who has since left the service of this Deponent and fled for fear of being murdered. That the horses were driven off the works by these men and their abettors, and the work brought to a stand. That the men were terrified and driven away, being afraid to work for this Deponent or stop in the neighborhood."[19]

Rowland went on to affirm his belief:

"… that it is the purpose and policy of these rioters, and of others who have acted in the same spirit elsewhere, to drive off the Railway Works the natives of the Province, and other industrious persons from other countries, and to secure to the Irish the complete command of the works."[20]

Rowland concluded by demanding the government take measures to protect the life and limb of his non-Irish workers:

"… unless the Government interfere, and make life and property and industry perfectly secure on the Public Works, all other labourers but Irishmen will be driven off or terrified from coming in from the distant Counties. That the monopoly thus created will place Contractors at the mercy of the riotous and unruly, raise the price of labour, lessen the competition among Contractors, and cost the Province very large sums of money before the railroads are completed."[21]

Howe's tirade in the press had been directed at one faction of Catholics, but his words stung the community broadly. He succeeded only in creating political ill will that would fester well beyond the trial of the offenders of the Gourley Shanty fracas, even after a court acquitted the men, and Condon proclaimed a moral victory in the *Halifax Catholic* newspaper. The political fracas was typical of North America at the time, where the large masses of Irish immigrants arriving to escape famine in Ireland immediately became grist for the political mills. Doggerel verse of the time described their plight:

> He slowly moves his rake, and swings,
> his pick with easy sweep;
> Seeming to be not quite awake, and yet
> Not sound asleep.
> We gazed upon the dreamy scene, and of
> Its beauty wrote,
> And could not help but realize the power
> of a vote.

The impact of the riot was, for the time being, short-lived. But the change in government that it provoked had a greater impact upon Forman's tenure. Annoyed by Howe's outburst, several of his party's Catholic supporters deserted:

"As the 1857 legislative session approached, William Young began to receive disturbing reports from his backbenchers about the likely secession of his Catholic members. The day after it opened Condon was dismissed – the price of Howe's continued support of the government – and the fat was in the fire. Two Irish Catholics, John Tobin and Peter Smyth, deserted the Liberals forthwith, but the government might have clung precariously to office if its Acadian and Scottish Catholic members had remained firm. It was not to be. Through the defection of eight Catholics and two Protestants representing seats with large Catholic populations it lost a non-confidence vote by 28 to 22."[22]

Young was another unfortunate victim of Howe's tirade, since he led the party in the legislature, and had prosecuted the rioters as the province's attorney general. The victors were to be James William Johnston, the Conservative leader who had defended the Irish navvies, and Charles Tupper, whose political ascendancy would begin on the day of the vote, February 18th 1857. The following day Howe resigned as chairman of the railway board, and Forman lost the clout of his strongest political supporter. Howe was replaced by James McNab, his brother-in-law and a fellow Reformer, but McNab had split with Howe over the railway policy, and was not as protective of Forman. "In the ensuing battle Howe lost both his seat in the Assembly and his post as railway commissioner. With him passed all hope of efficient construction and profitable operation of Nova Scotia's publicly owned railways."[23]

Charles Tupper was a stark contrast to Joseph Howe. Called variously the "Cumberland warhorse" for his support of the Conservative party, and the "Cumberland ram" for his frequent publicly rumoured dalliances with married women, the newspapers that opposed him knew him as "the Boodler" and "the great hater." James Wilberforce Longley, who wrote biographies of both Howe and Tupper, having known both of them well from his days in the provincial legislature, described Tupper in this fashion:

> "He never allowed himself to be cowed or bluffed; he boldly faced every situation and flinched not though hurricanes raged about him. He was sensitive of his dignity and never permitted undue familiarities. Some men attain popularity by being hail-fellow-well-met with all men; Tupper permitted no one to slap him upon the back." [24]

Tupper made enemies easily, and once his enemy, the offending individual was subject to a torrent of verbal abuse and political connivance. Opinions differ on the confrontations that took place between Howe and Tupper in the Legislature. Some

JAMES W. JOHNSTON (left)
His defence of the Irish navvies implicated in the Gourley Shanty riots won him political support at a critical time, and he paved the way for Tupper's political ascendancy.
(Nova Scotia Archives & Records Management Service, 53772)

WILLIAM YOUNG (right)
The first casualty of Howe's anti-Catholic tirade, he prosecuted the Gourley Shanty rioters, but found many of his witnesses suddenly reluctant to testify.
(Nova Scotia Archives & Records Management Service, 40807)

historians suggest that whereas Howe criticized on a reasoned and well-planned argument, Tupper sniped and heckled at every opportunity, frequently launching into defamatory statements that prevented him from being sued only by virtue of his protection of privilege in the public forum. Howe was Tupper's most prominent enemy in provincial politics (he would make many more when he entered the federal realm), and focus of his vitriol. Longley offers a contrary point of view, noting of Tupper:

"During the nine years he was compelled to confront Howe in the political arena, he was no match in humour and ridicule for that incomparable and versatile personality, but he offset this with dogged logic and a merciless appeal to fact and argument which were almost as effective with the masses." [25]

In Tupper's mind any friend of Howe's became his political and personal enemy, and Forman would be no different. Where Howe sought out the engineer as a symbol of Nova Scotia's innate ability to produce its own genius, Tupper saw him as a symbol of everything he despised in Howe, and was not above employing what may have been a deep-seated personal dislike of Forman to press his point home:

"When pressed, he was not scrupulous or fastidious in his means of extrication, and, in order to achieve his point, he would sometimes make declarations which suited the moment, but were liable to confront him inconveniently afterwards. His usual method was to secure the immediate triumph and trust to fate and his wits to meet any possible consequences." [26]

It was Tupper who provoked the members of Young's caucus to abandon him after the Gourley Shanty riots, and in retaliation for what he saw as the perfidy of the deserting legislators, Howe toyed with the idea of forming a political party to champion the

Left: Charles Tupper. Historians agree Tupper's political battles with Howe were of epic proportions and unforgiving animosity. With a reputation for his dalliances, could a woman have been behind his move against James Richardson Forman? (Jay Underwood collection)

Protestant cause. The idea was later dropped, but not before Protestants outside the political arena rallied: "A Protestant Association of Nova Scotia was formed, headed mainly by Free Church Presbyterian ministers, but the politicians appear to have ignored it and its influence was slight."[27] What the association managed to do was inflame passions even more, leading to in-fighting within the Protestant ranks, as evidenced by the battles between Howe and Tupper:

> "Otherwise it was a session of great bitterness revolving mainly around the religious controversy and the extension of the spoils system. Revolting in the extreme were the exchanges between the major rivals on the House, Howe and Tupper. Once Tupper regretted that Howe was not the richer for his efforts since he did not think that Nova Scotia was much the richer for them. Referring to recent innuendo relating to Tupper, Howe replied that no member of the Protestant Association had 'gained his education by a fraud of the basest character and almost caused a general set to.'"[28]

The Protestant Association was anathema to Catholics, made notorious by its founding in Glasgow in 1835. It is undoubtedly there that James Richardson Forman would have first learned of the association.

> "Impressed with the dangers of Popery arising from the Accession of Roman Catholics to power in the Legislature of the country, the manner in which that power is exerted, the zealous efforts made by the church of Rome to regain her ascendancy, the loose notions of religious principle unhappily prevalent among a large body of Protestants, and the magnitude of the Roman Catholic population in Glasgow, a number of ministers and laymen formed themselves, in October 1835, into an Association for the purpose, by public meetings and the press, of exposing the errors and pernicious tendency of the Popish system, extensively diffusing information respecting the character and history of the church of Rome, and arousing Protestants to the duties to which they are specially called."[29]

Such a mission would undoubtedly stir the passions of Catholics, many of whom took the news of the association with them when they went abroad. It was not, however, a political movement.

> "To guard against misapprehension, and at the same time better describe their object, they included the following resolution among the fundamental principles of the society:-
> 'That this Association disclaims all identity with party names and party interests, and presents a center of unity to as many as prefer the welfare of Protestantism to the objects of political faction, and desire to preserve that Protestant character of the constitution which has been recognized by Great Britain since the period of the Reformation.'"[30]

That statement alone could be construed as a threat to the Catholic members of the Nova Scotia legislature, who in the 1850s were just beginning to enjoy some political "muscle" after years of Protestant mastery.

It was James Richardson Forman's father who would precipitate his son's involvement in the organization. James Forman Senior was elected president of the Nova Scotia association (or Alliance, as it was also known) and was among the group that printed an inflammatory series of pamphlets pronouncing the Protestant "right" to rule the province, and decrying the evils of "Popery." The organization's aims were then made public in a series of letters to the press authored by Reverend Andrew King, Professor of Theology at the Free Church of Halifax, one of the Alliance's vice-presidents. The senior Forman also made it clear in a June 7th 1858 open letter to Tupper, published in the *NovaScotian*, that it was he, and not his son, who was behind the agitation:

> "Dear Sir, In your letter to the Editor of the *Colonist* this morning, commenting upon the Rev. Professor King's third letter, published on Tuesday last, you make the assertion – 'I learned from a gentleman of the highest standing in this city that Mr. Forman – 'the President' – had informed him that his name had been used without his consent.'
>
> I cannot now exactly remember the conversation which took place, but I meant to first convey the idea that my name had been *published without my knowledge*. I however added that I approved of the formation of the Alliance.
>
> I was not aware, at the time when the documents which seem to have created so much sensation and caused so great annoyance to yourself and others were read and ordered to be printed, that the names of the gentlemen who composed the committee were intended to be published. That course, however, having been pursued, I wish it now to be clearly understood that I consider no wrong act is to be imputed to any one, but on the contrary the appending of my name to these documents was in every respect justifiable, and that I have all along been aware not only of the nature and constitution of the Protestant Alliance, but that I endorse every one of its rules and regulations as having received my unqualified and cordial assent.
>
> I have not during my whole life been mixed up either directly or indirectly with politics, and for the last twenty-six years I have voted at but one general election, and on that occasion my votes were given for two gentlemen, my particular friends, whose political opinions were altogether at variance. I have never myself held any Government office or situation, received any Government pay in any form, nor been under any obligation to Government or any member of Government for assistance, and I think you must allow that under such circumstances, I am justified in saying that an unwarranted liberty has been taken with my name in dragging it on several occasions lately before the public to subserve the selfish purposes of political partisans, careless and indifferent whom they may injure, or whose feelings they may wound.[31]
>
> I am, Dear Sir, yours truly
> J. Forman."

Clearly the father was attempting to differentiate between himself and his son, both of whom were being made targets by Tupper as he stirred the sectarian pot. The "Colonist" referred to by the senior Forman was the *British Colonist*, the influential Halifax Tory paper over which Tupper exerted a great deal of editorial influence.

James Forman Senior's stand earned him a degree of respect among Protestant Nova Scotians, an aspect missed in Lotz's biography:

> "Mary, G. daughter of the first named Richard Black, was married to Elisha Gourley. He was a native of Colchester County, but lived for some time at Amherst, where, after his

marriage, he built the house now owned and occupied by Peter Etter, and lived there for several years. He afterwards removed to his native county where he, for many years, conducted the business connected with his trade. He now resides at Truro."[32]

The Gourleys, from the same family as the owner of the shanty, had six children, one of whom would memorialize James Forman in a unique and (at the time) complimentary way:

"They had six children whom they named Amelia, Bessie, Fitzallan, James Forman, Clarence, and Seymour Eugene.
James Forman, the second son of Elisha Gourley, keeps a large wholesale and retail clothing store in Montreal, and has seven agents in his employ. The business is said to be in a healthy state."[33]

In an ironic twist, with the Gourley's being related to the Blacks, Tupper was drawn into the story again. His family was related to the Blacks.

CHAPTER 3

Unexpected Developments

Past histories have paid scant attention to the Gourley Shanty riots, and some historians with better access to information have made some significant errors, especially with regard to the location of the major fracas. In 1916, David Allum noted in *History of Nova Scotia:*

"The work of track-construction on the Nova Scotia Railway had reached the Shubenacadie just beyond Grand Lake. Indeed it had progressed a little farther. 'Gourley's Shanty,' the scene of the unhappy incident about to be related, was located a little beyond Enfield. Of the navvies engaged in construction work, some were Protestants of the ordinary mixed Nova Scotia stock, others Irish Catholics. Except in working hours, racial and religious consideration led to a separate grouping. 'Gourley's Shanty' was a Protestant establishment. Whether there had been religious disputes and altercations in advance of what happened on Corpus Christi day, we are not informed. But on that day, some demon of discord impelled Protestants to jeer in a peculiarly offensive and objectionable manner with the most august and sacred article of the Roman Catholic faith. Instead of confining their indignation to verbal remonstrance, the Irishmen flew to cudgels, and in their attack on Gourley's Shanty shed blood and came alarmingly near actual homicide. Before the riots attack was quelled, personal injuries were inflicted, the marks of which the victims bore to their graves." [1]

B.W. Milner, associate archivist for the Dominion of Canada, echoes this point in the *Moncton Daily Times* of November 27th 1920:

"In 1856 occurred the Gourley Shanty Riot. North of Enfield, there were camps of railway navvies. There were groups of Protestants and Irish Roman Catholics, the headquarters of the former being Gourley's Shanty. A riot occurred at the 'Corpus Christi' procession, in consequence of the Protestants jeering and ridiculing in a most offensive way the most sacred rites of the Catholics. The Irish resented this scandalous conduct, not verbally, but with good cudgels. They went at it with as much good will as at a Donnybrook Fair. As the result there were many raw heads and broken bones, and the shanty was demolished. Except for its ulterior results the affair in itself was one of bad blood and of no lasting importance, but Mr. Howe elevated it into a place in Nova Scotia history by publishing a letter in a Halifax newspaper appealing to the Protestants of Nova Scotia to unite to resist the aggressions of the Roman Catholic Church." [2]

The major riot took place near what is today Lower Sackville, close to the road that leads towards Windsor Junction. The other common flaw of these histories is the assumption that the riot took place on Corpus Christi Day. That day is normally celebrated on the first Thursday after Trinity Sunday. May 26th 1856, the day of the vicious rioting, fell on a Monday, and therefore the earliest that the alleged taunting could have taken place was May 22nd 1856. This is significant in that it tends to support Howe's claim that the attack was undertaken with some planning, and not a spontaneous display of religious indignation.

There was much more to the events than these details allow, in spite of Milner's assertion that it was of "no lasting importance," and one detail has never previously been considered. From the viewpoint of railway history, the riot was notable for making Nova Scotia a link between the social conditions that had been created by the British railway mania of 1846 – when more than two hundred railway bills were before Parliament as speculators sought to cash in on the technological revolution – and labour strife that would develop in the United States some two decades later. It was a situation that Forman – despite his experience with navvies in Scotland (he certainly knew of the Stonehaven riot near Aberdeen in 1848, and at Penrith in 1846) – his novice engineering staff, the contractors and the politicians had never dealt with before.

Nova Scotians were not unfamiliar with navvies. The name comes from "navigator," the term applied to the labourers who fanned out over Britain to dig the canals that were, prior to the advent of the railway, the "new" form of transportation in the Industrial Revolution. Canal owners were to that day what railway barons would become less than a century later, and a great many canal owners, like the Duke of Bridgewater, would lead determined political opposition to the creation of railways, to no avail. Some navvies had come to Nova Scotia to build the Shubenacadie Canal. This waterway was to link Dartmouth, on Nova Scotia's Atlantic coast, with Maitland on the Bay of Fundy, by way of the Grand Lake. By this route, barges like *Lilly* and *Avery* would carry goods to and from places like Parrsboro and Saint John, New Brunswick.

"One of Thomas Telford's pupils, Francis Hall, was the engineer who designed the canal in 1826. In fact, Telford had some shares in the venture. Reasons for the lengthy construction delays were that the frigid winters damaged the locks, and money ran out for construction. Scottish and Irish stone masons had been brought over to construct the locks, and the poor souls had a very hard time when the company went bankrupt, and they were stranded here in the wilderness. However many of them eked out a living somehow, and their descendants still live in our area."[3]

The economic failure of the canal project was observed by 14-year-old brewery heir John "Jackey" Molson, who spent eleven days in Halifax and recorded his observations in a May 1841 diary:

"As we passed along, on the road we saw the remains of a canal. It was a most foolish undertaking and turned out in the ruin of many who invested their money in the stock. The most ridiculous part of it was their importing granite from Scotland for building the locks, although there was granite in Nova Scotia. If it was for some public building it would have been a different matter, but for canal locks it was the height of imprudence and extravagance."[4]

This was not the end of the Shubenacadie Canal, however, but even had it been a success, its days were numbered, since its eventual reconstruction would see the advent of the Nova Scotia Railway, which would – as railways had in Great Britain – reduce any canal to a secondary route of communication. Indeed, the railway later passed over the canal on a bridge at Grand Lake (Enfield) that was said to have deliberately been built so low as to prevent the passage of barges. The first bridge had been a moveable span, to allow the barges free passage through to the locks. The canal takes on greater significance later in this history of the railway.

The navvies worked in groups that would resemble armies. At the height of the railway craze in Britain, the largest of these would belong to Thomas Brassey, a contemporary of George Stephenson, who helped Brassey obtain a contract to build a railway viaduct. He later got one of the contracts to build the Grand Junction Railway linking Birmingham to Liverpoool, and in 1841 obtained the contract to build the Paris & Le Havre Railway in France. Over the next ten years Brassey's navvies were employed on railway projects in mainland Europe, and in England on the Lancaster & Carlisle Railway, the Caledonian Railway, the Great Northern Railway, the Tilbury & Southend Railway, and the Shrewsbury & Hereford Railway. In Canada, Brassey built the Grand Trunk Railway, and began working on the New Brunswick portion of the ill-starred European & North American line, just a small part of the more than 6,500 miles of railway (including one-sixth of the British network and over fifty per cent of the railways in France) that his "army" would construct.

This army was typical of the times:

"A third of the navvies were Irish, a third Scots, and a third English: that was the beginning of the trouble. Easy-going Roman Catholic Irish, Presbyterian Scots, and impartially belligerent English. The Irish did not look for a fight. As the *Scottish Herald* reported, they camped, with their women and children, in some of the most secluded glades, and although most of the huts showed an amazing disregard of comfort, 'the hereditary glee of the occupants seemed not a whit impaired.' This glee enraged the Scots, who then added to their one genuine grievance (the fact that the Irishmen would work for less pay and so tended to bring down wages) their sanctified outrage that the Irish should regard the Sabbath as a holiday, a day of recreation on which they sang and lazed about. As for the Scots, all they did on a Sunday was drink often and pray occasionally, and it needed only an odd quart of whisky and a small prayer to make them half daft with Presbyterian fervour. They then beat up the godless Irish. The Irish defended themselves and this further annoyed the Scots, so that by the middle of 1845 there was near civil war among the railway labourers. The English, mainly from Yorkshire and Lancashire, would fight anyone, but they preferred to attack the Irish. The contractors tried to keep the men, particularly the Irish and Scots, apart, employing them on different parts of the line, but the Scots were not so easily turned from their religious purposes."[5]

The value of this workforce to any great construction project cannot be underestimated:

"Their capacity for work was incredible. Brassey himself calculated the labour done by a typical navvy in a day and reckoned that each man would lift nearly twenty tons of earth on a shovel over his own head into a wagon. It was no ordinary man who could do such work. The unremitting intensity with which the gangs were expected to labour required much conditioning. No matter how brutal, how rough and rugged, how strong, how inured to savage treatment were the agricultural labourers who abandoned the land and turned up at the construction camps, not one of them found himself able to keep

Above: Enfield Bridge – the first bridge across the Shubenacadie canal – was a moveable structure, but this feature did not help the waterway overcome the competition from Forman's railway. The second bridge, seen in this photo dated 1889, was built low to prevent barges from using the canal.
(Nova Scotia Archives and Records Management Service, N-5304)

Below: Elmsdale station. Seen in a rare photograph, this building on the main line in Hants County was typical of the utilitarian stations planned by James Richardson Forman for the Nova Scotia Railway. (Courtesy Doug Fleming)

up with the gangs. It seldom took less than a year of continuous application and graft to turn a labourer into a navvy. For the first months he could not stand the pace for more than a few hours; slowly his capacity increased, as did his appetite and need for the meat and beer which comprised the navvy's sole diet. The apprentice navvy would consume what he could earn, month by month the quantity of both would slowly increase, until by the year's end he was about as strong as a man could be, and would eat and drink at the day's end quantities that astonished those who watched. Then he could spend all the hours of daylight digging and shifting and drink and fight all the hours of night. He had become the most extraordinary specimen of obdurate human brawn. These were men made almost into machines. Set to a task they would do it, like steam shovels of a later day; all they asked was to be fuelled up and have their heads set against a rock face and they would work till it was cut down. All they needed was to be fed their meat and beer and they would work as no men had worked before. You could not expect anything else of them. They would not be nice, nor polite, nor sing hymns when you wanted them to, nor go to church; they would not respect their social betters or acknowledge their existence in any way; they would not be obedient husbands or good fathers. They worked their way into the landscape, and they worked their way off it. Into the countryside of Old England they introduced a new social being – a mighty colossus of total and utter obliviousness and indifference. They disregarded all social conventions just as they disregarded the lie of God's land, cutting their ditches and embankments regardless of feeling or sentiment, or care for boundaries, or respect for ancient rights [sic]. Their appearance seemed to augur coming anarchy; their wildness and their barbaric ways of weatherproof life seemed to threaten the security and the composure of all the surrounding countryside, but in fact, wherever they went, they were only aware of themselves. Their wild debauches, their drunken riots were less alarming than they threatened. In a way they kept their disorder to themselves, not out of respect for the feelings of others but because what was not attracted to them in the way of drink, fun, and women they gave no thought to. They ravished no daughters; they broke into no halls; they embarrassed no congregations. If they scandalised local opinion they did not know it, or relish it; they lived entirely according to their own lights and by their own customs. If they threatened to undermine the social order, it was not deliberate. They were working men and once the work was done they disturbed the peace no more."[6]

As Coleman records in his book, one of Brassey's timekeepers noted with awe:

"I think as fine a spectacle as any man could witness, who is accustomed to look at work, is to see a cutting in full operation, with about twenty wagons being filled, every man at his post, and every man with his shirt open, working in the heat of the day, the gangers looking about and everything going like clockwork."[7]

It was to these men that Joseph Howe would turn to build his noble railway, following the philosophy outlined by George Pemberton. Ironically, some Irish immigrants had already had a bad experience associated with the name Joseph Howe, as this report of 1853 noted:

"Arrivals from 1st October to the 6th November: 'The emigrants arrived during the month of October have landed in good health, with the exception of those on board the *Fingal* from Liverpool, among whom thirty-four deaths occurred previous to arrival.

The greater part of the passengers by this vessel were transferred from the *Joseph Howe*, which vessel had sailed from Liverpool on the 12th August, but having put into Cork in distress, she was condemned, her passengers landed, and sent back to Liverpool, from whence they sailed a second time on the 5th September, in the *Fingal*, but, owing to this detention, the stores of many of the poor families were expended, and, being thereby without the means for necessarily renewing their stock, they became altogether dependent upon the ship's allowance. To this cause, added to a long and stormy voyage, may in a great measure be attributed the sickness and mortality; as, immediately on being landed at Grosse Isle, where they were detained a few days to wash their clothes, they were allowed a wholesome nourishing diet, and during these few days of detention no further cases of disease appeared among them.'

The great majority of these passengers were Irish families coming out to friends. One poor woman, with four children, was going to her husband in New Orleans. Several other families were going to relations in Virginia, Kentucky, and Missouri. Of 30 families found necessary to be assisted, there were but 12 male adults over 14 years, with 66 women and 70 children."[8]

The *Fingal*, carrying the wretched passengers from *Joseph Howe*, arrived in Quebec on October 22nd 1854 after some forty-seven days at sea.

The report continued with a list of railways already under construction, with which Howe would have to compete when ground was broken for the Nova Scotia Railway by LeMarchant in that same year:

"The following railways were under construction:
    The Quebec & Richmond - 100 miles
    The Montreal & Portland - 31 miles
    The Prescott & Bytown - 54 miles
    The Toronto & Simcoe - 66 miles
    The Great Western, from Hamilton to Windsor - 180 miles
Labourers were required for railway building and the lumber trade."[9]

Howe's competition was more local in nature, as the report of 1854 noted. New Brunswick's newborn railways were also importing labourers: "At St. Andrew's, 417 passengers were landed during the year, chiefly labourers for the St. Andrew's and Quebec Railway, the rest bound to Canada but driven in there by stress of weather, being too late in the season for Quebec."[10] Howe soon found that skilled navvies were in short supply, and he seized the opportunity created by the Crimean War to recruit his labour pool. This was spurred in large part by the man whom Howe had sought to avoid having build the province's railway, Sir Samuel Morton Peto.

It was Peto who approached the government to build the railway in the Crimea, and whatever his motive, Peto's method saved British honour, if not its army, from certain disaster, as Cooke has so brilliantly documented. It should be noted, however, that the success of the Crimean railway was not due to the military involvement, but to an army of patriotic and pugnacious navvies, recruited by Peto's partner, the dynamic Edward Betts:

"On 30th November (1854) Edward Betts... wrote to [Secretary of State for War] Newcastle saying they proposed to send 200-250 platelayers, navvies, and miners, ten gangers, twenty rough masons or bricklayers, eighty carpenters with three foremen, twenty blacksmiths and foremen, ten enginemen and fitters, four timekeepers, one chief clerk, one draftsman, two practical assistant engineers, and one Chief Engineer. He also stipulated that this force must come under the direct superintendence of the contractors' engineer. The men were civilians; they were not to be subject to military law, and were to be known as the Civil Engineer Corps.... Many of those engaged had already served for a while in Canada, on the Grand Trunk, as had Beattie, who was to be Chief Engineer of the Crimea Railway."[11]

Beattie was James Beatty, Peto's right-hand man on the survey for the European & North American line in Nova Scotia and New Brunswick, and the Grand Trunk in Upper Canada. Ever anxious for a fight, and just as eager to display their patriotism, the navvies responded overwhelmingly:

"Peto, Betts & Brassey advertised for men, and on Saturday, 2nd December (1854), and on the following Monday, their office in Waterloo Road, on the Surrey side of the bridge, was besieged by navies, masons, carpenters, blacksmiths, and gangers. They came in crowds, and the contractors could pick and choose. The outer room of the office was filled, and those out in the street tried to elbow their way in. It was like a theatre crush. Many of the men seemed to want to fight rather than shift muck.
'Hope we shall get out quick,' said one. 'Hope they'll hold out till we come.'
'We'll give it to them with the pick and crowbar, them Roosians, instead of the rifle,' said another.
On the second day the door was closed and a notice put up saying: NO MORE MEN WANTED. But some still lingered about, hoping to be taken on after all."[12]

This odd assortment of unlikely heroes, who had been reviled in the past by the press for their unruly and wicked ways, suddenly became the flower of British manhood, as *The Illustrated London News* proclaimed, and was repeated in the *NovaScotian*:

"The men employed in our engineering works have been long known as the very elite of England, as to physical power – broad, muscular, massive fellows, who are scarcely to be matched in Europe. Animated, too, by as ardent a British spirit as beats under any uniform, if ever these men come to hand-to-hand fighting with the enemy, they will fell them like ninepins. Disciplined and enough of them, they could walk from end to end of the continent."[13]

Inspired by this kind of hyperbole, and the evident enthusiasm of the British-based navvies, Howe may have been determined to do his bit for Queen and country, and decided the best way to assist was to raise a similar army of volunteers from the legion of expatriate navvies at work in the United States. It is more likely he never intended for them to go on to the Black Sea, and would hire them on the works of his railway once they were arrived in Nova Scotia. So it was he went south seeking his men. He was soon very quickly and firmly rebuffed by the Americans and came home under a cloud of political ignominy.

It was not that he was unsuccessful. A great many would-be Hectors downed their tools in the US and followed Howe back to Nova Scotia. There is a distinct possibility some of them participated in the Gourley Shanty affair. It is certain not one of them got aboard a transport ship for the Black Sea. It is equally possible that within Howe's mind, he foresaw the idyll of navvies from all corners of old England working in harmony on his railway line, perhaps toiling to the strains of the popular navvy song, "Ye Sons of Albion":

> Ye Sons of Albion, rise to arms,
> And meet the haughty band;
> They threaten us with war's alarms,
> And ruin to our land
> But let no rebel Frenchman *sans-culottes,*
> Nor the dupes of tyranny boast
> To conquer the English, the Irish, and the Scots,
> Or to land upon our coast,
> To land upon our coast.

It is just as certain not all of Howe's recruits were inspired by his love of the Empire, and that trouble would follow the Irish to Nova Scotia should not have come as a surprise. Desperation, and disillusionment with the unfulfilled promise of the American Dream, may have played a part in their exodus:

"In South Boston in 1850, the Irish slums were buildings from three to six stories high, with whole families living in one room, without light or ventilation, and even the cellars crowded with families....

Saloons were the curse of the neighborhood, and police records abundantly reflected this unhealthy condition. The death rate among the children of the Irish poor was alarmingly high. Disease, particularly during cholera epidemics, always ravaged the immigrants living in hovels in the western and eastern sections of New York City, worse than in other communities. Secret societies arose in the shantytowns among Irish laborers, with such names as 'The Corkonians,' 'The Connaughtmen,' and 'The Far Downs,' who engaged in bloody brawls and riots, which even the repeated denunciations of the Church authorities, seemed powerless to stop. In some of the 'better class' tenement houses in New York, Negroes were preferred as tenants, to the poor Irish and Germans. (There was a row of tenements in New York called 'Ragpicker's Paradise,' inhabited entirely by Germans with their dogs, who collected and sold rags, paper, and bones.)"[14]

The conditions Howe's navvies left in Boston were not much better than those that had forced them from Limerick, Londonderry, or Liverpool. The work promised by railway construction was not necessarily the panacea modern historians have supposed it to be:

"Newspapers friendly to the Irish immigrant warned him to stay away from the canal and railroad construction projects, for 'these railroads have been the ruin of thousands of our poor people,' and their workers are treated 'like slaves' by the railroad contractors. Wages were low, usually $1.00 a day, but often less; they were not clearly fixed and were paid partly in whiskey and 'store pay,' or merchandise, sold at high prices.

Friends of the Irish urged them to form protective associations, with objectives somewhat like the trade unions, in order to stop competition, rivalries, and fights between warring gangs that drove wages down in their competition for the available jobs. Above all, the Irish were advised to go to the country to work on farms, or squat upon government land in the West, to 'do anything,' in fact, in preference to railroading." [15]

Still, they came, and brought with them a lifestyle and history that Howe could not have ignored or been unaware of during his ill-fated recruiting trip:

"Irish workers had a bad reputation for rioting and brawling, and the newspapers of the middle of the last century are full of graphic accounts of their bloody battles. In 1853, for example, the eviction of an Irishman from a circus performance at Somerset, Ohio, for smoking a pipe, started a battle in which Irish railroad workers fought all night and into the next day. A company of militia had to be called from Zanesville to restore order....

The brawls were often efforts, however misguided and unwise, to achieve an improvement in labor standards at a time when the labor movement had hardly begun. There were strikes for higher wages on internal improvement projects, many of which led to a display of force, particularly when contractors later refused to respect the agreements they had been forced to accept....

In 1840, a serious riot broke out when the wages of Irish laborers on an aqueduct in New York City, were cut from $1.00 to 75 cents a day. There were similar disturbances, caused by wage reductions, on the Illinois Central, the Buffalo and State railroads, the Steubenville and Indiana, and other lines." [16]

Howe's labourers came at a premium, however:

"To add to the expense, the cost of labour, as was reported, was one-third higher than at any time during the previous twenty years....

The Engineer reported that during the year 1855, the average number of men employed daily was 630, the maximum on any one day being 1242.

[During 1856] the complaint was being made that labour and other commodities were costly, owing to a general rise throughout the markets of the world. Labourers were seldom paid any less than 5 shillings per day, and 6 shillings per day was a frequent wage. Masons usually made 10 to 12 shillings per day. The average number of men employed daily was 1622." [17]

It would appear from the newspaper reports of the Gourley Shanty affair that these wages were not sufficient for any of the Irish navvies, who were immediately singled out as the perpetrators of the dastardly attack, and the native sons of the eastern counties identified as the victims. The only other salient report on the events came in the June 3rd issue of the *Morning Chronicle*, in which it was tersely noted: "The detachment of the 76th Foot, which went up to the Railway last week, returned to the city on Saturday evening, bringing in some six prisoners." [18]

The series of incidents which occurred between Sackville and the end of the track at the Nine Mile River in Elmsdale, Hants County were not to be unexpected, given the leapfrogging of Catholic and Protestant churches along the route of the line. It began with St. John Vianney Roman Catholic Church and First Sackville Presbyterian Church on the Beaverbank Road in Sackville (closest to the site of the riot, as court testimony will later show), Saint Francis by the Lake Anglican Church at First lake in Sackville, Saint Rose of Lima Roman Catholic Church at Windsor Junction (now at Fall River), St. Margaret's Anglican Church at Oakfield, St. Bernard's Catholic Church at Enfield, and St. Matthew's Presbyterian at Elmsdale. Barbara Grantmyre notes the effects of the canal and railway construction on this area:

"Work on the Shubenacadie Canal and the railway brought more people into the area, particularly an influx of Irish construction men, some of whom settled near the 'Crossing' as it was known until 1862 when the name Enfield was chosen at the suggestion of Thomas B. Donaldson, after his native town of Enfield, Connecticuit [sic], U.S.A.

As Enfield became a center through which produce was shipped to market and was easier of access to the Roman Catholics of East Hants than their church, Saint John's, at Nine Mile River, this church was raised from its foundation and brought to Enfield." [19]

Grantmyre goes on to record the presence of the Presbyterian ministry in the area:

"Not the less devoted and hard working were the Protestant pioneer clergy who traveled by horseback, foot or boat hundreds of miles a year to minister to their flocks. Among these gentlemen of the cloth were… the Rev. John Cameron, from 1844 to 1879 pastor of Nine Mile River, Kennetcook and Elmsdale." [20]

Such was the state of the relationship between the churches that Nova Scotia was something of a sectarian tinder box at the time, and Howe, Condon and Tupper would all contribute to the stirring. It is interesting that in his response to Howe's provocative letter, Condon makes no mention of any slight made toward the Irish by Presbyterians jeering at the Corpus Christi parade. He reiterated his claim that Howe had in fact "entrapped" the railway labourers to come to Nova Scotia, always intending for them to work on the railway rather than battle the Russians in the Crimea.

"Disappointed, baffled, exasperated, by the action of the American Government and of the Irishmen in the United States who made the recruiting scheme the laughing stock and scorn of the world, and rendered the mission!!! [sic] abortive, 'tis natural that he should pour out the vial of his wrath and vent his long pent up spleen against them…." [21]

Condon crowed with delight at the subsequent unreported events of June 17th, after the soldiers had deposited their captives with the sheriff:

"Thank God, in this country, as yet, justice to an Irish railway labourer is as much due as to an Executive Councillor or even a Railway Commissioner, and notwithstanding all that has been said and written by Mr. Howe, to prejudge these poor men, notwithstanding that his letter of this day draws such a horrid picture of their barbarity, the public will be astonished to learn that the Judge, today, decided to take Bail for each man in what – the awful sum of *Twenty-five Pounds,* each, furnished by two securities." [22]

He went on to assert that Irishmen had a right and a duty to resist being inveigled into fighting for Britain, that they had no such duty to proclaim their loyalty to the British, and that they had every right to expect their homeland to rise to nationhood.

It was the Halifax *Catholic* newspaper which raised the incidents of taunting by Presbyterians as the cause of the violence, without giving specific details. Testimony at the trial of one of the rioters later indicated the animosity might actually have arisen in a dispute between a labourer and an overseer about the quality of the labourer's work. Unfortunately issues of the Halifax *Catholic* from that date are not contained in the collection of the Public Archives of Nova Scotia, and contemporary histories must be relied upon.

"The Halifax *Catholic* published a very mild article on the subject, not defending the Catholics, who were the aggressors, but deprecating the provocation which caused them to commit a breach of the peace; the editor only said, 'that knowing how sensitive the Irish people are to everything which affects their religion or the character of their clergy, Protestants of any nation, who are brought into contact with them, would show better their respect for the precepts of the Bible if they abstained from those taunts and provocations, and from actions in which they were too prone to indulge.'" [23]

It was this criticism that fuelled an indignant response from Howe, and moved the riots from being a railway labour issue to one of religious rights and provincial politicking. In any event, work on the line continued amid much tension, but with barely any significant delays. Indeed, according to the survey conducted by James and Edward Trout,[24] the work on the railway proceeded at a methodical pace. The Trouts list the dates of completion of each section as:

```
To Mile House.................... Feb. 1855.................... 4 miles
Mile House to Bedford.......... July 1855................... 8
Bedford to Grand Lake.......... Jan. 1857.................... 23
Grand Lake to Elmsdale......... Jan. 1858.................... 30
```

The trial of the first of the ten rioters took place Monday, December 8th 1856, presided over by Judge William Blowers Bliss of the Nova Scotia Supreme Court. James O'Brien had chosen to be tried separately, and it is from his trial that the salient details of the Gourley Shanty incident came to light, and on which most of the popular histories of the affair rest. The account of the trial was provided by the *Morning Chronicle*.

The first witness called was Thomas Gooley (the name was changed in subsequent reports to Gourley), the owner of the house in which the attack occurred. He described the shanty as being in the Township of Sackville between Long Lake and the railway line, the most definitive description of the location of the attack. Robert Easton of River John (his name was later changed to Gaston in subsequent reports, and both names are used here for sake of clarity) – a foreman on the line, and a resident of the shanty – testified that he had heard of a planned attack a few days previously, but did not believe the rumours. He was the only witness to positively identify O'Brien on the scene, with a stick in his hand and participating in the beating of the other men. He also testified that he had seen Patrick O'Brien, and men named Sullivan and Scanlan on the scene. Easton (Gaston) said he had been threatened by James O'Brien some time prior to the May 26th incident: "... he was a workman under me, and said he was going to thrash all the Nova Scotians on the road and I reprimanded him for it. He threatened me, and at last accomplished his design." [25]

Easton (Gaston) denied having sworn revenge against O'Brien for the threats. He noted the rioters spoke English and Irish, but most of them spoke in their native tongue at the time of the attack. Roderick McKay testified as the only man to have been spared a beating by the Catholic gang, because he had been ill at the shanty at the time, and had held a child in his arms to protect it from the attackers. His testimony then took an all-too-familiar course: "The witness was here called upon to identify any parties in court who were in the riot, but he could not prove any." [26]

The counsel for the Irish navvies, James W. Johnston, had insisted that all the accused be allowed to sit in the courtroom during testimony, placed among the spectators in order to ensure that they could be identified from a crowd. This proved to be a masterful defense, for only one other witness was willing to identify his attacker, while others said they knew their attackers, but noted that those men were not in the court:

> "Daniel McKenzie was at Gooley's house at the attack last May. Did not identify O'Brien as being one of the Rioters. Knew three of them but saw none of them in Court.
>
> Charles Robertson – was living at Gooley's Shanty at the time of the riot. Knew James O'Brien – did not see him there. I was down to the lake when the riot began. There were about 130 who broke in, went in the house and were there about 20 minutes after they pushed in. I escaped by one of the broken doors. I can speak of three of the rioters, but not of James O'Brien.
>
> Samuel Cameron, a young man was in Gooley's Shanty the day of the riot, but could not identify any one in Court as one of the parties. Don't know James O'Brien.
>
> Alexander McSellan was at Gooley's Shanty at the time of the riot – know two or three men who were present at the riot, Tom Power was one – can't see any body around the benches who was present at court." [27]

The final prosecution witness was John Martin, who claimed he spoke nothing but Gaelic:

> "... as he spoke nothing but Gaelic, the court could not examine him, for want of an interpreter [sic]. The Sexton of St. Matthew's Church being called upon, said that he did not understand Pictou Gaelic. He could not interpret the party's evidence, and was not sworn." [28]

At this point the prosecution, led by Attorney-General William Young (who was also the premier at the time) rested its case, and the *Morning Chronicle* reported that as the defense's opening testimony consisted of ninety minutes of evidence given in Irish, "the evidence was of no importance whatsoever."

The second day of the trial opened with the curious disappearance of several jurors, who were summarily fined ten shillings each. The first witness called was James Stewart Clark, who was present when beating victim Robert Easton (Gaston) gave his deposition to the justice of the peace, James Cochrane, two days after the riot. It was on the strength of this deposition that O'Brien and the other nine accused were arrested. Cochrane also testified, but Johnston focused specifically on the details of the difficulties the two men encountered in their trip from the Beaver Bank Road to the site of the attack. This would prove pivotal in O'Brien's defense.

Patrick Lyons testified he had spent most of the day with James O'Brien, at the home of Mrs. Lee, where he and O'Brien were boarders. He said the two men had played cards all day until supper. This testimony appears to contradict the *Catholic*'s claim that a Corpus Christi parade had been in progress on the day of the event, or at least indicates that O'Brien was not devout enough to be in attendance. Lyons claimed it would have been impossible for O'Brien to have been at Gourley's shanty on the day, for it would have taken him three hours to get through the bushes and swamps to the house. Easton (Gaston), Lyons said, had been O'Brien's overseer on work undertaken at Downey's cutting. On his recall, Lyons said he had had:

> "… a conversation with Gaston at a watering place on the Beaver Bank Road, and I asked him what reason he had for swearing against James O'Brien, John O'Brien, Patrick O'Brien, and Daniel Sullivan, and he said it was because of the dispute he had with them in Downey's work; and as he was a constable, he had the power to punish them. It looked as if Gaston would have his spite out against them." [29]

John Frier, a contractor on the works, testified O'Brien was "well behaved and a good workman.…" He testified it would have taken four hours to go from Lee's to Gourley's shanty. When Easton (Gaston) was recalled, he claimed the distance between the two houses could be covered in an hour and a quarter, faster if he was running, and that it was only five or six miles between the two, where the railway roadbed was flat and open. He went on to testify:

> "Patrick Cody, who said in court he could speak nothing but Irish, worked with me and spoke English freely. The statement that I was persecuting O'Brien and others out of revenge is an utter fabrication. I can't speak Irish and I could not have directed Cody to his work unless he understood what I said. I never met but one man on the Railroad that could not understand English, and the other men had to tell him what to do." [30]

This testimony was enough to split the jury on a 6-6 vote after only two hours of debate. The other nine accused rioters were put on trial together on December 12th, with much the same testimony, although Charles Robertson for the prosecution testified that a man called Kennedy (present at the trial) was one of the rioters, as was a man called Scannell, who was to appear in court. Easton (Gaston) appeared once again, and swore that the three O'Briens were at the riot and pointed to Sullivan and Landers, who were among the nine other accused. The verdict was much the same as in James O'Brien's trial. The *Catholic* was triumphant in passing its verdict:

> "It can be truly said that in this instance 'good has come from evil,' as had Mr. Howe not made this affair a subject of notice for his speech, in all probability the poor men would have been confined for six months in jail previous to their trial, and now very likely be in the Penitentiary. Mr. Howe's conduct saved those poor men from ignominy, and was the

means of arousing a sympathy in their behalf, which secured for them eminent counsel and friends who were determined that they should have a fair trial."[31]

The *Catholic*'s analysis, however, does not explain the apparently sudden inability of several prosecution witnesses to identify their attackers, or the inexplicable inability of two sworn witnesses to speak a word of English when they took the stand. Howe shot back with another irate letter in the *Morning Chronicle*:

"My speech at Temperance Hall was not made till some days after the attack on Gourlay's shantie [sic]. It was not made until I had spent two days on the Western and two days on the Eastern Road, talking with everybody who could give me any information. It was not made until I had sauntered around the town, and gathered unmistakable evidence that the rioters on the Railway were backed by the sympathies of some, at least, of their countrymen here. Then it was that I thought it time to speak out, and the miserable attempts at bullying and intimidation that followed convinced me that I was right. The results of the miserable farce played off in the Supreme Court have not surprized [sic] me. I was neither surprized [sic] at what was, or at what was not done, but this I saw from the commencement to the end, that the acquittal of all the prisoners was a foregone conclusion."[32]

The incident at Gourley's Shanty, and the tactics described by the Philips article, bear striking similarities, and it may be that Nova Scotia's Irish labourers were a precursor of those who would haunt the Pennsylvania coal fields in the two following decades, the notorious "Molly Maguires." Whether or not there was a society known as the Molly Maguires does not detract from the fact that such factions were operating in the Pennsylvania coal fields as early as 1854, the time that Howe was recruiting his navvies in the United States: "These Irish came to Pennsylvania as early as 1854, when lawlessness in Schuylkill county already revealed that there was a tough organization known as the 'Buckshots' – the forerunners of the 'Mollies.'"[33]

The same site includes another article that notes:

"At the time of the so-called 'Mollie Maguire riots' in the hard coal fields of Pennsylvania, the Mollies were declared to be members of the well-known secret and fraternal organization, the Ancient Order of Hibernians.
The AOH was a large and powerful Irish society extending throughout the United States. Outside the coal regions it seems to have enjoyed a reasonably good reputation....
In the early 1870s conditions grew extremely bad, when local miners did everything they could to scare away the 'scab' help imported to run the mines at times when the companies attempted to force wage cuts.
It was the common thing for a dozen or so ruffians to form a gang, arm themselves with all sorts of weapons, sweep through a mining camp and force all to join their party. As the numbers increased rapidly, few were inclined to resist....
It should be noticed at this point that there seems to be little or no evidence of lawlessness among the other nationalities employed at the mines – the Pennsylvania-Germans, for instance. It is worthy to note early in this account that the Mollies found

it convenient to 'pick a fight' or find cause to 'rub out' any who got in their way, which, as it appears by the accounts, usually accounted for men of English, Welsh, or German extraction....

The Mollies dictated to mine superintendents who they wanted hired, or fired....

The Mollies were not pikers – in a fashion – they had secret signs and passwords for use when necessary, but they seldom used such because their boldness obviated their need. If a Mollie was arrested he could obtain a hundred perjurers who would readily swear an "alibi," but not one single person could be found who would witness for the state....

During all this time none of the Mollies had been convicted of the crimes they had committed. Trials they had – but no convictions. Alibis were as readily obtained as weeds along the road." [34]

The true nature of this organization has become contentious. Jim (Seamus) Haldeman claims the Mollies were the invention of Franklin Gowan, president of the Reading Railroad, who called the major coal companies to a meeting in New York, in order to fix the price of coal:

"Not only were the miners being taken advantage of, but the general public was at the mercy of this cartel and its ambitious greed. Coal was fixed at a price of $5 a ton, thus being the first case of price fixing in the United States. As a result of that, the general public had no sympathy whatsoever for the miners and their plight. Clearly the miners were blamed for the outrageous price of coal. The Worker's Benevolent Association, to which most of the miners belonged, had made minor advances in achieving better working conditions and compensation for their toil. Their advances were abruptly halted by the Coal operators. In December of 1874 pay was reduce by 20%. Very soon after that another 10% cut was levied upon the miners. The miners went out on strike for 7 months, only to come crawling back at the demands of the company. Gowan had been informed that the miners were going to strike and he managed to stockpile enough coal to meet the cold winter's demands. Many of the men who supported the strike were singled out by the coal operators as trouble makers and would not be called back to work. In order to gain the support and sympathy of the populace, Gowan was quick to trump up charges that the troubles in the area were cause by a gang of ruffians known as the 'Molly Maguires.'

At this time there was no such known society in the United States, but Franklin Gowan made sure to re-invent this organization in order to recoup the sympathy of the citizens then living in the region, both German, Welsh, and Irish alike. Diabolically he linked the names of the men who led the efforts of the 'Great Strike' to the fictitious organization he called the Molly Maguires. Franklin Gowan wanted these men out of his mines and out of the area for good, to be punished and banished forever in the cold hard jails of the Commonwealth of Pennsylvania. It was then many of the men became extremely desperate and would cross the line of insanity to achieve their goals of a decent life for their families. Some of the men known as the Molly Maguires were probably guilty of many of the accused crimes against the state. They had been pushed to the wall and would strike back any way they could. In 1873 Mr. Gowan hired the monstrous thugs of the Alan Pinkerton detective agency to infiltrate the coal fields and expose the men who were at the core of all this mayhem. The most infamous of the successful detectives sent in was James McParlin, alias Jamie McKenna. In the 3 years McParlin was in the area he gathered and fabricated enough evidence to permanently remove 20 or so innocent Irishmen from their families and friends forever." [35]

Haldeman's article exhibits a certain pro-labour bias, however, as does Walter Boyle's examination of the relationship between the group and the Ancient Order of Hibernians. Boyle writes as historian of the Alec Campbell, Mauch Chunk Division of Jim Thorpe, Pennsylvania, The Ancient Order of Hibernians in America, Inc. He claims the Molly Maguires were the figment of a pro-capitalist newspaper editor:

> "In 1868, John Siney of Saint Clair, a native of Ireland, formed the Worker's Benevolent Association (WBA). Strikes were an effective weapon for the WBA but violence was also perpetrated against the mine bosses. And even though union leaders were black listed, sometimes assaulted and killed, by 1870 the mine owners grudgingly agreed to recognize the WBA as a legitimate bargaining agent for the miners. A minimum day wage was instituted along with a sliding scale of wages based on the prevailing price of coal.
> The handwriting was on the wall for the mine owners. Any improvement in the lives of the Irish came at the expense of their profits. Added to this was the deep-seated prejudice against the Irish and the Roman Catholic Church prevalent among the leaders of industry in America in that era. The coal and railroad owners found an ally in Benjamin Bannan, editor of Pottsville's *Miner's Journal*. Bannan wrote editorials against Irish Catholics, their union, and their political aspirations. It was Bannan who introduced the name Molly Maguires to America. Molly Maguire was a legendary figure in Ireland, an old woman who led a group of poor farmers in secret violent attacks against absentee landlords' rent collectors. Through Bannan's editorials, the name Molly Maguires came to symbolize lawlessness and violence to the average law abiding citizen. Every crime occurring in the coal regions was blamed on the Molly Maguires until the name took on a dread connotation, much like Mafia in today's society. By linking the violence in the coal regions to a phantom group named Molly Maguires and then branding the WBA as Molly Maguires, Bannan and the coal operators hoped to break the power of the union." [36]

The notion that Irish navvies were attempting to manipulate wages and competition for the jobs on the Nova Scotia Railway was certainly entertained by managers on the project, as Thomas Rowland of Shubenacadie, the superintendent of the sixty men on the works there had stated. Had the Gourley Shanty riot been an attempt by a nascent gang of Molly Maguires, it is likely they would have met with the same opprobrium that was meted out to the Maguires in Pennsylvania almost from the moment the organization was created:

> "In vain, Archbishop Wood of Philadelphia fought the Molly Maguires with the whole power of the Catholic Church issuing an edict excommunicating all members of the organization, depriving them of all spiritual benefits, and refusing them burial in Catholic cemeteries. In vain, the Catholic priests throughout the five counties, under Father Bridgeman of Girardville, seeing that not even the Church's curse could check the course of crime, formed an organization popularly called the 'Sheet Irons,' which was to oppose the Molly Maguires politically and in every possible way." [37]

There is no reason to believe the Catholic Church endorsed the actions of the Gourley Shanty rioters; indeed, it has been suggested by Beck and others that the established church in Nova Scotia regarded the Irish immigrants with disdain: "At this stage the Halifax Irish were receiving no support from the Scottish Catholics. Bishop Colin MacKinnon of Arichat told Howe that his recent denunciation of the editors of the *Catholic* had given 'great satisfaction in this quarter....'" [38]

There can be no doubt, however, that politics, religion, and the Nova Scotia Railway were inextricably intertwined, a fact made clear three years after the Gourley's Shanty incident, when Forman was dismissed. Had he not so mistrusted and despised Sir Morton Peto, Howe would have done well to have the navvies treated by the English contractor's example, for Peto's works were less plagued by navvy riots than any other. The reason is explained in an article in *Harper's New Monthly* magazine of 1874:

> "Christian philanthropy has not been oblivious of the condition of these navvies, equally dreadful to themselves and dangerous to society. Among the most interesting of all home mission work is that which has been carried on by ladies of the highest culture and refinement among these barbarians of civilization.
>
> The result of improved systems of administration by Christian contractors has been more effectual, however, than any direct and immediate efforts by lay missionaries. Of these the work of Sir Morton Peto may be mentioned as a type. He broke up the ticket system i.e., the payment of wages by tickets to be redeemed at the shop established by the contractor. He paid all wages weekly. He opened the way for house to house visitation by Christian clergymen and laymen. He provided clean barracks in lieu of their huts of turf or stone. He provided everyone who could read with a *Bible*, and organized clubs for mutual help in case of sickness or misfortune." [39]

The article also contains an observation pointing to the heart of the problem that helped create Nova Scotia's riot:

> "In this country the work of the pick and the barrow is largely performed by Irish laborers. Their temporary villages are familiar to every traveler on our roads. Their management requires, on the part of the contractor, peculiar dexterity to avoid the loss inevitable from wasted hours or misapplied energies. In brief, the railroad contractor has under him an army of men without the discipline of an army; he must exercise over them the control of a general without being invested with a general's authority." [40]

Still, the Gourley Shanty riot did not create such animosity that the province would sour on the notion of importing its labourers. In its August 30th 1856 edition, in the middle of the political ill will created by Howe's intemperate response to the attack, the *Morning Chronicle* was still advocating the use of immigrant labour: "Everybody feels that the country is suffering for want of an adequate supply of labour, and yet no effort is made to divert to our shores even the most insignificant portion of that tide of Emigration which is continually flowing from the Old world to the New." [41]

The newspaper went on to link the province's poor development of farmland as a symptom of this condition, but added:

> "[But] it is not only the Agricultural interest that is suffering for lack of labour. Almost every other branch of native industry is languishing from the same cause, and very many householders experience the most serious inconvenience for want of domestic servants,

male and female. We have ourselves known many a promising enterprise abandoned, simply because skilled labour was either not to be had at all, or if to be had, only at ruinous prices. We believe that at this moment there are scores of persons desirous of building within the City, and who are only waiting for a fall in the rate of wages and the price of materials. The want of labour, above all other things, is retarding the prosperity of the Country, for which the only effectual remedy is a sound and well digested scheme of Emigration." [42]

Ten years after the Gourley Shanty debacle, the provincial government was still looking toward the dispossessed of other lands to help build the province's railways. In his 1866 report to the legislature, immigration agent H.G. Pineo had noted:

"A very extensive emigration took place last summer from England and Scotland to the United States. This was induced by agents sent over from America who engaged men and women for special employment, advancing their passage money to America, the amount, by contract, to be gradually deducted from their earnings after arrival. I proposed a similar measure to the contractors on the line of railway from Truro to Pictou in May, offering to place the business in the hands of persons on whom perfect reliance could be had, should it meet their approval, but received no answer." [43]

The legislators were quicker to respond, with a resolution appointing more European agents, ostensibly to promote the mining industry:

"That owing to the great scarcity of labor for mining and agricultural purposes, and in relation to the construction of our public works, the Executive Council are of opinion that the prosperity of the country may be increased, and a large saving of public money effected, by the introduction of able-bodied immigrants at the present time, and with that object and for the purpose of diffusing information touching the resources of this province and of contributing to lessen their passage money of immigrants to this country, propose:

That an advance be made to Captain Liebman of $200 towards his expenses in visiting Germany as an immigration agent, and, until further notification, he be entitled to receive $10 for each able-bodied immigrant landed in this province;

That Henry Boggs, esquire, in London, Alexander Campbell, in Glasgow, and James R. DeWolf, in Liverpool, be appointed immigration agents for Nova Scotia, with the understanding that they are to receive $10 for every able-bodied immigrant landed in this province, until notified to the contrary." [44]

Boggs, DeWolf and Campbell produced a compelling pamphlet to sell the allure of Nova Scotia, and while it aimed to attract miners and agricultural workers, it offered the promise of work for the immigrant navvy:

"To Emigrants –Tradesmen and Laborers Wanted in the Province of Nova Scotia....
... The population consists chiefly of the descendants of immigrants from England, Scotland, and Ireland, and partly of those from France and Germany. They are engaged principally in farming and the fisheries, and now mining is becoming a most important branch of business. The commerce of the province is rapidly advancing, and the revenue yearly increasing.

… Labor, both at the mines and for agricultural purposes, is very scarce, and wages are high.
… Ninety-three miles of railway are completed, and in operation.
… Fifty miles are in process of construction, and over
… One hundred and fifty miles additional are now under contract. These works are creating an excessive demand for labor, skilled and unskilled. Laborers are paid in specie, at the rate of 4s.stg. a day; masons, 8s. a day, and other mechanics in proportion. Boarding may be had at from 8s. to 10s. stg. per week." [45]

It should be noted that the wages being offered to the prospective employees of 1866 amounted to about two shillings per day less than the Gourley Shanty rioters had received.

It is ironic that the unrest between rival groups of navvies should occur on the Nova Scotia Railway, when other navvies were at work constructing the Shubenacadie Canal at the same time. Although the canal promoters had seen the mortgage on their project foreclosed in 1851, a new company rose from the ashes in 1853, and work began anew under the direction of engineer Charles William Fairbanks. This put canal and railway navvies at work in close proximity to each other. In Britain such competition would have spurred classic confrontations and bloody brawls (called "Randys"), but this does not appear to have occurred, even when the canal was presented with the provocation of the Grand Lake Lock bridge at Enfield. In his 1856 report, quoted in Grantmyre's work, Fairbanks noted:

"The Provincial railway passes over the Canal above the Grand Lake Lock. The Bridge has three spans, 2 of 30 ft. I understand there is to be no draw on this bridge….
… I know not what is to be the height of the Bridge over the River. I think they should be drawbridges and that Tow paths should be formed around the abutments. The Railway will not interfere with the Traffic on the Canal in any way. It will, in my opinion, add to the value of the Canal; in fact the works will aid each other. The Canal will carry many articles which the Railway cannot take…." [46]

It was perhaps this cockeyed optimism that allowed Fairbanks to maintain order among his workers, or it may be that they were motivated by a greater self-interest than the railway navvies, for he noted later in his report:

"… the men employed on the Company's works with very little exception have been remarkable for their good conduct, many of the mechanics and workmen are owners of the land on the banks of the canal they therefore have an interest in the work and are very desirous to see it in operation." [47]

The canal lingered until 1870, when the discovery of gold at Waverley obliged the government to seize the property and, as with the lock at Enfield, place the low, fixed railway bridge over the water, rendering the canal useless except to recreational traffic. The railway – and the legacy of Gourley's Shanty – remains.

Above: Shubenacadie Canal. Via Rail's *Ocean* crosses the bridge over the Shubenacadie Canal at Enfield, Nova Scotia. This site is unique in that Highway 102 passes over the railway, which in turn passes over the canal, all at the same point, while aircraft above make their approaches into Halifax International Airport, located about five miles away.
(Jay Underwood)

CHAPTER 4

Laurie's Report

Throughout the furor of the Gourley Shanty affair and the subsequent political uproar, the railway's cost overruns were reaching the point where they could not be ignored, having totaled £70,000 more than either Forman's estimates, or the budget, had anticipated. There were several small and almost inevitable problem sites along the two branches of the railway. In her history of the Dominion Atlantic Railway (which was later to inherit the use of the Windsor Branch), Marguerite Woodworth noted that two men had died in the collapse of a cutting near St. Croix.

Forman's real headaches, however, were at Little Meadow Brook, near St. Croix, on the Windsor branch, at "Third Lake" on the Windsor branch, and Grand Lake Station on the main line. (The "Third Lake" reference is misleading, for although the name appears in Laurie's report, there is no railway embankment across what is known as Third Lake – at Windsor Junction – today. The reference must have meant to indicate Fenerty Lake near Mount Uniacke, where there is a substantial fill.) At Little Meadow Brook, a trestle had been planned to cross the deep ravine of the brook, but finding footings proved a problem for the contractor, who asked to be allowed to use a fill instead. It is a common misconception to think of a trestle as the more expensive option, but where contractors were paid by the cubic yard for fill, embankments were quite commonly more expensive.

According to his testimony before the Legislature's railway committee, Forman noted he had told the contractor, Cameron, that the fill option could be used, as long as its cost did not exceed that of the trestle. Cameron would later tell a legislative inquiry that a railway commissioner assured him his excess costs would be paid. These large fills were not unexpected. The final route for the Windsor branch was the most direct, and as such ran over some difficult ground, but Forman – and his surveyor, George Wightman, for that matter – were not alone in underestimating those difficulties. Two other engineers surveyed the area to determine the best location for a junction for the railway, yet neither of them gave much more than a cursory examination to the route eventually followed. Once again, time and money were the determining factors.

In their reports to Howe in May of 1851 (tabled in the session of that year), Charles Fairbanks and William Faulkner presented two different routes, both on the eastern side of the highway now known as Route 215. Fairbanks did not agree with any of Wightman's findings; indeed, he objected to Wightman's route as being set on too high ground at several points, and yet neither did he attempt to find any route to the west:

> "I did not explore with a line of levels the four valleys to the west of the little river or Scott's valley. The best information I could obtain, joined with my own judgment, induced me to try Scott's and Temple's valleys. It would have cost a larger sum of money to cut through the woods in the other valleys than I felt justified or authorized to expend. The chances are against a good line being found except a very deep cut or tunnel be used at the summit height."[1]

Fairbanks suggested the junction of the Windsor branch and Truro main line should be at Shubenacadie Grand Lake, some twenty-five miles from Halifax, close to present day Enfield (then known as Horne's Settlement). Faulkner submitted a survey for his line (leaving the main line at Elmsdale, and following the course of the Nine Mile River) with the warning: "The limited period of time allotted for this service, and my previous engagements with government, precluded the possibility of a more than hasty run over the extended surface of country necessary to form an accurate judgment on this important matter." [2]

Third Lake (actually Fenerty Lake) posed more of a personal problem for Forman, for a fill was again used as a substitute for a trestle, where a footing could not be found in the soft mud. The soundings in the lake were performed in part by Forman's younger brother, Robert, who had no apparent qualifications. The water was not deep, according to testimony given later at the railway committee inquiry into the claim for compensation, and the mud's appetite for additional fill should have been anticipated. The soundings, however, were made in the winter, when the permafrost gave a false indication that firm footing was only a few feet beneath the surface.

Faulty soundings taken during a winter survey were also made at Grand Lake. There were three such areas on the short stretch of line between what was then known as Shultze's (Grand Lake Station) and Oakfield Park. The track on its northward path crossed two bays of the Grand Lake, and on the shore side the depth was determined to be about thirty feet. What the surveyors failed to measure, however, was the lake-side depth just a few feet from the shore, where the water was more than one hundred feet deep. With the fill amounts calculated on the thirty-foot sounding, the contractor, Spencer Sutherland, soon found the fill being swallowed at an alarming rate by the deeper water.

His problem was compounded by the mud along the shore of Gaspereaux Lake (now known as Fish Lake) several hundred yards further up the line. Those depth measurements were taken during the winter, with similar results: the seasonal frost made the bottom of the mud in the lake appear solid at just a few feet. What Sutherland found, to his chagrin, when the embankment was being made during the spring and summer, was that the mud seemed almost bottomless, consequently swallowing many times more cubic yards of fill than the specifications allowed. Sutherland, who had experience building lines in both Scotland and Canada, testified before the railway committee that embankment No. 3 on his section at Grand Lake, the first embankment half a mile past Shultze's:

> "…required 54,000 yards [of fill] by the schedule. We think we put in double that quantity…. At embankment No. 6 we were told that there was mud, as marked on section, about 5 feet, but it turned out there was 49 feet…. Embankments No. 4, 5, and 6 had mud at the bottom as well as No. 3. We did not sound at all until after we had begun to work. No. 6 exhibits on the section 5 feet of mud, but on sounding we found 49 feet. We used iron rods with the pressure of two men – it was not deep water like the lake, but rather dry – a great many trees were put into embankment No. 6 to keep it up." [3]

Sutherland complained that upon his arrival in Nova Scotia in November of 1855, he had just two days to see the ground on which he was tendering. On cross examination, however, he was obliged to admit his son Donald had arrived ten days before, and gone over the ground. His sometimes contradictory testimony also damned his own business practice, which he based on his experience on the Grand Trunk Railway in Upper Canada, for he admitted he had not done a thorough examination of the ground, as the contract had required:

> "I went along the line with my own sons, and an engineer belonging to the office, who went to show us the ground. We made no measurements but what we took off the section. I compared the section with the schedule. I went over to see what ground [sic] was like....
> ... I placed my dependence altogether on the figures in the schedule; I had no cause to dispute them."[4]

He then went on to identify the engineer who approved of the extra work: "A great deal of extra work was done on embankment No. 6, for which Mr. Mosse allowed."[5] These developments proved alarming to the members of the Legislature, especially those with an axe to grind against Joe Howe. On April 18th 1857, just two weeks after Johnston became premier and Tupper had taken up his post as the new provincial secretary, a resolution was passed: "... to employ competent persons to examine the books and accounts in the several public departments, including the accounts and contracts touching all public works and their condition, and to report thereon...."[6] Johnston, the new attorney general, proposed the resolution. He had become a leading opponent of Howe's scheme, but in August of 1851 had been able to muster only ten votes against the railway bills.

Johnston's role becomes that of a political chameleon, for he had been a delegate to the Portland Convention of 1850 when advocates of the Annapolis Valley railway had attempted in vain to muster support for that route, linking Halifax to Saint John, New Brunswick. A lawyer with a practice in Kentville and Annapolis, Johnston had every reason to back that proposal, yet it appears he was somehow prevented from doing so in April of 1836, when Lawrence O'Connor Doyle's motion to subsidize a survey for a railway through the area was defeated by a single vote. Johnston's name is not recorded in the division, even though he was the MLA for Annapolis County at the time. In the spring of 1853 he had protested the sweeping nature of Howe's plan (320 miles of railway linking Halifax to Windsor, Pictou, and the New Brunswick border) and "... accused him of inoculating 'the public mind with extravagant and unrestrained ideas.'"[7] It was clear that Johnston now had allies on the executive council, for it appended a minute to the resolution on June 16th 1857 requiring:

> "...the employment of a competent engineer, unconnected with the railway works, for the purpose of affording the fullest and most authentic information to the public with reference to the railway, the amount of money already expended, the sum required to complete the line to Windsor and Truro, the cost per mile, and detailed statements of the accounts, with the particular services for which the money has been expended."[8]

A September 28th 1857 letter from Tupper to inquiry chairman James Laurie, showed that the investigation would be given the broadest possible latitude:

"Your report will also be expected to notice any defect that may come under your observation, and in fact, to present a statement of the operations, that the legislature and the public may be enabled fully to understand the whole subject, and resolve any doubts as to the permanence or stability of the work."[9]

The apparent perfidy of the Johnston government's proposal was not made clear until the *NovaScotian* of March 29th 1858 pointed out that the original resolution was intended to initiate an examination of the spending surrounding all public works, not the railway alone:

"… that when the Government changed hands in 1857, among other things it was asserted that the Railway Commissioners and their Accountant, Mr. Morrow, were keeping the accounts of the department in some unintelligible manner, and it was more than insinuated that if a strict examination should take place, it *might appear* that all the public money which had come into their hands had not been faithfully and properly accounted for.

Thereupon one of the first acts almost, of the new Government, was to prepare a Resolution to be passed by both Houses of Parliament, authorizing the Lieutenant Governor 'to employ competent persons to examine the books and accounts and contracts touching all public works, and their condition, and to report thereon – and also upon the system in which the books and accounts were kept, and on any changes in the system of receiving monies and keeping accounts, that may be beneficial for the public services.' This was intended, as its terms plainly enough point out, as authority to examine the books of accounts, and the mode of keeping them, *in all* the public departments – having especial reference, however, to the Railway department, although not

Left: James Laurie, the Scottish-born American civil engineer who reviewed Forman's administration of the railway, became the target of Howe's political allies in the press.
(Courtesy American Society of Civil Engineers)

mentioned, and at which the Resolution was leveled. It was to be done by 'competent persons' – and the fact is, that in discussing, debating, and passing the Resolution, a commission costing possibly £100 or so, composed of competent accountants, it was expected, would be appointed, who would thoroughly examine and report.

Now Halifax could have produced two or three accountants, we believe, equal to this task – and not inferior to any on this side the Atlantic. And it was but natural to suppose that such a course would be pursued. But mark what was done. Instead of this the Executive Council, *professing to act on the Resolution,* on the 16th of June, some two months after its date, met and passed a minute of Council requiring 'the employment of a *competent Engineer* unconnected with the Railway works, for the purpose affording the fullest and *most authentic information* to the public with reference to the Railway, the amount of money already expended, the sum required to complete the Line to Windsor and Truro, the cost per mile, and detailed statements of the accounts, with the particular services for which the money has been expended.'

This the Provincial Secretary declares was done, *'under that Resolution.'* See his letter of 28th September 1857 to Mr. Laurie to be found in the preface to Laurie's Report.

If a bushel of coals cost nine pence, what will a pair of tongs cost? Lads of the junior school classes are often puzzled with this question; and the premises and conclusion sought are quite as relative as is this Resolution and Minute of Council. Tupper's letter to Laurie, in point of fact, contains a *glaring falsehood* upon the very face of it, as any body may see by comparing the Resolution and the Minute of Council." [10]

This scathing attack might be construed as an indictment of Howe's tenure at the head of the railway commission, for as Stevens noted:

"During his last months in office a rot had set in. It had taken the local business men and their political friends a little while to discover how to make a good thing out of a government enterprise. In those days promotional opportunities were few and in dealings with the Nova Scotian government they could scarcely be said to exist, for all official services – land registry, tax collection, the mails and education – were on a small scale, patchily administered and pinched for funds. But with participation in railway development the provincial government, expropriating land, hiring labour, buying a wide range of miscellaneous supplies, became the biggest business in the province. It was in a position to reward its friends and to chastise its enemies. This it had proceeded to do.

Railway expenditures suddenly had given party allegiances a cash value: voters thereafter had other reasons besides family tradition for being Whigs or Tories. As political loyalties in the Nova Scotian backwoods were rabidly and almost religiously sustained, those fortunate enough to be members of the party in power viewed the largesse of railway spending as little less than a sign of divine favour. They hastened to enter their claims for the first easy money (or in some instances the first money) that ever came their way. Nor did government officers who controlled the spending feel any scruples in rewarding the faithful. 'It stands to reason,' declared a Colchester County spokesman stoutly, 'that a Grit is more honest and more worthy than a Tory....'

... However Argus-eyed Howe and his fellow commissioners, distance and the ignorance or dishonesty of their subordinates had betrayed them. It was difficult to keep in touch with what was happening even a few miles away; when railway construction moved afield, there followed a lamentable loss of control." [11]

It is ironic that at the same time that he was retaining an engineer to investigate Forman's construction of the railway, Tupper was asking Forman and engineer Henry G. Hill, by letter dated June 9th 1857, to investigate the quality of the construction of the province's lunatic asylum by Robert Davis and Messrs. Richardson & Son, at Dartmouth. It is not known if engineer Hill was related to the family of James Richardson Forman's wife.

This inquiry was another aspect of Johnston's intent to show the public the folly of Howe's profligate spending on public works, and the public debt that had accrued as a result. Forman, however, was too involved in the railway project to contemplate an assignment to which – as his contract with the government would attest – he had not agreed. Hill reported back to Tupper (September 12th 1857) that, aside from two days on the site in July, Forman had not been active in the inquiry:

> "The time required to estimate the extent of brick work executed, the quantity of material on hand, and the value of the building as it now stands, being more than Mr. Forman could properly spare from his many duties – Mr. Hill undertook to make up those details...." [12]

Hill went into the investigation with credible tenacity, examining everything from the drainage around the site to the quality of the sand being used to manufacture the bricks on site. He also found problems with the manner in which Davis' book keeper, a man named Chambers, charged out costs for the work: "A considerable number of days' work has been charged by Mr. Davis, but he does not say on what the labor was performed, in the years 1855, 1856, and 1857. Mr. Chambers gives us no account how or where Mr. Davis expended the labor." [13] This complaint would come to sound similar to that of Laurie as he investigated the accounts of the railway construction, and perhaps points to what might be considered a common business practice of that era.

Also similar was the discrepancy in the estimate of just how many bricks were necessary to complete the section Davis was building, since it could not be reconciled accurately with what he was charging for the bricks being made. Those bricks, supplied by the board of works from a site located near the shore, were made of sand that contained a high proportion of salt, resulting in soft stones that absorbed moisture easily. By November 10th 1857, James Laurie's name had been added to the head of what had become a tribunal on Davis' work, and the report recommended six remedial measures to bring the asylum construction up to an acceptable standard.

When Davis protested the findings of the trio (November 17th 1857) and attempted an explanation of the difficulties he had faced – including having to import brick from New Brunswick to substitute for the inferior bricks provided by the government – he was promptly told by Stephen S. Thorne, chairman of the board of public works:

> "Your reply to our communication of the 12th instant (enclosing the "commissioner's report" on the foundation walls, etc., of the asylum) is not at all satisfactory.
>
> The board do not deem it necessary to enter into particulars at present, but have to repeat the request: 'are you prepared to proceed at once with the work, as recom-

mended in the report above referred to, in reference to the walls, and at your own cost?' – An explicit answer is required. If you are not, the board will be compelled to have the necessary work done, and call upon you for the amount so expended, as they do not intend paying anything extra for the work."[14]

The final outcome of the dispute has no further bearing on Forman. The report of December 26th 1857 was signed only by Laurie and Hill. The events, however, beg the question why was the government not as aggressive in its cost-recovery with the railway contractors as it had been with the asylum contractor. The disparity in the government's approach lends credence to Forman's later claim that government members were extending preferential treatment to the railway contractors.

As the head of the inquiry into Forman's performance, James Laurie was a worthy choice, as his biography published by the American Society of Civil Engineers indicates:

"James Laurie (1811-1875), the first President of the American Society of Civil Engineers, was born near Edinburgh, Scotland. He came to the United States in 1833, quickly becoming engineer or Chief Engineer on many early railroad projects in the Northeast. Among his earliest professional engagements were appointments as an Associate Engineer on the Norwich and Worcester Railroad, and as a Consulting Engineer for railway location and surveys, dams, bridges, and wharves (ca. 1848). Living in Boston, in July 1848, he helped to found the Boston Society of Civil Engineers, the oldest existing engineering society in this country. This initial experience with setting up a professional engineering society proved beneficial years later in the establishment of ASCE. Perhaps Laurie's greatest work was the design of the bridge across the Connecticut River at Warehouse Point on the line of the New York, New Haven, and Hartford Railroad. As the Chief Engineer for the railroad, he had the iron work for the bridge's structure imported from England, creating a notable American example of riveted bridge work whose span was more than 177 feet long. The bridge remained in use to the early part of the 20th century."[15]

At the time of his appointment in Nova Scotia, Laurie was working from offices on Broadway in New York City. His report – in the Journal of the House of Assembly for 1858 – has been construed as a scathing indictment of Forman's performance, a litany of errors and professional misadventure that would certainly have demanded the removal of the chief superintendent. Stevens offers the most charitable point of view:

"Laurie, an intelligent and honest officer, had found both good and shoddy workmanship. In some instances specifications had been too vague. In other cases the bidders, not knowing their jobs, had accepted work at unremunerative figures. On the whole, however, the roadbed was satisfactory. The superstructure was not; British-style chairs and keys did not stand up to the Nova Scotia winter; often it was necessary to dispatch a crew to replace the wedges which had been jarred loose by the passing of a train.

Yet the construction, declared Laurie, was a more creditable performance than the operation of the line. Maintenance of way had been let out to private contractors, who had undertaken to keep the railway in first-class condition in return for fees which averaged five shillings per mile per day. (This upkeep charged was declared to be two thirds of similar costs in Great Britain and less than one third of average American costs.) Under this plan all sections of the line had tended to descend to the lowest common denominator of upkeep. Laurie also found the running of the trains to be haphazard and the railway accounts to be in a hopeless muddle. Station agents, conductors, and others pocketed a substantial portion of gross receipts. Already the idea was abroad that publicly owned service should be conducted upon a basis of unlimited credit."[16]

The evidence given before the select committee on the railway over the course of hearings held in March and April of 1858, indicates both Howe and railway commissioner Jonathan McCully were guilty of interfering in the process. Donald Fraser told the hearing he had discussed the heavy embankment necessary at Grand Lake with Howe and McCully:

"I came with you [Howe] from Grand Lake, and said that it was very strange that the formation levels and plans were not correct, and the contractors had to pay for extra work. He [Turnbull] said it was very strange, and there was a good deal in it, and he thought they would hear more about it. Mr. McCully told me to go on with the work, it would be paid for."[17]

Spencer Sutherland likewise implicated Howe:

"I told you [Howe] at Richmond that the lake [Grand Lake] would take more stuff. You said full justice would be done me – this was in September, 1856. I think the board had acknowledged an error in this particular embankment. If Mr. Howe had said, I would not be paid for extra work."[18]

Eliakim Creelman, another of the contractors who quit the work (Contract 3 on the Windsor branch), also testified to McCully's assurances that he would be paid for extras:

"Mr. McCully told me that it never could be intended by any board to deceive the contractors, and though they were excluded by the clause in the contract from recovering extra claims, still it never would be supposed that their claims would not be considered. This was after he left the board."[19]

On the basis of such supposed promises, Creelman, Sutherland, and Cameron continued to dump tons of extra fill into embankments that kept sinking right before their eyes. (It never seemed to bother Tupper's opponents in the press – perhaps it never occurred to them to check – but Creelman was the son of Hannah Tupper, Charles Tupper's niece. Hannah Tupper Creelman's father, Samuel Tupper, was the politician's brother. Eliakim Creelman's brother Samuel was a member of the Executive council from February of 1851 to 1856, and served as financial secretary and on the board of revenue during that time… but he was a Howe ally.)

William Baillie Smellie, a young engineer recruited by Forman in Scotland, where they had worked together, attended almost all of the meetings where re-measurement of the disputed contracts took place. He was adamant that no one on the engineering staff led the contractors to believe they would be repaid: "I have been about four years in railway office – saw a good deal of contractors. Everything that was said was the reverse of leading the contractors to believe they would be paid for their extra work." [20]

McCully's denial was unequivocal, and it set a precedent to have a member of the Legislative Council, appointed by the Lieutenant Governor as a non-elected advisor, give an account of his actions to members of the House:

"I am quite sure I never told Mr. Fraser that he would be paid for every yard of his extra work. I never thought any of the contractors had any legal claims beyond their contracts and Mr. Donald Fraser must have been mistaken in stating so. I have always been of the opinion that where there were great mistakes in quantities and embankments, the claim for the extra work done in consequence was a fair matter for consideration when the work was done. The intention of the board in framing the contracts, was to exclude all claims for extra work, except under the restrictions written in the contracts themselves." [21]

Indeed, McCully went on to place some of the blame at the feet of the contractors:

"I remember John Cameron giving me as a reason for his tender being so high, that there was a bog which he had sounded and found a considerable depth – this was on the contract close to Ward's. This led me to believe that the contractors made soundings and surveys for themselves; the board always gives a reasonable time in their advertisements, so as to permit contractors to make a pretty accurate survey, and we thought they did so." [22]

McCully then went on to praise Forman, and further defend his own involvement in the contract process:

"Mr. Forman, in my opinion, treated all the contractors with equal justice and fairness. I drew up the memo on which the transfer of Cameron's contract to Blackie & Johnston took place, and it was guarded so as to protect the province from any loss in consequence. I am not aware of any loss accruing to the province in consequence of the transfer of Creelman & Tupper's contract to Johnston & Blackie – I do not think I was in Halifax at the time. I would not have consented to any transfer of contracts which would put the new contractors in a different position from the old one. When I left the railway board I do not think I left a dispute there. All the claims had been equitably considered and settled, and I do not recollect any dispute existing with the contractors at that time." [23]

Forman told the committee the problem between the different amounts claimed by the contractors and those recorded by his engineers may have been in the fact that the contractors were not using engineers to do their measurements. One contractor on the Windsor branch used a man who had been trained as a mason; another contractor complained that to hire his own engineer would have cost him more money. In this regard, the contractors fell victim to what George Wightman called a "great evil." Wightman felt that the orderly development of roads was essential to a "new country:"

"None have paid greater attention to this matter than that of Nova Scotia, but it is to be regretted that they had not originally been guided by a better system in laying them out. This defect has been attributed to the great expense of employing skilful engineers.

One great evil derived from this source is the idea, that as the expense of employing regularly educated engineers cannot be afforded, no middle course remains – that one person may nearly as well be employed in laying out a road as another – that because expensive instruments cannot be afforded, roads must be laid out without instruments, altogether; and persons who would not be entrusted to lay the floor of the most insignificant building, are employed to construct a floor, for miles, upon the irregular surface of the country, and one which is to go down to distant posterity, as a monument of the skill, or of the ignorance of the present generation. The consequences need not be pointed out; they are seen on almost every road in the Province."[24]

Forman also noted that his own staff was competent, but insufficient for the task:

"I think if engineers had longer time to lay out the works it would have been better – or if I had more engineers. The first I heard of anything wrong with the sections, was a rumour that at Nine Mile River, the depths were not correctly taken. This was in 1855 before we laid off No. 3, main line."[25]

He offered only tepid defenses of some members of his office, however:

"Mr. Bradley was recommended by Mr. Chesboro; he was a young man; so was Fulsom. I heard them state they located roads in the States. Faulkner is a country surveyor; he used to run preliminary lines for me. I always found him very accurate in that sort of work. I think the staff of engineers was sufficient. I would not be content to lay out a road like this with such a staff – the work was too hard upon me...."[26]

He went on to remind those who had been privy to his appointment that the duties with which he was tasked were not those for which he signed on:

"... I came out as a Consulting Engineer to the government, and not for the purpose of construction of the road. It was then thought that English companies would construct the road. When the work was commenced, we took the best skill in the province we could get. Mr. Mosse was engaged from the first – also Mr. Faulkner and Mr. McKay, accurate and skilful men in their departments.... Mr. Bradley and Mr. Fulsom were afterwards brought in from the States as the work progressed, and I thought they understood their business, and I had no reason to doubt their accuracy and skill – they brought very satisfactory certificates which were filed by the board. Mr. Smellie was specially recommended by myself – he had been a professional engineer since 1846, and was with me after six months from the commencement of the work. Mr. Ramsay, from New Brunswick, also assisted me, and appeared most well versed in the use of instruments for engineering. I was anxious to economise as much as possible, and to do with as little engineering staff as possible."[27]

Still, he acknowledged that some inexperience, especially on the survey of the Windsor branch, led to difficulties:

"The surveys on the Windsor branch were mostly made in the winter – those on No. 3, entirely so – and there was no difficulty as respects bogs. Persons of experience and practical skill would, by walking over a bog, have a pretty correct idea of its general character....

... The young men employed on the work were those who were articled to me as my pupils for four years, for the purpose of learning engineering. They were all a year in my office before the board allowed them any remuneration for the duties they performed."[28]

Once again it seemed the entire board of commissioners – and the legislators who had created the establishment – had, at least in part, their own frugality to blame for some of the problems. Forman had omitted to mention that one of the men working on the Windsor branch survey was his brother Robert, neither an engineer nor a surveyor.

In the aftermath of the committee inquiry, Laurie noted in his report that Forman had co-operated fully, and lost amid some of the often complex jargon that defeated Tupper's supposed quest to make the line's problems understandable to the public, was a defence of his fellow engineer:

"Every facility and assistance has been afforded me by the Chief Engineer in obtaining the data as relates to the characteristics of the road, and otherwise, when the information was in his power, but as he keeps no general account of the expenditures or cost of the railway, mostly all the information of this kind has been derived from the books kept in the commissioners office, and from quarterly accounts and vouchers rendered to the financial secretary."[29]

This is a clear statement that the responsibility for the financial mess in which the railway found itself was not Forman's alone. Indeed, Forman could hardly have been at fault for an accounting system that moved vouchers once listed as being for excavation by contractors, to a second list showing the same expense for office furniture. Unnamed in the report, but equally culpable for mismanagement were Morrow, the accountant, and James Mosse, the superintendent who was nominally responsible for the day-to-day operation of the road. Laurie also laid some of the blame on the railway's self-imposed frugality:

"It may be proper to state that I consider the engineer department of the road as having been organized on too limited a scale, originating no doubt in the laudable desire of economy, but in this it is quite possible to go too far. The force employed has not been sufficient to give the requisite levels and stakes during the progress of the work, and we consequently find at several places the grading out of line – the excavations and embankments too wide, and others not wide enough, improper ballasting used, and other matters of detail imperfectly executed. Some of the bogs and lakes, which have swallowed up large quantities of material, could have been partially or wholly avoided, and no doubt would have been, had proper soundings been taken to determine their depth on the original surveys. The services of one or two well qualified assistant engineers in addition to those who have been employed on the road, to have given a personal superintendence to the work, would have saved large expenditures at many points – expenditures which, although nominally borne by the contractors, have generally in the end to be made up to them in the shape of allowance or otherwise. The duties of Chief Engineer are such in the office as prevents his spending much of his time upon the line during the construction of the road." [30]

Among those duties was the supervision of training engineering students. This was not to suggest Forman was left to his own devices. The railway report of 1859 indicates there were three assistant engineers hired during his tenure, but the engineering staff in general had increased markedly by the time of this report. Much of Laurie's report focused upon the disputed contracts on the Windsor Branch, a mere thirty miles of track. Forman had warned in 1856 that the branch would present difficulties:

Before determining upon the line to Windsor, it appeared judicious to explore all the routes previously proposed; surveys were therefore made along the valleys of the Nine Mile, Herbert, and Meander rivers. The valleys through this part of the Province are narrow and crooked, and the country contiguous to them is generally much broken: in some instances their descent is great, while in others a dead level is maintained for a consider-

Below: Map of Nova Scotia Railway

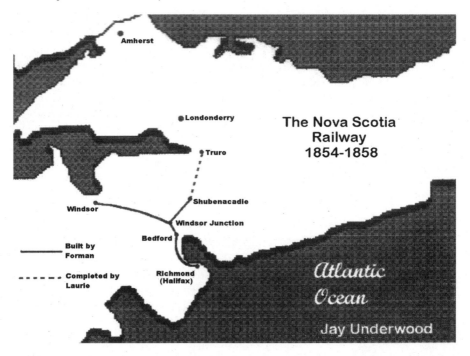

able distance. The streams are subject to rapid changes in their volumes, in the steep portions of their courses the rush of water is formidable, and in other places they overflow their banks, including the flat ground on either side. The construction of a railway under these circumstances would be attended with difficulty and at a large cost."[31]

The cheaper option was therefore the logical course for the line:

The selected line, by taking advantage of the rising ground on the west of the public road near Windsor, passes over the Ardoise hills with good grades, and having none of the disadvantages above enumerated, is generally of easy construction, and effects a considerable saving in distance. The following may be adduced as the reason for its selection: First, it is the shortest; Second, the least expensive to construct; and Third, the cheapest to uphold."[32]

As Laurie noted, however, there was a danger in taking economy too far. The route turned out to be a veritable quicksand of bogs that swallowed many times more of the fill than estimated, leaving contractors lobbying for compensation for extra work not stipulated in their contracts. He offered some observations that reflected equally upon the engineering of the line as they did on the lawyering:

"On other sections of the road, difficulties of another kind are encountered in endeavoring to make an estimate of the cost, originating in a difference of opinion between the engineers and contractors as to the meaning or construction to be put on certain clauses and stipulations in the contracts.

In earth cuttings the contracts specify that the slopes shall be one horizontal to one perpendicular, and the quantities exhibited at the time of the letting were estimated on such slopes. During the progress of the work, however, they were found insufficient, and were in some instances reduced to one and a half horizontal to one perpendicular – the engineer in some cases having made agreements and given orders to that effect; while in others the contractors reduced them, or removed the material which had fallen into the cuttings to enable them to complete their work, but without instructions from the engineers; and for removing such extra material, they claim to be paid.

Again, on several of the sections where the track crosses lakes and bogs, the bottom being composed of soft mud, 10 to 50 or 60 feet in depth, large subsidences have taken place, and much larger quantities of material have been required to fill them than was anticipated or shown on the schedule of work – and for the excess over the schedule quantities, the contractors claim to be allowed. Several of them also make claim for extra material required to supply the waste and shrinkage in making embankments on which there was no subsidence."[33]

Laurie noted that the contractors bore some responsibility in the matter, for the terms of the contract clearly specified they must check the estimates drafted by the province's engineers, and satisfy themselves of the accuracy of the surveys before taking on the job. Any fill material was to come from the cuttings made on site, and any additional fill needed due to any inaccuracy in the estimates was to be gleaned from side cuttings along the works. He also pointed to a contradictory clause cited by the contractors:

"The contractors hold that the above clauses refer only to the profiles and quantities and plans exhibited, and do not cover inaccuracies of survey and soundings; and that so far from every care having been taken to insure accuracy in the quantities, no cross sections nor proper soundings had been taken, and that there are large discrepancies between the amount of work exhibited in the schedule and that actually performed. That by the contracts the commissioners reserve to themselves the right of making alterations, and of requiring extra operations of any kind to be performed by the contractor, and, that it is specified that – 'such alterations or any additional labor shall in no way affect the contract entered into further than that the same shall be paid for extras at like rates as other work, and they reserve a like right to withdraw any portion of the work, and thereupon to make a corresponding deduction in payment.' And that annexed to each contract was a schedule of quantities referred to in the specifications as follows: 'The contractors shall fill in prices for the several descriptions of work enumerated in the annexed schedule,

BIG BOG BROOK (left)
Spring floods could wreak havoc on railway lines in low-lying areas as the washout at Big Bog Brook near Ellershouse, Nova Scotia in 2003 indicates. Had the original trestle been built according to James Richardson Forman's specifications, this disaster might not have happened.
(Courtesy Gary and Shirley Ann McCabe)

GRAND LAKE (right)
VIA Rail's *Ocean,* crossing one of two small bays near Grand Lake Station, Halifax County. The depth of the lake (on the left-hand side, mid-way down the train) is a mere thirty feet; on the right-hand side it exceeded one hundred feet. As a result of faulty soundings, several thousand cubic feet of extra fill was needed to carry the line.
(Jay Underwood)

and by these rates the value of any extra or altered work shall be fixed, and the contract price increased or diminished by the amount thus ascertained, as the case maybe, but should there be any extra or altered work for which no price has been given, then in these instances the value shall be decided by the engineer.'"[34]

This is an indication that the government's lawyers had not been as clear as they had intended in the practical execution of the contracts, and that both sides had entered into the work with a different understanding of their own liabilities. This could not have been the fault of James Richardson Forman, but the cost of unexpected cartloads of gravel were only a part of his headache. Laurie then went on to tackle the issue of additional damages sought by the contractors:

"Other claims, such as damages for not being furnished with iron rails, for alterations made in the grade and line of the road, and for other items, are also made.

The whole amount of extra work which has been recognised and allowed by the board of commissioners and engineer under the foregoing clauses, over and above the sums specified in the contracts, up to December 31st 1857, is about £41,000. The additional claims which have been presented by the contractors, and which are now in dispute amount to over £70,000.

It would perhaps, be premature to go much into detail on the merits of these claims, although I am free to confess that for some of them – such as for additional material removed by reducing the slopes – the contractors are, in my opinion, entitled to be paid; for although the contracts provide that 'the contractor shall be bound to construct the railway, with the breadths and side slopes specified,' this in clay and earth cuttings – such as are met with on this road – is impracticable. The slopes originally ought to have been not less than 1 to 1; and at a few places a flatter slope even than this will be required to prevent the road being obstructed by slides. On equitable principles, I can see no reason why the extra sloping, where actually required, should not, as a general rule, be embraced under the clauses referring to extra work and extra operations."[35]

Having made this important concession, Laurie then ruled in favour of the government in a minor dispute:

"The claims of another class, however, for additional material excavated, beyond what was shown on the profile and schedule, to make up for the waste and shrinkage in making embankments, in my opinion, ought not to be allowed. The contracts specify that 'embankments shall be made from the material taken out of the excavations as far as it goes, and the deficiency shall be made up by side cutting procured and deposited at the contractors' risk and expense.' I see no construction that can be put on this to raise a doubt or give the contractors a claim; they were bound to make all due allowances for waste and shrinkage in making their calculations."[36]

The issue of greatest importance to the credibility of Forman's stewardship, however, was disposed of in a short but damning statement:

"The important item, however, in these claims, is that for the additional material required to fill the bogs and lakes. The quantities estimated and shown on the profiles and schedules of work, at the time of the letting, having proved erroneous, is the origin of these claims.

The contracts undoubtedly mean to put the risk of quantities with the contractors, but it is under the representation that 'every care has been taken to insure their accuracy,' and although the contractors are required to satisfy themselves on this point, it could scarcely be expected that they were each to have surveys and soundings made of the entire line – some reliance must have been placed on the soundings made and the quantities estimated by the engineer; especially under the representation above quoted."[37]

Forman, not having had time to get out of his Halifax office to survey the line personally, had been forced to rely upon earlier surveys by George Wightman, who had promoted the eastwardly and indirect line between the Meander and Sackville rivers, and by his students. Laurie found fault with both the engineers and those who drafted the contracts:

"It is difficult to understand how – where the bogs and lakes were so numerous and where it was so evident to anyone passing over the line that the bottoms were soft and yielding, and that large quantities of material would be required to fill them – that no distinct understanding was had between the parties – that no special mention or clause in the contract occurs in relation to them. The only mention made of subsidencies or settlements is under the head of upholding the road for twelve months after completion, and the prices attached to this item sufficiently show that the contractors did not allow for subsidencies of the character in question.

Notwithstanding, therefore – by the strict letter of some of the stipulations of the contracts, the risk of quantities appears to be with the contractors, still, taking the whole matter in view – the general scope and spirit of the contracts, which assume that the quantities estimated are substantially correct – I consider it a fair subject for settlement on equitable principles, depending on the facts and special merits of each claim. Some of them are undoubtedly extravagant, but as to others, a re-measurement of the work would be necessary in order to arrive at any satisfactory conclusion. If the approximate estimates made by the engineer, of the additional quantity of material involved on the sections, are correct, at least one half of the total amount claimed would be stricken off."[38]

Laurie's criticism overlooked one detail with which even he was unfamiliar. Many of the soundings of the bogs along the route had taken place during the winter months, when the frost had penetrated deep into the soft ground, leaving the surveyors with the impression a firm footing had been found. Neither Forman nor Laurie (whose experience in North America was limited to the New England states) had any previous encounters with this condition, one that would bedevil British railway engineers in Canada until well into the 1890s. Of all the engineers involved in the survey, only Wightman could have been expected to know. But Wightman, whom Howe had called "a skillful and scientific Civil Engineer [sic]," had done only a cursory examination of the western route:

"The reason for this preference is, that it is lower by eighty feet than any pass Westwardly of it.... Another reason for the preference given to this line is that by crossing the main road leading from Newport, Rawdon, and Douglas, towards Halifax, it will attract more of the business of these Townships, both in freight and passengers, than if it went direct from Windsor, and the direct route is too barren to afford any compensation for the loss of this business." [39]

Wightman's findings were examined and approved by an independent American engineer, who would have been known to Laurie. Ellis Sylvester Chesborough, who had also recommended that Bradley and Fulsom be added to Forman's staff, may have been related to Wightman, but his qualifications, as evidenced by his later work, were beyond question.

The considerations raised by Faulkner and Fairbanks were cast aside by the railway commissioners as time and cost became their overwhelming criteria. With both in mind, Forman was ordered to undertake a hasty survey of the direct line. Had Howe's timetable not been so enthusiastic, surveys in warmer weather would have made the problems more evident and avoidable.

Another delay over which Forman had no control was in receiving rail for the prepared roadbed. Laurie made note of this problem, which stemmed from the suppliers in England "countermanding" orders. The rail was produced from two foundries, one at Merthyr Tydfil in Wales, the other near Liverpool, but both were under increasing pressure to meet the demand for rail not only in Great Britain, but Upper Canada (for the Grand Trunk Railway), India, and the Crimea. It appears Nova Scotia's orders were given a lesser priority on more than one occasion.

The province's purchasing agent in Liverpool was one William McCully. William McCully was a native Nova Scotian, the brother of Jonathan McCully, and a partner in the firm of Patterson, McCully & Co. of Liverpool, although it appears he travelled regularly between Great Britain and his hometown of Amherst, Nova Scotia, where he died, December 8th 1866.

When rail did arrive, it suffered from its own misadventures. A fully laden lighter sank to the bottom of Bedford Basin on one occasion, carrying its cargo of bridge iron, chairs, and spikes with it. In August of 1856, the ship Glide, carrying rails, chairs, and spikes from Halifax to Windsor by way of the Bay of Fundy sank, and without insurance to cover it, some £2,140 worth of material was lost. At the same time, with the demand for iron so high, track spikes and chairs were in short supply. Laurie noted the shortfall was quickly made up from foundries at Halifax, which produced a superior quality product than the English mills. It did little good with no rail available.

The public reaction to Laurie's report was immediate and predictable – immediate because the report was printed and released to members of the House of Assembly, the press and the Halifax reading rooms long before it was tabled in the Legislature, as proper procedure required. The pro-Conservative newspapers, the *Express* and Tupper's *British Colonist,* hailed it as proof of the government's commitment to fiscal responsibility. The pro-Howe *NovaScotian* and the *Morning Sun* found plenty of reasonable grist for their mills.

History has since given more credence to Laurie's report (see G.R. Stevens' history of Canadian National) with little regard to the legitimate concerns of his critics. The fact that the report was in the public domain before it was tabled lends weight to the suspicion that it was part of a deliberate campaign to discredit the railway board and

Forman equally. This notion was given voice by a correspondent under the pseudonym "A Hants Man" in the June 29th 1858 edition of the *NovaScotian:*

> "Sir: There are some people silly enough as not to believe that the present Government are determined to destroy the Railway, and prove to the world that, in the hands of the 'Government' it must become a failure. But the most skeptical on this point are beginning to have their eyes opened to the fact, when, by practical experience, they are enabled to judge of the management and system upon which the working of the concern is carried on. It is obvious that everything is so *mismanaged* as to disgust and annoy the people, and force them to the conviction that, after all, a Railway is a most expensive affair, and its benefits in no way to be compared with the cost. *The present Government are preparing and paving the way to first destroy the character* of the road, and then sell it to the first 'Jackson' speculator who may come this way, sell the people's Railway for a mess of pottage."[40]

This was not an exaggerated claim. One of the members of the executive council had been Adams G. Archibald, the Truro lawyer who had been the Nova Scotia agent for Peto, Jackson, Brassey & Betts when they were submitting estimates for the railway contract. Archibald managed to remain aloof from the storm that swirled about Forman and Laurie, and forged his own career as Lieutenant Governor of Manitoba when he was also a shareholder in the Canadian Pacific Railway.

Within weeks of the report's release, however, the *NovaScotian* was already baying at the government's heels and attacking Laurie's professional credibility in the March 29th edition:

> "In voluminous tables never perused, nor to be perused, resembling Bowditch's navigation or a treatise on logarithms, it professes to give the curves and the grades over the whole line, but Mr. Laurie has *never had an instrument on the works*. The whole of this information, right or wrong, he got, it appears, from Mr. Forman. It professes to furnish a statement of the present condition of the works. For this, his only authority is either the contractors themselves, the local Engineers in the Board's employ, or Mr. Forman's office. Mr. Laurie has never measured the works. He has had no opportunity of doing so. His report is a pompous display of figures truly – but they are not his own. He does not know to-day, whether they are right or wrong."[41]

The editor continued his attack relentlessly in other parts of the paper, linking Laurie's credibility to that of Johnston's administration:

> "But Mr. Laurie has not only attempted to pass himself off as an accountant, but he has done worse – he has prepared a report at the instance of the government, by the same rule, and in the same spirit, in which the Financial Secretary prepared his public estimates the other day, and which has since been all scattered to the winds."[42]

The *NovaScotian* clearly saw a plot involving the government, the pro-government press, and the avarice of the contractors claiming the extra money:

> "The press of the city supporting the Government, the *Colonist,* the *Recorder,* and the *Express,* are all crying down the Railroad, and crying up the Contractors. They are all using

their best efforts to weaken the hands of the present Board, and to strengthen the claims of Messrs. McDonald, Johnston, and Blackie, and Sutherland & Sons – with their claim of £70,000 before a Committee of the Assembly – a Committee not one of whom have the slightest knowledge of Railway matters except as they pick it up during the discussion.

Let the Government then overrule and override their own Board – let a one-sided Committee report against the decision of the Commissioners, and then what? Why the Board must resign. No gentleman of spirit we take it, would hold his seat a single day to disburse the public funds contrary to his own better judgment."[43]

The gauntlet having been thrown down, the *NovaScotian* concluded its argument, but not before having given an indication that much more was to come:

"Already we have the absurd anomaly of one Engineer appointed by the Executive Government without authority, reviewing and condemning the acts of another Engineer, a public officer. More, reviewing and criticizing the acts of the Board, and their Accountant, on subjects of which he is as palpably ignorant as the Bushman from South Africa or a Bedouin of the desert.

And now we have discharged a duty, we feel that we owed to the people of this Province – and with these facts before them we leave the public to draw their own conclusions.

That the Railroad will cost more than was originally contemplated it were vain to deny; that it ought to cost anything like the amount named by Mr. Laurie, we have we think, plainly disproved. But in the hands, and under the control of persons who evince every desire to *ruin the whole enterprise in order to gratify their revenge upon their political opponents,* who, instead of sustaining their own Board and officers, seem to be seeking every plausible means for *overruling their decisions and degrading them before the country,* it were difficult to say what the Railroad may not be made to cost, or what the country may not yet be required to pay."[44]

Despite the inquiry into his management of the project and the furor that Laurie's report ignited, 1858 should have been a year of triumph for Forman. In June the railway officially opened its branch to Windsor, fulfilling a promise made almost exactly four years earlier with the ceremony at Richmond, and the twenty-year promise made to the people of the town. Marguerite Woodworth describes the events:

"To celebrate the opening of the Windsor Branch, June 8th 1858, was declared a public holiday in Halifax by His Excellency the Earl of Mulgrave. All shops and offices were closed and the inhabitants had a full day of festivity.

At 5:30 AM the people were amused by 'a merry peal from all church bells;' at 6:30 AM any laggards were reminded of the occasion by a royal salute of 109 guns by the Royal Artillery from the Grand Parade; at 10 AM there was 'a Grand Review of the Troops, ending with a Sham Fight' on the Common; a yacht race took place at 1 PM, and the ceremonies ended with a grand ball at Government House."[45]

And, perhaps to the irritation of Johnston and Tupper, Howe was there to steal some thunder:

"During the day half-fares prevailed on the trains between Richmond and Windsor, at which latter place another demonstration was held. The morning train to Windsor had carried Joseph Howe, accompanied by over 300 of his friends and admirers, who wished not only to celebrate the opening but to do honor to the man who had first conceived the idea of the Windsor Branch. The depot was gaily decorated for his reception, flags and bunting adorned the houses of the village, and the streets were hung with evergreen arches. At the end of many long and eulogistic addresses, Howe was presented with a draft for £1,000 as a mark of appreciation for his public services."[46]

This account contradicts other contemporary reports, however. The Halifax *Morning Sun* suggested there had been more lively graveside services, and the *NovaScotian* observed in its June 28th edition that small towns in Spain had done more to celebrate their railways:

"We read an account in an American paper a few days ago of a Railway celebration somewhere out West, at which the bulk of the population was present, and upon which a small corporate city spent $10,000. This is the way they do things in democratic America, and although varying perhaps in the mode, we find the same spirit at work among semi-

despotic nations in Europe. For instance: 'The Alicante railway inauguration took place on the 25th of May, and was a complete success. Four Ministers were present. M. Mon made a speech. There was an illumination in the evening.'

This was in Spain. Four Cabinet Ministers were present, and one of them made a speech. Think of that Mr. Johnston. Ponder over it Doctor Tupper. The poor, ignorant and besotted Spaniards of Alicante had their day of rejoicing, and an 'illumination' in the evening, to celebrate the opening of their Railway. Everybody rejoices on such momentous occasions except poor Blue Nose, who, having handed his railway over to its enemies, is in no heart to enjoy himself.

Then M. Mons made a speech. How suggestive. Where was the Attorney General when the Windsor Branch was opened? Where the Provincial secretary? Four Spanish Ministers assisted in the inauguration of the Alicante Railway; surely one Nova Scotia Minister at least might have honored the Windsor opening with his presence. As for a speech, we could hardly expect one from its enemies – from those who opposed our Railways in their inception, and who have over and over again predicted that bankruptcy and ruin would follow in their train. We dare say there might have been an 'illumination' if the Glebe House people had not expended so much light when they celebrated the fall of Sebastopol." [47]

Left: Lord Mulgrave, also 2nd Marquess of Normanby, was new to Nova Scotia politics when he agreed to the dismissal of James Richardson Forman.
(Nova Scotia Archives and Records Management Service, 383 #34)

CHAPTER 5

Defensive Measures

DESPITE the ensuing onslaught of political invective upon his abilities, Forman's technical genius did not escape the notice of his peers, even though he was practicing in far-off Nova Scotia. The Monday February 2nd 1857 edition of the *NovaScotian* triumphantly carried this endorsement:

"At a time when some people professing to be Nova Scotians are trying to detract from the merits of our Railway and its prospects, it is really refreshing to hear what persons who know something about such matters as these think on this subject. The subjoining article from the *London Mining Journal* is the best possible answer that can be furnished in refutation of the suicidal sneers of the Editors of the *Catholic* as regards our Railway:–

'During a hurried tour in the course of this summer, I was struck with the wonderful difference between their railways and those with which I was familiar in this country. In general the works are not only ill-constructed, but there appears to be a want of engineering skill, or at least, a great disregard of many things which are considered essentials in England. Decidedly the best railway works which I saw anywhere were in the Province of Nova Scotia, where railways are still in their infancy.

'I landed in the little town of Windsor, on the Basin of Minas, from which I made the journey by coach to a place called Sackville, at the head of Bedford Basin, and about ten miles from Halifax, the capital of the Province. At various points along the road I saw the works in operation, and on my arrival in Sackville, a delay of an hour gave me an opportunity of inspecting the railway which is finished in that place. Across the river, which here falls into the Basin, I found a box-girder malleable iron bridge that would have done credit to any country. It is supported on massive stone pillars, of great height, and, whether for beauty, or design, or solidity of construction, I have seldom seen anything superior. I was the more surprised at this, because I had been told that the Engineer, Mr. Foreman [sic], was a young man and native of the Province. The railroad from this place to Halifax follows the windings of the shore, presenting many beautiful points of view, but what interested me the most was the skilful manner in which the engineering difficulties had been mastered. It was a sad disappointment in me, on my arrival in Halifax, to find that Mr. Forman was absent, and would not return before my embarkation, but I confess it was with no little pride I learned that, although a native of Nova Scotia, he had been regularly educated and drilled in the old country, and in a school which has sent out some of the best practical railway engineers. Since my return to this country [*viz.* the United Kingdom], I have had occasion to visit the neighbourhood of Glasgow, where Mr. Forman was for many years employed in the construction and working of railways, and where he amply justified the Government of Nova Scotia in placing their interests in his hands.

'The railroads of Nova Scotia are constructed entirely at the risk and expense of the Province under the superintendence of a board of commissioners, of which Mr. Howe is the chief. The funds are provided by the sale in England of bonds guaranteed by

Above: Sackville bridge, crossing the Sackville River, at what is now Bedford, Nova Scotia. This print was made by Edward John Russell, for the *Canadian Illustrated News,* October 7th 1871. (Canadian National Library/Archives)

Below: Sackville bridge today. VIA Rail's Halifax-Montreal train, the *Ocean,* crosses the bridge at Bedford in 2005. It is still the largest bridge on Canadian National Railways' Bedford subdivision. (Andrew Underwood)

the Province, which are now at a considerable premium, and there can be no doubt that the railways, when completed, will greatly increase the prosperity of this valuable colony.'"[1]

Founded in 1835, and despite its title, the *Mining Journal*'s weekly edition was the leading journal of the engineering profession, focusing equally upon mining and construction. In 1856, when the railway built its station at Sackville (the community singled out by the *Mining Journal*'s correspondent), the name of the community was changed to Bedford, in honour of the Duke of Bedford, who had been Secretary of State for the Colonies when Halifax was founded. Ironically, the Sackville River bridge – virtually unchanged and on what is now Canadian National Railways' Bedford Subdivision – is still one of the most imposing structures on a Nova Scotia railway, the equal of the Folly River viaduct (at East Mines, Colchester County) and the River Phillip bridge (near Oxford, Cumberland County), both of which have been significantly altered over the years. Tourist literature frequently made mention of the spectacular bridge, although today's urban blight has reduced its allure somewhat.

The *Mining Journal*'s glowing pronouncement came in an edition of the *NovaScotian* that epitomized the controversy swirling around Forman and his railway. Other pages of the paper carried stories of continued violence among the navvies: a young man who was collecting ties for a contractor was mistaken for a sheriff's deputy, come to arrest an Irish navvy on charges of assault. The young man was stabbed by a gang of the navvy's mates, to the continued outrage of the Protestant community. On another page was a letter with the familiar complaint that the route from Halifax to Windsor was not the most direct line – even though the line itself was just months from completion. Clearly with his administration of the work under scrutiny by Laurie and the government under attack for having subjected him to the professional indignity, Forman would be offered no opportunity to speak publicly on the completion of the Windsor portion of the line.

That did not prevent the *NovaScotian* from speaking out on the issue of the railway's management, in the August 18th 1858 edition that carried another salute to Forman:

"The *Canadian Railway and Steamboat Guide,* a periodical published at Montreal, and exclusively devoted to the advertisement of that class of interests which its title indicates, contains in a number for July, an account of the presentation of a service of Plate to S.P. Bidder, Esq.....

... We know nothing of Mr. Bidder, personally. The Grand Trunk Company *[sic]* has, by one means or another, and some of them far from scrupulous, succeeded in accomplishing extensive improvement in Canada, as regards inter-communications. It has become a great institution, to use an American phrase, and is already a kind of East India Company, an *imperium in imperio* in the heart of that noble Province.

But it was not to discuss the policy which brought the monster Company into existence or by which it influences and is in turn influenced, that we grasped our pen on the present occasion; it was for an entirely different purpose, as will presently be seen, and to this we address ourselves.

Mr. Bidder states that 'it is now *twenty-four years* since he first entered the Railway service.' He must, therefore, be a man of long experience, and practical knowledge, and, we should suppose, understands the making and Management of Railways."[2]

Although the very name of the Grand Trunk was anathema to Howe and his supporters, they were not above quoting the devil to prove their point:

"Among other things Mr. Bidder says: 'There is nothing, gentlemen, in which *perfect harmony* and *good feeling* between employees are so necessary as in the working of a Railway. The *safety of the passengers* and the *success of the road* depend chiefly upon them, and the Superintendents, I am sure, will give me credit for never having missed an opportunity of calling their attention to the importance of *unity and harmony, always existing between them and their subordinates*. (Hear, hear.) There is nothing more likely to create a bad feeling amongst those engaged on great undertakings than *departmental institutions*. These should be avoided in every possible way. Managers, Superintendents, Locomotive Foremen, and the men under them, *should go hand in hand in everything*, and feel that the success of the one is necessary to the advantage of the other. The lowest laborer should be taught to feel that he is cared for by his superior, and that his good conduct will be noticed and rewarded. (Hear, hear.)

'These principles, gentlemen, I have always endeavored to inculcate, and I hope they will take deep root in the management of the Grand Trunk Board, for *where discord reigns, no man can manage a Railway with either satisfaction to the public, himself, or the Company he serves*. (Hear, hear.) I know my worthy friend and successor, Mr. Shanley, fully concurs with me in this belief – (Cheers) – and will do all in his power to secure that harmony of action so essential to produce the results which you are all striving to accomplish, *viz.,* to make the Grand Trunk Railway a dividend paying concern. (Cheers.)'"[3]

Acknowledging that the italics had been added by its own editors for emphasis, the *NovaScotian* agreed with Bidder's analysis of the principles of running a railway, principles the newspaper felt were lacking in the Johnston-Tupper administration's stewardship:

"We have thrown some of the more important paragraphs and phrases into italics.

About the mode of building a Railway, we differ from the views of the advocates of the Grand Trunk, as wide as the Poles, but as to the *manner of working a Road* – and it is of this that Mr. Bidder is discoursing – we entirely agree with him. 'Harmony and good feeling,' among those employed in working a Railway, are indispensable to *its safety,* as well as *its success.*

Now, if Mr. Bidder be authority on this subject – and we must believe that he is – it is utterly impossible that success can attend the working of the Nova Scotia Railway, as at *present managed.*"[4]

The newspaper then launched the first in a series of attacks on the reputation of Laurie, which would grow more rabid with each edition:

"First, then, as Chief Engineer, holding an office of the very highest responsibility, is James R. Forman. Under the former Administration, in addition to the construction of the Roads, he held pretty much the same situation to the working of them that Bidder did to the Grand Trunk. But while he still retains this position *nominally, virtually,* in both departments, Mr. Forman has been superseded. In the Construction department, Mr. Laurie is, to all intents and purposes, placed over him. The Government consult Mr. Laurie, instead of Mr. Forman, and he has been, and is at this moment, a kind of spy, as well as a dead weight upon the public works of the Province. He has lately been commissioned, it appears, to locate the line from Truro to Pictou. Dr. Tupper announced this fact at the Hustings at Windsor on nomination day.

Now, in the first place, we believe that we are justified in saying that this Mr. Laurie never saw a mile of English Railway in his life – that he left Scotland at a time when nothing better than *tram roads* were in use in Great Britain. So much for his great experience, and thorough knowledge, about Railways. The public will easily understand from this, why he condemned the English double-headed rail, and recommends the American T-rail instead.

About the only thing in his report which had any merit of originality (Mr. Forman and his office contributed all else, except the mistakes), was a disquisition upon the powers and capacity of Nielson's Scotch Engines, and here he made an egregious blunder, as we have been given to understand – one so palpable and unpardonable that Nielson has thought it proper to remonstrate, and correct his errors – showing clearly that he was incompetent for the self-imposed duty."[5]

The case was then made to support a growing belief that Forman was being unceremoniously ushered out office:

"While, then, it was contrary to all faith with Forman – virtually an *American Engineer* – to put this stranger over his head, for he (Forman) has a written contract entered into with the Government, in which his duties and emoluments are distinctly defined; it is worse – it is a personal insult, deliberately and, as we believe, intentionally offered him by the Government – done, probably, with a view of ensuring his resignation and retirement, and if that does not accomplish its purpose, the public should not feel greatly surprised if some more effectual means were soon taken, some *excuse devised*, to place a more versatile and servile Engineer upon the works – one who can be secured by Contractors to report such sums of money in their favor – £70,000 in one item – as the Government for the time being may desire. *It looks like it*. This, then, is the sum and the head of Forman's offending. He never *would*, he never *will*, depend upon it, while he holds his office, sacrifice the public interest to please any Government, or any Contractor, whatever. And the best proof that he is acting fairly and honestly in beating back Contractors and their dishonest claims, is to be found in the remarkable fact that the Board, with the Chairman of the Government's own appointment, *sustain* him, *uphold* him. McNab, Pryor, and Anderson – men of honesty and integrity, hitherto reputed – to their credit be it spoken, believing him right, (and who so well can know?), have steadily backed up the Chief Engineer against these foreign Contractors; while, on the other hand, it is well known that the Attorney General, the Provincial Secretary, the Solicitor General, with others of their own Government, and of Government supporters, have as continually, and as steadily and systematically sought to weaken the influence of the Engineer and the Board, and to find plausible excuse for paying the extravagant, unfounded claims of the Contractors. The more the roads could be made to cost, as a matter of course, the more their old opponents are gratified."[6]

The *NovaScotian* railed at the cost of the tactic, pointedly noting the irony that Johnston's government had created when it made cost efficiency the motive behind the investigation:

"We have therefore *two heads* in the Construction Department. Mr. Forman, at a salary of £937 10s. per annum, and Mr. Laurie – unless some new contract has been entered into with him, and we have heard of none – at a salary of £500 a month, or £1500 per annum. Surely, surely, this is scandalous. How can our railroads pay, or what but disastrous results must follow, from such monstrous extravagance? More than the road money for any county for a year, to pay the salary of *one man*. What would be thought of having two Governors, with £3000 stg. each per annum, and how long would they go on harmoniously? Or two Attorney Generals, with £600 each? And yet it is just as necessary, and just as reasonable as two Chief Engineers over Nova Scotia Railroads, and far less dangerous to travellers."[7]

Overlooking its faulty mathematics, the *NovaScotian* then introduced a new villain to the plot, in the form of James R. Mosse, the railway's newly appointed superintendent, who had been hired as Forman's lieutenant in 1856:

"But this is not all. The Government having ceased to locate any more Railroad, and Mr. Mosse's services being no longer required in the Engineering Department, about the end of last year a new office was created for his special benefit – namely that of 'Superintendent of Working Department.' This was a service, which had been performed by the old Board of six, and afterwards by the new Board, assisted by the Chief Engineer. Mr. Mosse, we believe, received £450 per annum, and still receives it, in this new office – and if we are rightly informed, keeps the lines and the works in a beautiful state of confusion. His duties, it would seem, have never been defined. It would be a difficult thing to do, and the consequence is his finger continuously in some body else's dish.

The road, up to the autumn of 1857, as remarked, had been worked by the Board. They, assisted by Mr. Forman, had fixed the times of starting the trains, regulated the tariff, ordered rolling stock, given directions to station keepers and locomotive foremen (except that after the change of the administration, the patronage of nominating to new offices, and supplying vacancies in old ones was very improperly wrested from them by the government) – and consequently the difficulty has been to know what duties really devolved upon Mr. Mosse. And now at this hour, the whole thing, as far as we can learn, is in a state of dispute and wild uproar.

As a single illustration, *we happen to know* that a short time ago the Board contracted for a freight house at Richmond. It was raised near the north platform, and was progressing rapidly, when Mr. Mosse interfered with the contractor, ordered him to cease, and said the building was too near the edge of the platform, and must be removed back. The locality had, it appears, been selected by the Board, or the Chief Engineer, or both and a grave council was forthwith called. The Board refused to give way – and there is no doubt they were right – the building proceeded, and Mr. Mosse, chafed and annoyed, was overruled, and ran off to the Government as usual with his complaints.

Not a day it is said, passes by, but that the pockets of the conductors are crammed with letters of instructions, and counter instructions from Mr. Mosse, who has rigged himself up an office at Richmond station, and furnishes an excellent illustration of *the very opposite* of what Mr. Bidder so emphatically recommends. In him, and the Board, we have theretofore *two heads* to the working department, and one of these days the probability is, there will be an apt illustration of the practical operation of such a system at the expense of the lives of a train filled with passengers. These *collisions* which hitherto have been confined to the *department,* the existence of which Bidder so strongly deprecates, and among their officers, will be transferred to the line and the locomotives, producing a smash up, unless some speedy remedy is prescribed."[8]

What followed would today be considered a political bombshell, but has gone unobserved by historians, and apparently raised few eyebrows at the time:

"This Mr. Mosse, the nephew of Attorney General Johnston, happens, unfortunately for himself, and still more so for the public, to be the Engineer whose errors in sounding lakes, and measuring quantities to fill them, have caused the principal difficulties hitherto, and given rise to the greater portion of the disputes, which were under examination by that celebrated Committee, of which, Mr. Henry was chairman. Mosse has been transferred by the Government from *construction department* therefore, and placed over *working department* – never having had any proper experience or training for it, so far as we can ascertain, and hence the mischief and confusion.

Then again, the continued interference of the Government with the action of the Board, the Chief Engineer, and the difficulties along the line keeps the whole thing in a fever. The Contractors are everlastingly appealing from the Board to the Executive Government, who are as perpetually inter-meddling with the independent action of the Board. Mosse and Laurie are the Government favorites, and act as a kind of vigilance committee upon Forman and the Commissioners, and instead of what Bidders so strongly enjoins, that – 'Managers, superintendents, locomotive foremen, and the men under them should go hand in hand, in everything, and feel that the success of the one is necessary to the advantage of the other' – nothing could be more diametrically reversed than the management of the Nova Scotian lines. Jealousy, discord, and the want of confidence obtain, and abound on all sides, from the Executive Government down to the lowest laborer – the Board only and the Chief Engineer continuing to work harmoniously.

Now we put it to the community, how can a Railway be expected to pay, under circumstances like these? Mr. Laurie in one department, and Mr. Mosse in the other (their combined salaries being about £2,000 per annum), dead weights, useless – worse than useless both."[9]

Perhaps in its most unkind rebuke, the newspaper likened the Johnston administration's management of the railway to what might have expected from Jackson, Peto, Brassey & Betts, who were then linked to similar difficult operations in New Brunswick and Canada:

"The road to Windsor has been earning, it is said, about nearly £500 per week, but the expenses of working the line must be consuming all these earnings, or very nearly so. Whereas 50 per cent of the gross earnings *ought to pay* the expenses on any well-managed Railroad – Jackson, we remember, put it down at 45 per cent.

We may have no higher or more exalted opinion of the present Board of Commissioners, perhaps, than we ought to have, and yet we will do them the justice to say, that if the Executive Government would let them alone, would refrain from all interference with them, would allow them, upon their own responsibility, to deal with the roads, *with the Contractors,* with the Engineers, and with the operatives – to appoint such officers as they needed only, and to dismiss all the *blundering,* useless, supernumerary, *officious,* and *mischief-making individuals,* the roads would soon assume a new and healthy aspect, and realize what their projectors originally anticipated from them.

Managed, or rather *mismanaged* as they now are, they bid fair to be as ruinous, as their greatest enemies ever predicted, or could ever desire." [10]

One can only imagine the relish Howe would pour into his terse letter to Mosse dated March 22nd 1860 when, as the newly-returned Provincial Secretary (having vanquished Johnston's administration), he informed the railway superintendent:

"The Hon. Mr. McCully having reported to the Government that your services are no longer required by the Department committed to his charge, I am commanded by the Lieutenant Governor to acquaint you that your appointments are to be considered as revoked after the 31st March ensuing." [11]

Mosse responded with a short letter, expressing no surprise at his sudden ouster. The euphoria of the Windsor branch opening would be short-lived, and the government would be forced to acknowledge that its plan to oblige Forman to resign had failed. On August 25th 1860, little more than a month after the Windsor line opened, Forman was dismissed and replaced by Laurie. Tupper's letter of dismissal to Forman was short and to the point:

"Sir, His Excellency the Lieutenant Governor having obtained the assurance of the Commissioners and yourself in the early part of the summer that the extension of the railroad to Truro should be accomplished on or before the 1st day of November next, had reason to expect that with every facility at the command of the Chief Engineer, the public would not be disappointed, but, from the several reports you have recently submitted, and the verbal explanations made by you in presence of the Council and Commissioners at Government House on Tuesday last, it being manifest that under your management the work will not be completed for several months beyond the time limited for its accomplishment, His Excellency has commanded me to inform you that with the advice of his Council, he has reluctantly decided upon removing you from the office of Chief Engineer.

His Excellency regrets the necessity which compelled him to adopt this measure, but he is impressed with the conviction that in reviewing the Railroad operations since their first inception under your auspices, it is manifest that they have not been conducted as judiciously, economically, and expeditiously as the interests of the public demand, and feels himself bound to employ an Engineer whose energy and skill command the entire confidence of the administration.

You will, therefore, be pleased to hand over to the Commissioners all the books and papers and other public property in your possession connected with the office of Chief Engineer.

I have the honor to be, Sir, Your obedient servant.
Charles Tupper." [12]

Sir George Augustus Constantine Phipps, then Lieutenant Governor, was new to the position in Nova Scotia, and took his cues from the executive council. He was a career bureaucrat with royal ties, having been Treasurer of the Royal Household before his arrival in Nova Scotia. As such, he was a complete contrast to Sir John Gaspard

LeMarchant, who had appointed Forman to the engineer's post, and there is reason to believe that, had LeMarchant remained in the vice-royal position, Forman would probably not have been dismissed.

The former Governor was a career soldier, having entered the British army at seventeen and spending £10,000 over the following twelve years for his commissions. He became one of the youngest officers ever to command a British regiment. In 1846 LeMarchant reluctantly accepted the governorship of Newfoundland, thinking it would improve his prospects in the army:

> "With no prior experience in colonial administration, LeMarchant faced a difficult situation. Severe economic difficulties were compounded by potato blight and the impact of a hurricane the previous September. St. John's was being rebuilt after the great fire of June 1846, and there was much dissension surrounding the administration of relief funds. The new Governor did little to ease the situation. Taking the view that far too much had been spent on direct relief, he diverted funds to public works, mainly in St. John's, including repairs to Government House."[13]

LeMarchant, despite his unpopularity in Newfoundland, clearly understood the value of public works projects, and the time and cost involved in such undertakings. He had been a ready supporter of the railway, having donated the land for the Richmond terminus in Halifax's north end.

The railway commissioners responded to Tupper's letter on August 26th 1860, the following day, with a short letter to Forman, apparently intended to console and encourage him:

"Sir,
As your connection with the Railways of which you have been Chief Engineer since their commencement in this Province has ceased, and as your conduct in that capacity has been constantly under our observance since the year 1854, we conceive it an act of simple duty to record our opinion of your unwearied diligence, energy, and skill, and our unabated confidence in your integrity. Our intercourse with you has always been of the most friendly and confidential character, and in the emergencies that have from time to time arisen, we have found you fully competent to the duties of your office. We have often marked your anxiety to push forward the works with all possible celerity, and to economize the public money, and in parting with you, beg to assure you of the sincere regard and esteem with which we remain.

Your very truly,
Jas. McNab
W. Pryor Jr.,
Jno. H. Anderson"[14]

Clearly the view of the board of railway commissioners was at variance with those of the Lieutenant Governor's council, and to emphasize the point, Pryor and Anderson resigned. The *NovaScotian* reacted with predictable outrage:

"The day it was discovered the Formans – father and son – were members of the Protestant Alliance, that day the doom of James R. Forman was a fixed fact. We never doubted it. An upright, honest, unassuming religious man, he has been victimized to gratify Roman Catholic cravings for revenge, and the hatred of a batch of dishonest Canadian contractors."[15]

It is this single statement that has been promoted by historians to explain Forman's failure, but it was made with no previous reference to his father's membership in the Alliance, or to any of the rancour created by the Gourley Shanty affair. Indeed, at this point, the newspaper's arguments began to lose all reason, and devolved into ranting marked by xenophobia, sectarian vitriol, and outright defamation of character:

"A man eminent in his profession, of the very highest moral standing, one who has conducted the public works for upwards of four years, who has planned, put under contract, and well nigh finished a hundred miles of railway in Nova Scotia, who has certified to the disbursement of three quarters of a millions of money without a stain or shade of suspicion as to his integrity, (or capacity, except where his successor or other interested parties are concerned) – this young man, on the very day that his native City was wildly welcoming home one of her sons whom the Turks and Barbarians abroad had united to honor, this young man is struck down by a corrupt and tyrannical Administration. And all to make a place for an adventurer, of whom little or nothing is known, farther than that being schooled in American tactics, he has at last succeeded in undermining a brother Engineer. Forman has been sacrificed for his independence. No money could be paid to dishonest, servile contractors, fawning upon the Government, without the Certificate of the Chief Engineer. Thousands and tens of thousands of pounds will probably pass now into Contractors' pockets – money never earned – in consequence of this change of officers – and Roman Catholic malice will be abundantly gratified."[16]

The newspaper's conspiracy theory grew to add the contractors to the Catholics and malicious Conservatives they saw being at the root of the plot:

"We deeply regret Mr. Forman's dismission, because his known integrity was a guarantee against fraudulent certificates and dishonest Contractors. Whatever sums the Chief Engineer certifies must be paid – a dishonest Engineer and a fraudulent Contractor may rob the Province to any extent with impunity. A great misfortune has happened to Nova Scotia. And although it will so very materially strengthen the Opposition, for the Country's sake we deeply regret the loss of Mr. Forman. Were his successor an entire stranger, we should have more confidence in him. But the underhanded manner by which he has succeeded in displacing the former Engineer marks him as a man unworthy of his office – one who deserves not, and never can command, the confidence of the people of this Country. We have no faith in him. He has reached his position and supplanted a rival, by means which merit every honest man's contempt."[17]

By its September 6th edition the *NovaScotian* had returned to more reasoned arguments against Laurie, but could not quite break away from sniping at his character and credentials. The article in question offered some well-documented refutation of some of the assertions made by Laurie in his report:

"The conduct of the Government in dismissing Mr. Forman and appointing in his place Mr. Laurie, has created an amount of dissatisfaction in this city for which, we are frank to admit, we were not prepared. Men of all politics do not hesitate to condemn the act in the most unqualified manner. Without a moment's warning, so far as we can learn, the first intimation of their determination having been communicated to the Board and to Mr. Forman after the act was done, no wonder the public generally denounce it as one of the most tyrannical measures that ever disgraced any Government.

Mr. Forman, and the Board, and the public, are all taken, it seems, by surprise. We cannot say so much for ourselves – although we were as uninformed as to the actual determination of the Government as others, but we plainly foresaw that Mr. Laurie or Mr. Forman must soon leave the country. There could not be two Kings in Brentford. And knowing how anxious the Government were to pay the Contractors, and not insensible to the amount of influence their Counsel has with the Administration, we anticipated, as we have already shewn, that Mr. Forman would be sacrificed.

It has been done. And now another fact, as we have all along contended, is manifest. The Board of Commissioners and their Chief Engineer have been steadily co-operating together in harmony, on the one side, and the Government and the Contractors (their Counsel), and Mr. Laurie, on the other. This fact is now evidenced by the action of the Board. Their resignation, that is, those of Messrs. Anderson and Pryor, follow *with promptitude* the dismissal of the Chief Engineer, so that whatever the Government may think or say, in the eyes of these two members of the Board – and mark, two gentlemen of the very highest standing in the city, re-appointed by the present Government, and not liable to be suspected of any improper leanings in favour of the Opposition – we repeat it: in the opinion of these gentlemen, Mr. Forman has been *unfairly and improperly dismissed*. As to the Chairman of the Board, we make *no remarks at present;* we want to see what course he adopts. We know pretty well what he thinks of it all; in fact, everybody in the city knows, but we prefer that he should be judged by his actions.

We have not the slightest doubt, and we say it here openly and publicly – we have no doubt whatever, that, one after another, the whole staff upon the entire works, or nearly so, is about to be dismissed, or their situation made so uncomfortable for them that they will be *compelled to resign*." [18]

The "contractors' counsel" referred to by the newspaper was Jonathon McCully. The *NovaScotian* then returned to its xenophobic theme, the "Americanization" of what it still considered to be a British railway:

"Not only so, but the whole system of operations is to be altered. The entire *treatment,* to use the language of the Doctor, is to be changed with the *physician.* The English double-headed rail was changed last winter for the American T pattern, by Mr. Laurie's recommendation, and the boast is that the latter costs £100 less than the former." [19]

To their credit, the *NovaScotian*'s editorialists had done some thorough research, and were prepared to quote chapter and verse of any document that supported their argument. In the case of double-headed rail, the newspaper referred to a recent report from the Franklin Institute, a Philadelphia-based organization that still exists today, promoting invention and mechanics. The report showed that the operating cost for railways based on the US pattern (including maintenance and renewal of the right of way, engines and management) were twice that of railways based on the British pattern. Using Laurie's experience against him, the newspaper repeated the institute's finding that from 1855 to 1857, the average cost of operating railways in Massachusetts was 26.9 cents per mile, while in Great Britain it was 10.56. In New York State, where Laurie also claimed to have experience, the cost for 1857 alone was 70.5 cents per run mile, as opposed to 36.5 cents in England:

"The climate of England, though not presenting such trying circumstances of frost and snow and severe summer heat, has nevertheless, some severe peculiarities, as compared with that of the United States. There is an average annual fall of over 60 inches of rain, much of which falls upon a treacherous clay soil, rendering liable frequent slips, besides soaking and settling of road beds....

... The price of labour and iron were on an average two-thirds of those in the United States. Cross ties (sleepers) on the other hand cost from four to five times as much and ballast nearly double.

Allowing for all these circumstances, the conclusion arrived at is, that there was *an absolute economy of from 30 to 40 per cent over the corresponding results on American railways;* attributed chiefly to superior construction, embracing the earth and drainage, ballast, distribution and preservation of sleepers, *the make and form of rail, rail joints, etc. The rails of England were mostly of the* DOUBLE HEADED FORM."[20]

The *NovaScotian* accused the government and its new engineer of "quackery" and derided the *British Colonist* for its defence of the T rail, which had been offered on the 19th of that month. Tupper's newspaper had claimed:

"We next come to the T rail, which one would suppose from the editorial was a new Yankee device – whereas it is an alteration of the English rail, made necessary by the difference of climate, and has been consequently adopted either entirely or with some modification under the name of the Bridge rail, both in Canada and New Brunswick. It is therefore better suited for Nova Scotia, *and withal, it costs over £100 per mile less – or £40,000 in 100 miles of railroad.* What do our readers think of this as a specimen of the practical advantage of American experience united with the British, over an experience exclusively British. We beg every one who has the means at hand to read at large what Mr. Laurie says in his admirable *General Report,* pp. 35, 36 on this subject."[21]

The *NovaScotian* then returned to its favourite target, James Laurie:

"Laurie's admirable report was got up, as is now manifest, with a view to getting Mr. Forman's place – the *Franklin Institute Report* is got up with no such object, and is a paper of first rate American authority. Now the public probably begins to discover – and when it is too late, that a fatal mistake has been made even in this respect. Mr. Forman brought with him the latest and most approved patterns of rails, switches, engines, and everything else known in England and Scotland when he left. But as we remarked not only the rails, but the whole system is to be altered with this Mr. Laurie, and thousands upon thousands of pounds will be thrown away in consequence – and all added to the cost of our roads, which of course will be just so much more capital for the enemies of railroads to charge to the construction of our public works. It will be duly added to the per mileage bye and bye. Had Mr. Forman been continued on the works another twelvemonth, we should have had the best one hundred miles of railroad – with all the *principal bridges of stone and iron – to be found in America.*

With a new Engineer, who has spent just twelve months in the colony, devoting his energies to the task of destroying confidence in a brother officer, with a view of obtaining his position and place in which he has but too well succeeded, what can the public expect but that he will condemn everything, misrepresent everything, and so try to erect a reputation upon the ruins of his rival.

What is Mr. Laurie's report now? Who does not discover the object and aim he had in view throughout? And of him, as Hamlet says to his queen, one may say –

'Look you now what follows,
Here is your *Engineer;* like a mildew'd ear
Blasting his wholesome brother.'" [22]

The pro-government newspapers, in the meantime, had been indulging in their own attacks on Forman's reputation. In an issue prior to his dismissal, the *British Colonist* had apparently misrepresented Forman's qualifications, as he gave them before the railway committee's hearings into the overpayments to the contractors. It appears the *Colonist*'s editor was willing to give Forman some measure of forbearance, when it allowed him space in its September 6th 1858 edition to correct the "errors":

"Sir – May I ask you to insert the following few lines in your next issue, in answer to that part of your editorial of Thursday last, which refers to the evidence taken last winter before the Railway Committee.

As this evidence was not correctly reported, and a considerable portion of it was not taken down at all, and as that which was reported was not read over before I left the witness box, and no opportunity afterwards given for making corrections, errors were inevitable, more especially as the subject was so foreign to the customary duties of those who were employed to perform the task." [23]

What followed was Forman's précis of his resume, recorded in the opening pages of this work. At that time, Forman had referred to his association with another well-known engineer at work in Canada: "I would further add, that the present Chief Engineer of the Great Western Railway of Canada – an important line and well known in this community was a pupil at the same office in Glasgow as myself, only he was several years my junior." [24] It appears Forman was referring to Roswell G. Benedict, who died at the age of forty-two in New York, on February 6th 1859. As it would turn out, any comparison was odious. The Great Western did not enjoy a good reputation for the quality of its construction:

"The Great Western was equally unsafe, but it never suspended service. Between the beginning of operation and 1st November 1854 – a period of less than 12 months – 17 accidents involving a loss of life occurred. After the most serious of these accidents, when 52 passengers were killed near Chatham [Ontario], the Government appointed two commissioners, W.F. Coffin and M.C. Cameron, to undertake an investigation of the line. A Chatham newspaper, with rather grim wit, reflected the low esteem in which the railway was held by the public, when it noted 'the accidents on this line have become of such frequent occurrence that even Mr. Cameron, the government commissioner, declines to travel upon it without his coffin.' The report of the commissioners, subsequently rendered, was highly critical of the deplorable state of the Great Western:

> 'At the opening of the road, the embankments and cuttings were in a dangerous state; the ties and sleepers were laid without the stay or support of gravel on the surface; the road-crossings and cattle guards were unfinished.... Neither grading nor superstructure were in a fit state to hazard the prosecution of traffic in the face of contingencies of the coming winter and spring in this climate and country.'" [25]

The Great Western's managers had succumbed to the temptation to cut corners and reduce both the cost and time involved in opening the line to traffic, to the detriment of the entire work. Forman could never have been accused of the same practice. In his letter of defence, Forman went on to note:

> "To a professional man of any standing it is distasteful to be obliged to bolster up his position by referring to his past employment, as it is presumed that his standing and the position he occupies is a sufficient guarantee for his qualifications....
> ... The comparisons made between Mr. Laurie and myself are anything but creditable. Surely it is not necessary, in addition to the other unfounded reasons given, to detract from my reputation in order to find an apology for handing over my plans of the Pictou branch to that gentleman." [26]

They would be the last civil words exchanged by the engineer with the *Colonist*. The newspaper's next missive appears to have been written in defence of an administration that had been set on the defensive, and amid a split within the caucus over the propriety of Forman's sudden dismissal. Tupper was also again beset by a scandal surrounding the financing of his medical degree, which had delighted his opponents and thoroughly infuriated the doctor. It was perhaps to take the spotlight off Tupper that an anonymous member of the executive council penned a counter-attack upon the *NovaScotian* and Forman in the August 31st edition of the *Colonist*. The gloves came off:

> "We are not surprised at the tempest in a tea pot which this act has created.
> Let the public read carefully the correspondence which was submitted to the House last winter, touching the delay in opening the Windsor Branch – let them attentively peruse the evidence taken before the Railway Committee, especially that of Mr. Forman himself – let them read Mr. Howe's speech at Windsor on nomination day, exhibiting the mismanagement of the whole work, and the article on Railway management in the *Morning Chronicle,* and they must be blinded and prejudiced indeed if they do not arrive at the conclusion that the radical camp have good ground for dismay and sorrow at seeing Mr. Forman removed from a position in which he was serving their cause most effectively, to one in which he will be impotent for mischief.
> The fact stands boldly out on the face of the public records that the Government were trifled with and deceived as to the progress of the works last summer, and the promised opening of the line to Windsor. Ultimately the fact was revealed, that Mr. Forman could never have intended to accomplish that object, as no preparations were made on the line for traffic, nor was locomotive power provided to work it.

The testimony of the late Chief Engineer before the Railway Committee itself proved that he located the line to Windsor contrary to the valuable decision of Wightman, Chesborough, Sykes, and Beattie, through interminable rocks, swamps and lakes, with enormous grades and sharp curves, in complete ignorance of the Engineering difficulties, and without the remotest idea of what the line would cost." [27]

The *Colonist* then turned the tables on Forman, accusing him of being a servant of Howe's political agenda:

"Worse than this, from his own testimony it can be shewn that he certified as finished a contract of Cameron's contrary to the fact, and paid him thousands of pounds for work which he had not done, besides other acts of favoritism of no small amount, which have been recently repaid by Mr. Cameron polling from 50 to 100 of his navvies against the Government.

Admirable arrangement, truly, for Mr. Forman, with every means at his command to enable him to press these works to completion, lying a dead weight upon their advancement, while Mr. Howe could harangue the people on the indisposition of the Government to push them forward, and the *Chronicle* day by day obtain from him and through him grounds for assault upon the administration, who have struggled in vain to get him to discharge his duty with faithfulness and vigor.

We can hardly wonder that the Executive, notwithstanding the many proofs of Mr. Forman's inconsistency from the time he declared that our roads could be built for £4200 per mile down to the present hour, blundering from step to step, would be slow to believe that any man could be guilty of such baseness and treachery, until the fact forced itself upon them that this power of obstruction must be taken away, or the present season would end in the same disappointment to their efforts and hopes which characterized the last.

What the Government will have to answer to the Legislature and the country is not why Mr. Forman has been removed, but why he has been so long retained. We know how desirable it is to have these large Railway contracts closed up and scuttled by the same Engineer who has supervised them from the first, and we suppose that having the advantage of an Engineer of undoubted skill at hand to aid by his counsel on matters of moment, the Government were determined to give Mr. Forman every consideration and opportunity of retrieving his character. It is well known that without the cordial and devoted co-operation of the Chief Engineer, who is necessarily the life and soul of such a work, nothing can be accomplished." [28]

Tupper's newspaper launched a new salvo in the sniper fire of character assassination that was to mark Forman's removal from office, accusing him of theft of government documents to cover his alleged unprofessional execution of his duties:

"The public will scarcely be prepared to learn that Mr. Forman has given, since his removal from office, proofs of the most unequivocal of downright dishonesty, by purloining and obstructing documents from the Railway office which belong to the department, and are essential to carrying on the works with promptitude.

Up to Saturday night we understood that Mr. McNab, the Chairman of the Board, although making the most determined efforts, had been unsuccessful in effecting their recovery.

Of course the obstructives, who daily shew that in their hungry greed for office they would like to see the Railway and Province sink together, will be delighted at any rascality by which the public works may be retarded, and that dreadful man, Mr. Laurie be thereby prevented from exhibiting the energy and skill which his undoubtedly high character warrant us to expect.

We hope that gentleman will know how unworthy of the slightest regard the radical press is considered. A perusal of the low filthy Billingsgate abuse with which the *Morning Chronicle* and the *Presbyterian Witness* have teemed against every man upon whom they desire to pour their impotent venom, from His Excellency the Lieutenant Governor (who is continually dragged before the public in an insulting manner) down to their brutal attacks upon private life, must render these journals objects of unfeigned disgust and contempt."[29]

Quite ignoring its own participation in the skirmish, the *Colonist* attempted to counter the anti-American feeling toward Laurie by emphasizing his Scottish ancestry:

"With characteristic veracity Mr. Laurie, born and bred in Scotland, and always continuing a British subject, is denounced as a foreigner. Do not these people know that the rabid profuseness of their abuse renders it harmless? It is only the other day that Mr. Howe pronounced a report signed by Mr. Forman on the construction of the Lunatic Asylum, worthless and unworthy of credence. It is only the other day that the Inland Navigation Company, in which the leading liberals are largely interested, sought and obtained the services of the same Mr. Laurie to examine their works and report on their condition and prospects.

The opposition press may puff Mr. Forman until they are tired, and decry Mr. Laurie to their heart's content, but the Legislature and to a large extent the people of Nova Scotia have had testimony upon which they can rely, that the former has plunged us into ruinous losses and difficulties the most disastrous, while the latter has every hour obtained the confidence which his large experience and high standing are calculated to inspire.

Never was Government hemmed in by greater difficulties than ours has been in connection with this great work, but let them go fearlessly forward and discharge their duty to the country independently and irrespective of clamour, and they need not fear the result. They will be sustained by the voice of an intelligent people."[30]

In a second item in the same edition, the *Colonist* went on to attack Howe with equal ferocity:

"The *Morning Chronicle* of August 28th says touching Mr. Forman's dismissal:-

'We deeply regret Mr. Forman's dismissal, because his known integrity was a guarantee against fraudulent certificates and dishonest contractors. Whatever sums the Chief Engineer certifies must be paid. A dishonest contractor, and a fraudulent engineer may rob the Province with impunity.'

We recommend our friends of the *Chronicle* to turn to Mr. Howe's speech [sic] at Windsor, as published in his issue of the 14th, in which the want of an energetic and able Engineer is pretty fully illustrated. Mr. Howe said, speaking of contractors' claims: –

'Those claims were presented to the Legislature last session, and after 34 days of mystification and humbug it was discovered that nearly £20,000 more had been paid to those contractors than they were entitled to under their contracts – a sum large enough to cover all that they could justly claim, even assuming that to some extent they were entitled to consideration. This startling fact, concealed by the Government – never reported by the Committee – induced the House to resolve that no more money should be paid to the Contractors till the roads were finished. In defiance of that resolution the Government has been paying money to these contractors all summer.'" [31]

In a new twist, the *Colonist* attempted to separate the government from the board of railway commissioners:

"What will our readers say when, with these two statements before them, we assert that the Government have never paid the Contractors a shilling? That the money that was advanced to them was paid by the Board, on the recommendation of Mr. Forman, and that this money which Mr. Howe declares has been paid to them this summer improperly in defiance of the resolution of the house, has been paid by the Board on the 'certificates' of the Chief Engineer. The *Chronicle* people may take whichever horn of the dilemma they choose.
  Mr. Howe also asserted in the same speech: –
  'There is not one contract finished yet. The parties are everywhere insufficient, and the whole summer is rapidly passing away. The little work that is being done is done with the Board's engines and new platform cars, which are wanted on both lines to do the work of the country.'
  The law places the management of this work in the hands of the Commissioners and Chief Engineer. The means furnished by the Government have never been abundant. Was it not time then, if there was any truth in this picture, that there should be an overturn somewhere? That somebody should be found who would infuse a little life and vigor into the dry bones, and prevent the whole summer from passing away without anything being done?
  Does not everybody know that, anxious as the Government have expressed themselves to have the wharf at Windsor put in a condition that would not excite the curses – deep if not loud – of the passengers to and from [Saint John], nothing could be accomplished to remove that fertile and just cause of attack from the opposition press? Procrastination and incapacity have everywhere along the line stared us in the face. Yet this was just what the opposition papers wanted, that they might continually assail the Government who had no means of doing anything to alter it save by their ineffectual remonstrances with the Board and Engineer, which was immediately communicated to the *Chronicle*, and trumpeted forth as unwarrantable interference.
  This deep game has been pressed a little too far for some of the parties principally concerned, and we now congratulate the Government and the country upon being shaken clear of Howe's incapables who were sinking them." [32]

While the author of the letter remains a mystery, Tupper is the prime suspect. He was a frequent contributor to the newspaper, using it in the same way that Howe used the *NovaScotian* to advance his political agenda. The *NovaScotian*, however, painted the entire executive council with a broad brush:

"We never remember to have read or witnessed such a savage, scorpion-like attack, made by a Government upon a public officer – and all within a single week after his dismissal – as has been made upon Mr. Forman.

We think Mr. Forman is quite right to treat the article in the last *Colonist* as the act of the Executive Government. Nothing is more certain than that the Government either authorized one of its members thus to vilify and slander Mr. Forman, or some one member, having access to the public correspondence, has done it on his own responsibility.

It is more correct and constitutional on our part to assume that it has been done by and with the advice of His Excellency the Lieutenant Governor, than that it has been done by any member unauthorized. Now we are not disposed to drag His Excellency into any political warfare unnecessarily, but we think Mr. Forman has a right – to the protection the Constitution gives him, in this class of case, and one of these rights is, that those who have access to Executive Correspondence shall not, with impunity to himself or his Government, garble and use it to injure and defame private individuals.

But happily for Mr. Forman, in this case, he is beyond the shafts, and the barren malice, and the malignity of Mr. Attorney General Johnston and his colleagues. None but a man whose soul was steeped in gall, whose conscience was seared and crisped, and whose heart was black as Hades, would write the article which appeared in Tuesday's *Colonist*."[33]

The editorial then took a clear aim at Tupper, identifying him as the creator of the *Colonist* articles:

"If Mr. Forman had been as bad as the individual who now stands convicted of fraud by the verdict of a jury of his country, and yet sits in the Executive Council, *side by side with His Excellency*, to assist in preparing articles like the one in question, he could not have been treated with more coarse contempt or more bitter contumely.

No sooner had the Government decided to dismiss Mr. Forman, who has been their own officer for now *upwards of eighteen months*, than they charge him with almost every crime in the Calendar. He is accused of 'incapacity,' 'falsehood,' 'favoritism,' 'baseness,' 'treachery,' 'rascality,' and last, with 'downright dishonesty, in purloining and abstracting documents and papers etc.'

Now, from a correspondence very recently conducted with the Government, a copy whereof is upon our table – but which, for wants of space, we cannot give in this issue – we select a CERTIFICATE, given by the members of the Railway Board before any of them had resigned, to this same Mr. Forman, and if ever nine men stood convicted of infamous conduct, of low, mean, dastardly falsehood, of wretched truckling and treachery – *if the Railway Commissioners are to be believed* (AND THEY WILL BE BELIEVED) – these nine men are the nine Executive Councillors of Nova Scotia, who signed the order for Mr. Forman's dismissal."[34]

The newspaper then reprinted the letter to Forman from McNab, Pryor, and Anderson, thanking him for his sterling service. Without waiting for the new commissioners, S.L. Shannon and Archibald Scott, to prove themselves, the *NovaScotian* served notice they too were under suspicion by virtue of their alliance with the government:

"We are not aware of the antecedents of either of these gentlemen, which are supposed to qualify them for the discharge of the onerous duties of their new offices. Their qualifications, to say the best of them, must be sadly in contrast with those of the men who have sat there going on five years, and whom they have succeeded. There is one thing to be learned, however, from the fact of their acceptance of these offices when tendered they thereby endorse the act of the Government that dismissed the Chief Engineer – and they condemn the conduct of Messrs. Pryor and Anderson who resigned in consequence. They go into office, Messrs. Scott and Shannon do, as the nominees of a Government whose proclivities are now notorious, and far from acceptable to the great majority of the Protestant population. They accept their situation substantially at the hands of those, upon whom the Government rely principally for political support. They embark in that boat, and must have been chosen rather for their known approval of the acts and policy of the *office-closing, half-mast flag-Administration,* than for any other known qualifications. If it be true as commonly reported, that the offices had well nigh gone a begging, and it must be admitted that it rather looked like it, the Government are, perhaps, as much to be pitied as to be blamed on this account."[35]

Despite the *NovaScotian*'s acidity, Samuel Leonard Shannon would not suffer any political damage from the comments. A Halifax lawyer, he went on to be elected MLA for the county's western division in the election of 1859 (in which Johnston, along with his party, was ousted from office in favour of Howe), and served with distinction as a Liberal-Conservative Confederate with Tupper, appointed to the Executive Council in 1863, and receiving the title of "Honourable" by special permission of Queen Victoria, as a reward for his services in promoting Confederation.

By this point, Tupper was almost certainly irate over the fact that Forman had successfully challenged the council's order for him to hand over all documents in his possession related to the railway, and was able to use his access to them to mount his own defence, which he did in the September 6th edition of the *NovaScotian* and the *Morning Chronicle*. Prior to the outburst in the *Colonist,* the heated exchanges between the government, the board, and the engineer, had been limited to private correspondence. The animosity – and the full extent of the government's attempts to unseat Forman – became very public, outlined in the engineer's letter, which the *Colonist* refused to publish, but found daylight in the *Chronicle,* and was reprinted in the *NovaScotian:*

"Halifax, 3rd Sept., 1858
To the Editor of the *Chronicle*

Sir:- The following letter in reply to the *Colonist* Editorial of Tuesday last has been refused by that paper, notwithstanding the infamous language made use of in that article. Under these circumstances, will you give me space in the columns of the *Chronicle?*

I am, Sir,
Your obedient servant,
James R. Forman"

"Halifax, 1st Sept., 1858
To the Editor of the *British Colonist*

Sir, – In your leading article on Railway matters, which appeared in your issue of 31st August, there are certain statements which I cannot allow to pass unnoticed; they are so distinctly personal attacks upon myself, that I must claim space to reply in your columns.

You assert 1st. 'That the [Lieutenant Governor] was trifled with and deceived as to the progress of the work last summer, and the promised opening of the line to Windsor. Ultimately the fact was revealed that Mr. Forman could never have intended to accomplish that object, as no preparations were made on the line for traffic, nor was locomotive power provided to work it.'

This statement is utterly untrue, and no one knows it to be so better than Doctor Tupper. My correspondence, which I intend to publish, shows that the whole blame rests entirely with the present Government. The Windsor branch last year was to a considerable extent taken out of my hands, and Mr. Mosse, at the special request of the Government, was placed in charge of it with instructions to report the progress made, and with every facility, so far as I was concerned, at his command, and with no other duties to perform – his remonstrances failed to secure the completion of this branch, notwithstanding the many favorable reports submitted by him.

The contractors at this time had the complete control of the works; they were using *gratis* the engines and cars belonging to the Province; they were holding frequent conferences with members of the Government and the Board, entertaining the latter with promises never to be realized, and for the purpose of affording the Government an excuse for casting aside my authority, reports were circulated that I had determined that the line should not be opened, and this state of matters continued so long as there remained an engine on the road to be destroyed by the contractors.

2nd. 'The testimony of the late Chief Engineer before the railway Committee itself, proved that he located the Railway to Windsor contrary to the valuable decision of Wightman, Chesborough, Sykes, and Beattie.'

I was not bound by anyone's opinion, no matter how valuable you may think it, but the Government well know that all the explorations made by the above Engineers were under consideration, and full advantage taken of them before the position of the present branch was determined. As each Engineer had a line of his own, probably you could tell which was most valuable. This subject has been considered in the correspondence referred to.

3rd. You state: 'Worse than this, from his own statements it can be shewn that he certified as finished a contract of Cameron's contrary to fact, and paid him thousands of pounds for work which he had not done, besides other acts of favoritism of no small amount, which have recently been repaid by Mr. Cameron polling from 50 to 100 of his navvies against the Government.'

The Chairman of the Railway Board can testify to the utter untruthfulness of these statements. Mr. Cameron's works were paid as far as they advanced, and on the measurements and reports of the resident Engineers, the proper deductions being made, and approved of by the Board, until his contract should be finished. The remainder of the paragraph is beneath notice.

4th. 'And the *Chronicle* day by day obtains from him, and through him, grounds for assault upon the Administration who have struggled in vain to get him to discharge his duty with faithfulness and vigor.'

It would not be easy to string more falsehoods together than are contained in the above paragraph. I distinctly deny ever having, during the whole period I held office, contributed directly or indirectly to the columns of any newspaper or having in any way whatever furnished grounds for assault upon the Administration. The Government knows that it never assisted me in the discharge of the duties of my office, but on the contrary threw every obstacle in my way.

An attempt has been made to turn certain statements in Mr. Howe's speech at Windsor into an admission that the Railway was in need of an able and energetic engineer.

You represent Mr. Howe as saying 'that nearly £20,000 more had been paid to the contractors than they were entitled to under their contracts, a sum large enough to cover all they could justly claim even assuming they were entitled to some consideration. This startling fact concealed by the Government, never reported to the Committee, induced the House to resolve that no more money should be paid to the Contractors till the roads were finished.... In defiance of that resolution the Government has been paying money to those contractors all summer.' On this you remark, 'what will our readers say when, with these two statements before them, we assert the Government never paid the contractors a shilling, that the money that was advanced to them was paid by the Board on the recommendation of Mr. Forman, and that this money, which Mr. Howe declares has been paid to them this summer improperly in defiance of the resolutions of the House, has been paid by the Board on the certificate of the Chief Engineer.' But I ask – what will your readers say when I tell them that these large sums of money have been paid without any certificates under the contracts... that *the present Government made alterations on the Contracts,* and I was then called upon as Engineer, contrary to my expressed opinions, to give certificates in accordance with *these alterations.* That some of the contractors have been paid on account of their claims under instructions conveyed *direct to the Board by Mr. Laurie,* before the sections were completed, and that the Contractors often transacted their business with the Board through members of the Government, instead of with the Board through the Engineer, and that whenever they desired it, Government pressure was exerted on their behalf.

You say also 'Does not everybody know how anxious the Government expressed itself to have the wharf at Windsor put into a condition that would not excite the curses – deep if not loud – of the passengers to and from [Saint John]. Nothing could be accomplished to remove that fertile and just cause of attack from the opposition press.' On this subject there is a story to be told, and it is this: – A Member of the Government about the time immediately before the Hants election ordered some work to be given to Mr. MacDonald at Windsor. On this being represented to me, owing to the attitude assumed by that contractor and the unsatisfactory condition of his sections, I remonstrated with the Board, and stated that this work ought to be done by tender and contract. The Board felt the force of my remarks, but did not feel themselves in a position to resist the pressure brought to bear on them, and the alternative which they considered best was to reduce the work to the smallest possible quantity, in the expectation that the contractor would quit the ground and leave them free to pursue that course which recommended itself as proper and for the interest of the Province.

I am not party to the transactions between the Government and the Board, neither am I responsible for doings over which I had no control."[36]

In a separate letter, Forman defended his tactic of having retained the papers Tupper had ordered McNab to recover, and the reason would become abundantly clear in the longest letter Forman wrote on the topic:

"Sir, – As members of the Executive Government of this Province, not content with dismissing me from the situation I lately occupied as Chief Engineer of Public Works, have commenced a system of base detraction with a view of injuring my private reputation – I refer now to the Editorial contained in the last *Colonist*, prepared and published by the advisers of His Excellency the Lieutenant Governor – *for it were impossible* that the Editor of that paper could have possession of the facts necessary to make the disclosures he does, unless furnished by command of His Excellency – I must solicit of you the favour of publishing the annexed correspondence. I do this in self defence, owing principally to this passage in the *Colonist* Editorial of the 30th inst., prepared as will be admitted by all candid persons, as soon as they read the correspondence, by the parties, and for the ignoble purpose already described.

'The public will scarcely be prepared to learn that Mr. Forman has given since his removal from office proofs of the most unequivocal of downright dishonesty, by purloining and obstructing documents from the Railway office which belong to the department, and are essential to carrying on the works with promptitude. Up to Saturday night we understood that Mr. McNab, the Chairman of the Board, although making the most determined efforts, had been unsuccessful in effecting their recovery.

Of course the obstructives, who daily shew that in their hungry greed for office they would like to see the Railway and Province sink together, will be delighted at any rascality by which the public works may be retarded.'"

Forman was emphatic in his insistence that he had not stolen the government documents, as Tupper had claimed, and spelled out his reasons for keeping them in his possession:

"The 'documents and papers' in question, are *the only vouchers* I possessed, for the vindication of my reputation. Without them, or access to them, I should be entirely defenceless. My enemies, unscrupulous as they are – as these extracts already *prove them to be,* might overwhelm me with impunity, but for the evidence these Books and papers contain. In order to conduct a correspondence now going on between myself and the Government – and which I shall immediately lay before the public, with my reply to other portions of the Editorial thus published by the Queen's printer and by authority – access to the Books in question were indispensable.

With any proper regard to my own reputation, how could I have done otherwise? In acting as I have, I may also add that I have done so under the advice and sanction of such of my personal friends as I have been able to consult. I deeply regret that His Excellency the Lieutenant Governor should be advised to allow such uses to be made of the correspondence conducted by individuals with public officers and Heads of Departments – and that garbled accounts of public matters, so deeply affecting private reputation, should receive such sanction as has in this instance been given to them. I am, therefore, now required to defend myself as I best can, against a Government that is but too obviously bent on crushing, by most unfair means, those whose reputations they may not otherwise be enabled to destroy. I may have to trouble you still further on the subject of the Editorial in question. In the meantime the correspondence to which I refer, and which was in the possession of the Executive Government when they so wantonly assailed me through the Queen's printer in the *Colonist,* and to which they make not a passing reference, is now appended and numbered.

Halifax Aug. 31, 1858"[37]

The facts recounted by the engineer provide damaging testimony regarding the government's determination to manufacture a reason to dismiss Howe's man from the post. The letter is so explicit and eloquent that it cannot be paraphrased without obscuring the detail:

"My removal from office as Chief Engineer of the Provincial Railways, and the terms in which your letter of the 25th ult. is couched, ought not perhaps to have surprised me. The temper of the present Government had been sufficiently disclosed by their previous conduct and the tone of their correspondence – yet as I had successfully refuted the numerous charges – many of them equally frivolous and unfounded – that had been from time to time brought against me, I did not believe that the Government would have proceeded to this final step and done me so great an injustice. That my dismissal was a foregone conclusion, and that my successor was brought here for the purpose, is now abundantly obvious, and I regret that I am compelled in justice to my own reputation to review the steps of this very singular transaction."[38]

Forman obviously knew who wrote the *Colonist* article, since he refers to previous attacks made on his abilities in letters exchanged between the Executive Council and the railway board:

"Not content with the blow you have struck in the first paragraph of your letter, you proceed in the second to attack the Railway operations under my auspices from their first inception. A charge of a similar kind and in still more offensive terms was contained in your letter to the Hon. Mr. McNab of 17th June last, and I will extract a paragraph from my reply of June 26:
'As it has become so unexpectedly necessary to defend my professional character and conduct from grave imputations, His Excellency the Lieutenant Governor, I trust, will permit me to state that I have now been employed as an Engineer for a period of eighteen years, mostly in Scotland. I have had charge of several important works as Chief Engineer and General Manager, and under Directors who held the highest social position, and my professional skill has never been questioned before; on the contrary, I have always received the warmest expressions of good will and approbation from all who sought my professional aid. In coming to Nova Scotia, which I was induced to do only from the circumstance of my being a native of the country, I gave up a lucrative post with the certain prospect of advancement in my profession, for an office that did not pay me better or even so well, irrespective of my prospects otherwise.'"[39]

Despite the claim that he could have found better-paying employment elsewhere, it is clear from this statement that Forman had bought in to Howe's concept of the railway as great patriotic undertaking for his colony, to which Howe always referred as "my country." The engineer went on to use portions of the documents he had retained from his office, to support his argument:

"In this Province I have exerted myself to the utmost for the satisfactory completion of the railways, and I can confidently appeal both to the present and former Boards that this has been the case, and that I have labored most assiduously, both from the warm interest I have always taken in the success of this great enterprise, and from a just regard to my own reputation. I can point to the road as it now stands, to its general finish, its durability, and its bridges, with some pride, as the best evidence of the skill and care that have been bestowed upon it.

It is indeed a remarkable circumstance, if I were incompetent to my duties, that from the 12th April 1853, when I was appointed by a Minute in Council, I enjoyed the entire confidence of the Executive Government till the late change in the Administration; that I had the confidence of the former Railway Board till they were broken up, and that I retained the confidence of the present Board till the hour of my abrupt and summary dismissal. I insert here with a feeling of pride the letter which the Chairman and the other two Commissioners constituting the Board gave me on the day after your letter of the 25th, and presenting certainly a striking contrast to it. The opinion thus expressed by gentlemen who have had the best opportunity for judging of my qualifications and conduct, and who, independently of their official position, are men of the highest character and standing in this community, is a sufficient offset, and perhaps a sufficient consolation for the disapproval which you have thought to express." [40]

Here Forman included the verbatim of McNab's consolatory letter to the engineer, and thereafter his account takes on a defiant tone:

"The Board also, in their letter to you of 30th June stated 'that in their opinion the Chief Engineer has had difficulties to contend with of an unusually harassing nature, inseparable perhaps in conducting a work of such magnitude in a new country, and they feel it but due to him to say that, in their judgment, he has done all that could be done under the circumstances to promote and facilitate the works under his charge, and the Board continue to feel that he is still doing so.'

The Government is well aware that from the hour they took office they never gave me their support, and that in place of aiding me, they left me to struggle, alone and unsustained, with all the difficulties of my position. Before the Committee of the assembly last winter I was assailed with impunity, and imputations, which there was ample evidence to repel, were permitted to remain unanswered. It was the feeling and interests of the contractors alone that were cared for in that inquiry.

Your letter indeed of the 5th July contained this passage:

'His Excellency further commands me to say, that he is aware of the importance of continuing the works under the management and direction of the same Engineer, and that while it will give him unfeigned pleasure to learn by the rapid and efficient progress of the works, that Mr. Forman possesses the skill and energy required by his position, he and the Board may confidently rely upon the continued cordial support which the Government have on all occasions hitherto given them.'

And my letter of the 12th of July, I wound up in these terms:

'In conclusion, His Excellency, I trust, will permit me to say that I am extremely gratified by the assurance in the letter I am now replying to, of the cordial support of the Executive Government. My duties are at all time sufficiently arduous, but with the aid of that support, and more especially by a determination, while dealing justly and liberally with the Contractors, to hold them strictly to their engagements, I confidently trust that the object which His Excellency has so much at heart will be accomplished, and the line to Truro completed, and opened for traffic by the first of November next.'"[41]

Forman continued, expressing his suspicion that an apparent inability to complete the railway by the deadline was not the real reason for his dismissal. His letter shows, however, that he had no knowledge of what the government's ulterior motive might have been, other than to repeat his claim that it was conspiring with the contractors:

"You now state 'that it is manifest that under my management, the work will not be completed for several months beyond the time limited for its accomplishment,' and you make this the ground of my removal.

Now I believe that this is by no means the real ground, and that other influences are at the bottom, which the public and I perfectly appreciate, and the government have not the courage and manliness to resist.

I assert further that there is only one difficulty in the way of the completion of the line to Truro by the first of November, and that is the extraordinary position and influence which the Contractors have been permitted to assume and exercise, since the advent of the present government, and against which I have so often remonstrated in vain."[42]

To back this claim, Forman referred to the papers that Tupper had tried in vain to recover when the engineer was sacked:

"My letter of the 26th June last, contained this passage:
'It is true that during the last year I have had many difficulties to contend with, into which I forbear from entering. The chief of these has been the insubordination and the position assumed by the Contractors, who asserted a practical independence, and seemed to think that they would be upheld in disobeying both the Board and myself. In this I trust they are now undeceived, and if they are kept in their proper place, and the government give me the same generous and cordial support which I have always received both from the former and present Board, I have no reason to doubt that the railway, which I am unwilling to abandon, will be successfully and vigorously prosecuted to its completion.'

The Board in their letter of the 30th June, expressed their regret, 'that there has been so much delay in the completion of the contracts, but the government are familiar with the difficulties they have had with the contractors, in compelling them to finish their sections, as well as those which prevented the works being taken out of their hands.'"[43]

Forman then presented the most damning indictment of the Johnston government's culpability for the cost overruns and delays, showing that he had urged his political masters to press the contractors to accelerate the pace of their work:

"Till the year 1857 there was little or no difficulty with the Contractors – since that time the letter books are filled with repeated applications to them to get on with their work, and fulfill their obligations, and with every variety of expostulation and warning.

My report of 17th May last, in reference to the Windsor Branch, contained these passages:

'I feel it is necessary to urge that the measures to be adopted for the completion of the work be properly taken....

'The time heretofore lost in negociating [sic] has occasioned a great deal of delay, and often led to no result....

'The condition of these works is so unsatisfactory that I find it impossible, judging from the experience we have already had, to say when they will be fully completed by the present Contractors....

'The Contractors, in my opinion, should be called upon at once to proceed with all the works simultaneously and not to defer commencing one portion until another is completed....

'Three gangs of platelayers should be employed on each section, and the deficiencies in the embankments over the whole road should be made up as nearly as possible at the same time....

'Vigorous measures are necessary to prevent disappointment to all who may be interested in the opening of this branch.'

In my report of 20th May, on the main line, I stated, that 'To insure the opening of the road this season, the bridge at Shubenacadie should be pushed forward with all possible dispatch; all the piers and abutments should be proceeded with at the same time. I estimate that at least twelve masons can be employed with advantage upon this Bridge, and ten on the Stewiacke Bridge, exclusive of quarrymen, stonecutters, and laborers, which should be in proportion to the number of masons. The other works on these contracts present no difficulties, but unless vigorous measures are at once adopted with No. 8 Section, and with the Shubenacadie and Stewiacke Bridges, it will be impossible to complete the road to Truro before winter.'" [44]

The reference to the Shubenacadie bridge (in reality this was the second bridge across the river; the first was at Enfield) is significant in that it contradicts conventional history. Such history holds that it was Sandford Fleming, the Chief Engineer of the Intercolonial Railway, who first championed the use of iron bridges, a move placing him squarely at the centre of confrontation with the four-man commission appointed by the federal government in 1867. What conventional history overlooks is that Forman was using iron bridges a full decade before Fleming arrived on the Intercolonial, and did so with the full support of his overseers, the commissioners of the Nova Scotia Railway. Forman also planned an iron bridge across the Stewiacke River, since it possessed a tidal stream similar to that of the Shubenacadie, capable of ripping apart the traditional stone and timber cribwork used as the foundation of other bridges (such as that across the Nine Mile River) and wider than a conventional timber bridge could reasonably span.

The engineer continued his defence, reiterating his conviction that it was the contractors who were at the root of his problem:

"In my report of 29th June, I pointed out in detail all the steps that were necessary to accomplish the opening of the road for traffic by the first of November – that on contract No. 8, the number of men at work should be at least doubled – that on No. 9 the contractor had been called on largely to augment his forces – that judging from the then condition of the works, I felt pretty certain that the bridges across both the Shubenacadie and Stewiacke rivers, would be ready by the first of November – that the site for the station house at Truro had been determined, and the plans were in the course of preparation.

In my detailed report of 24th July, I stated that, having walked over the works to Truro, I found they were progressing more satisfactorily than at the date of my last report. Still I suggested at one place more vigorous measures were necessary – that on another section the operations on embankment No. 1 had ceased from November last, and I regretted I was unable to report, notwithstanding the contractor's attention had been called to it, that anything had been done since that date – that the excavations on No. 10 and 11 ought to be completed in two months – and that various other things were required to be done, so that the Railway should be opened for traffic by the first of November.

In my letter of 2nd August, I stated that 'the present mode of completing the Windsor branch contracts is far from satisfactory, and I take the liberty of calling attention to the desirableness of taking these works out of the hands of the contractors....

'Almost all of the rolling stock used on this work is supplied by the Board, and notwithstanding this, the schedule rates are paid for earth work not nearly so costly as the average cost of excavations on the sections, and for which these rates were originally intended to apply, and as these payments are made in addition to the contract price, I am decidedly of opinion that it is for the interests of the Province, that these sections should be taken out of the contractors' hands and finished by the Board.'

Now, Sir, let us pause here and reflect for a moment on the relative position of the Chief Engineer and the other authorities of the Government. In your letter of the 5th July the Government define it to be the 'first duty of the Chief Engineer, not only to furnish plans of the work when required, but to exercise such a thorough and constant supervision of the whole work in progress, as to ensure their completion within the time specified in the several contracts, keeping the Board always in possession of the information necessary to enable them to accomplish that object.'" [45]

At this point Forman condemned the lack of foresight shown by Johnston, McCully, and the commissioners who framed the contract process within which he was obliged to work:

"It will not be pretended surely after the above reports, and with the known and exclusive devotion of my whole time and thoughts to the business of my office, that I neglected my duty as so defined. The Commissioners have given me the most ample testimony, the Government themselves know that I did not neglect it. But of what avail was the performance of my duty if the Attorney General and the Government did not do theirs? It was not part of my business, nor had I the power to enforce the fulfillment of the contracts – to compel the contractors to employ an adequate force – and to induce their obedience to my representations and entreaties.

They set these entreaties and the wishes of the Board equally at defiance, and having the ear of Government, were beyond our control. I saw plainly, therefore, that the work would not be done – that I was to be held accountable for a supineness and neglect which I could not remedy – and that in my own vindication it was necessary to speak out." [46]

To emphasize this point, Forman referred to a letter he had written August 6th 1857, following a review of various sections of the work between Truro Road (now Lantz) and Truro, complaining about the attitude of contractors MacDonald and Johnston:

" If the contractors will, as they promise, put on the additional force necessary to execute the above works during the present month, and which only requires ordinary exertions, there will be no difficulty in securing the opening of the road by the time named, 1st November, but to ensure this they must be compelled to employ the labor, and as under the contracts this power is vested in the Board, it must remain with them to give effect to these reports by exacting the penalties, or by enforcing the stipulations of the contracts, and it is because this has not been heretofore done that the present difficulties exist in getting the road urged on to completion. The Board are aware of the treatment several of their officers have received from the contractors when in the discharge of their duties. Mr. MacDonald threatened the inspectors at different times if they interfered with his section, and yet Mr. MacDonald is continued on the road, and additional works are entrusted to him. Mr. Johnston threatens to kick a second inspector off his section." [47]

There is nothing to indicate that this Johnston was in any way related to the premier, but had he been, it is unlikely it would have created any more furor than the acknowledgement that Mosse was the premier's nephew. Forman continued to use the government's own documents, to which it now seems likely Laurie did not have access, to condemn Johnston, Tupper, and McCully:

"Contractors plant held for advances made under my letter of 27th November 1857, [should be 5th October 1857] is taken out of the country in defiance of the remonstrances of the Board, and notwithstanding these Contractors are supplied with the material and Engines belonging to the Province, to the serious permanent injury of the rolling stock and are paid scheduled prices for work done irrespective of its actual cost and beyond the terms of the contract.

Had sufficient security been taken with making the advance on the 27th of November [should be 5th October 1857], and had the terms of the agreements been afterwards enforced, there would have been no difficulty in completing the Windsor Branch last season, and I feel satisfied that it requires but the execution of the proper power to secure the completion of the Truro road by the time named, and I now call upon the Board to give effect to my reports or the result must entirely rest with themselves.'

The document next in order is a letter of 9th August, from Mr. McNab to you, which runs as follows:-

'I have the honor to enclose a report from the Chief Engineer on the state of the Main line yet to be completed to Truro. If the works required by Mr. Forman are done within the months he sees no difficulty of having the line opened by November, and on pointing out to the Contractors the requirements, they promise to put on a sufficient force to accomplish that object, and say they will have no difficulty in doing so – but from past experience the Board do not place implicit dependence on their promises; they will, however, urge them on by every means in their power, and the inspection to take place a fortnight hence will show if they are in earnest.

The Board beg to call to your attention to the concluding part of the report from which you will not fail to perceive the difficulties that have been and are still existing to prevent the completion of the work, and they would respectfully suggest that the Contractors be notified that unless the works be put in running order by the time named, that their claims for extras will not be entertained or paid, and that any sum due from that source will be held to meet the damage sustained for want of the road – this is the only effectual means the Board know of by which they can be compelled to complete the works.'

Letters were addressed on the same day to Messrs. Johnston & Blackie, Sutherland & Sons, and Walker & Co., as follows:-

'I enclose an extract from the report of Mr. Forman to the Board, of work required to be done on your contract (8-11) within the month of August, so as to ensure the opening of the road by the 1st November 1858, and as this has been arrived at after a careful inspection and you concurring that there was no difficulty in having the works required completed within the time, they require and trust that you will use every energy in your power to accomplish it, and hope on an inspection to be made next week such an amount of work will be found done as to insure its completion within the time specified.'

On the 13th August, your Deputy addressed a letter in reply to Mr. McNab's letter of the 9th August – a copy of which I have not retained. Its purport, however, may be gathered from mine of the 16th as follows:

'I have read the Deputy's Secretary's letter of 13th August, and in reply I have to state that it was not my intention to imply neglect of reproof by the tone of my report towards to the Board, as such a course would be altogether unsuited to our relative positions, but simply to state that I could not be held responsible for the completion of the contracts unless effect was given to my reports, and the terms of the specification enforced. The Windsor Branch, and the difficulty in getting it completed last year, was referred to, because these circumstances were stated in the Hon. the Provincial Secretary's letter of 13th inst., and to which my letter is now in part a reply.

'The Board are aware that I have all along been averse to continuing the works in the hands of several of the present contractors, and especially that the mode adopted to complete the Windsor branch and main line did not agree with my views expressed time after time, and which were not followed.

'I have considered it my duty to carry out the wishes of the Board though opposed to my expressed opinions, but I certainly object to any responsibility being attached to me, as to the result of these views, or in the event of their involving additional cost in construction.

'The treatment the inspectors receive, and the removal of plant by the contractors is well known to the Board.'

On the 19th Mr. McNab wrote to Mr. Keating acquitting me of any intention to reflect on the Board, and stating that both they and the Chief Engineer had used every effort in their power (short of taking the work out of the hands of the contractors) to push forward the works, and that they still hoped to overcome all difficulties, and open the line to Truro this season.

On the 17th, having inspected the main line in company with a member of the Board, I sent in a report shewing that the contractors in the weeks ending on that day, had fallen far short of the quantities they had engaged, and declared it was easy to perform, the quantity of excavations and ballasting to be done per week, on the four contracts under my report of 6th August, 26,601 cubic yards, and the actual quantity put out for the week being only 8,687 cubic yards."[48]

If anything, Forman's greatest flaw may have been his naivety. His letters make it clear he felt his concerns were being taken into consideration by the commissioners, that the commissioners were passing these concerns on to the government, and that in the absence of any contrary communication from Johnston or Tupper, he was getting the support he sought:

"On the 24th the meeting took place between the Government and the Commissioners and Engineers, which is referred to in your letter and from which I retired with a conviction in common with the members of the Board, that the numerous objections there taken had been completely refuted, and confidence restored.

You may judge then my surprise, and that of the Board, when I was handed your letter of the 25th announcing my removal. You state in that letter that every facility for finishing the road to Truro on or before the first day of November next was at my command. I may well ask you what is the meaning of this phrase – what facility had I, or what power over the contractors? What could I have done that I did not do? Was it possible to exercise greater diligence, to pay more assiduous attention than those reports display? Could these be more explicit or more importunate? And is not the only facility that was wanting, the facility of bringing some pressure to bear upon the contractors, which the Government neglected or refused to apply.

You tell me every facility was at my command, and you withhold the only facility I required." [49]

CHAPTER 6

Exoneration Delayed

If his letters offered Forman any relief from the frustration he must surely have been feeling, an even more crushing blow would follow his dismissal. On October 19th 1858 his oldest son, James Hill Forman would die at the age of nine. The death was recorded in the *Presbyterian Witness* of October 23rd, but no details were given. There were three likely causes: typhoid or diphtheria, both of which had spread through the province earlier that year, or influenza, which was rampant worldwide at the time. His personal loss would still outweigh whatever emotions he felt when the railway – his railway – was opened from Halifax to Truro on December 15th of that year:

"When the first run was operated between Halifax and Truro, the people of the area showed very little excitement. Only a few flags decorated the town, and not many people were on hand to watch the first passenger train come in. The official party on board the 'inspection train' included Dr. Charles Tupper, an English railway tycoon by the name of Lord Bury, the Lieutenant Governor (Lord Musgrave) [viz: it was Lord Mulgrave] and other dignitaries. The train left Richmond Station behind the locomotive 'Mayflower' on the morning of December 6, 1858. It is said that one of the two English gentlemen in the special party sat behind the engineer blowing the whistle and the other behind the fireman, ringing the bell. The group had lunch at McKay's Hotel, visited the Normal School, and returned to Halifax at the reported speed of 35 MPH! A special excursion, limited to 450 persons, was operated on December 13th, with regular service beginning on Wednesday, December 15th."[1]

The political developments in Canada may have made the railway opening seem like a second-rate accomplishment. The line had originally been intended to continue on to Amherst and link up to a railway across New Brunswick. The alternative option was to proceed eastward to Pictou County's coal mines and a link to the ferries between Pictou and Prince Edward Island. Political bickering between the three colonies over who should pay how much for an inter-colonial railway left the Nova Scotia government with no real choice but to pursue the Pictou link. Laurie was directed to survey a line eastward, even though several lines had already been surveyed by Forman.

Laurie's appointment was not without a price, or opposition, particularly from Joe Howe. In its March 28th 1859 edition, the *NovaScotian* reported on Howe's speech in the Legislature during the debate over extending the line to Pictou:

"Mr. Howe objected to the lavish expenditure of the Railway Board, and thought it might be largely reduced. He did not believe that the people of Nova Scotia would consent to pay Mr. Laurie, or anybody else, except the Governor, £1500 per annum. They could only afford to pay £1000 to the Venerable Chief Justice. His successor would receive much less. A retaining fee of £500 secured them the services of a gentleman of the rank, talents, and experience of the Attorney General to lead their government and conduct the business of the Crown Office. Why should they pay £1500 a year to an Engineer, when half that sum would secure the services of a competent officer? The people would pay no such sum to any public officer. Nor should they. If borne down by such salaries, and others in that proportion, the railroads could not pay, nor would there ever be a fund to build the road to Pictou."[2]

The Halifax *Morning Sun*, opposed to the appointment of an American engineer, calculated that Laurie's report, including his expenses and salary, the salaries of all his assistants and the publication of the 55-page booklet, had cost Nova Scotia taxpayers £23 10s. per page.

Laurie's appointment did not end the impact of Forman's time on the project. Even before he was dismissed, Forman was dealing with the claims made by various contractors for payment for work not stipulated in their contracts, resulting from changes in the route or the nature of a particular work at a certain location. The disputes involved a complicated process of arbitration and exchanges of letters from engineers, lawyers, and commissioners. The resolution of the problem would be left to Laurie. Much of the focus was on the claims of Donald Cameron, who had won the original contract for No.4 section on the Windsor Branch, but had it taken from him by the board and placed with the firm of Johnson and Blackie, who likewise sought compensation for extra work done on the section.

Left: Jonathan McCully was described as an unoriginal thinker, but he was nevertheless indispensable to leaders of all political parties. His term as lone commissioner of the railway put the project back on a sound financial footing. (Library and Archives Canada, PA 025271)

One of the men who had a hand in drafting the contracts was Jonathan McCully, the Amherst lawyer and railway commissioner who never held an elected office at any time during his lengthy political career. He was appointed to the powerful Executive Council in 1848. Although a Liberal by politics, he had a personal association with Charles Tupper, having been Tupper's teacher in Amherst, and an apolitical connection with Howe. Upon his appointment to the council, he moved to Halifax to be near his work. He served consecutively as solicitor general, commissioner of railways, and as government leader in the council. For eight years he was editor of the *Morning Chronicle*, one of the leading newspapers in the Maritime Provinces, and later followed Howe as editor of the Reform-minded *NovaScotian*. He would distinguish himself as a Father of Confederation, and be appointed to the first Senate. McCully was the counsel referred to in the *NovaScotian*'s September 6th editorial.

James Wilberforce Longley was as charitable as he could be about the alliance between the two men: "Probably Dr. Tupper did not altogether regard him as a *persona non grata*, Mr. McCully not being either an amiable or popular man, but he had ability, and could not fail to be a source of strength to a body of statesmen dealing with any large question."[3]

Dalhousie University historian Paul B. Waite paints an unflattering portrait:

"[McCully] was always a slow, rather unoriginal thinker. Nor was he a great orator. He spoke with force and directness, often with homely allusions laced occasionally with slang, but neither in force nor in metaphor, nor in his public presence, was he the equal of Joseph Howe, whom McCully seems much to have admired....

...McCully was not a remarkable man; one of those people who could not do things by halves, he climbed, not very elegantly, up through colonial society. He disliked humbug or pretence; he had none of those arts himself. He cared little for public opinion; his course on confederation took courage: there were not many who would have done what he did. Yet somehow he remains an unlovely figure. With McCully, instincts answered for ideas, and his advocacy did not always help a good cause. He was in this respect like Charles Tupper, but without Tupper's cleverness or agility. McCully's stubbornness and pugnacity, his capacity for work, took him a long way – farther perhaps than his talents really deserved."[4]

McCully had set his sights on Forman, resigning from the railway commission in order to act as the solicitor for Cameron (who sought to recoup losses incurred in filling the Big Bog Brook near Ellershouse, rather than build the viaduct specified in the contract). In this, Cameron had received agreement from Forman, but the engineer had made it clear that the cost of the fill must not exceed the contract price of the trestle. Cameron would later claim that this agreement was made with one of his lieutenants while he was "out of the country," and that he could not be expected to abide by Forman's stipulation.

There is evidence to suggest McCully exacerbated the problem. His letter of January 26th 1859 to provincial secretary Tupper exhibits a certain exasperation with the railway commission's chairman, James McNab. Having received no immediate reply from McNab about the status of his client's claim (for £1,350), McCully demanded that Tupper take up the matter immediately with the Lieutenant Governor and his executive council:

"On the 14th January instant, I requested Mr. McNab, as chairman of the board, to consult with the executive government, and inform me if he would accept service of a writ of summons to be issued out of the supreme court, and submit the case to a court and jury on its merits, as was done in the case of Hill & Fraser, where the present attorney general prosecuted for the plaintiff. Receiving no reply to that letter, on the 20th instant I again called his attention to the subject, and was then informed by him that my letter of the 14th had been handed to the attorney general for the decision of the government, but that no reply had been received.

I have now, sir, to request that you will be pleased to remit this application thus renewed, to His Excellency in council, and to move His Excellency on the subject at the earliest opportunity.

If His Excellency in council prefer it, Mr. Cameron, who seeks only what is right and reasonable, would be perfectly willing that the case should be submitted to arbitrators to be mutually chosen."[5]

McCully then let fly with his impatience:

"It seems to me so contrary to all sense of right and justice, and equity, that a subject having such a claim as Mr. Cameron prefers, with such admissions of its correctness, should not only be refused payment by the government under which he lives, but refused a tribunal where he shall be permitted legally to establish its validity if he can. I will not, in the mean time, suppose such a wrong will be done him.

Asking you to remind His Excellency Lord Mulgrave, that a delay of justice in certain cases becomes substantially a denial of it, and several months have now elapsed since this money is claimed to be due, and soliciting an early reply to this application,

I have etc.
J. McCully"[6]

His temper was not calmed when Tupper responded, January 28th 1859, asking McCully to have his client furnish the Lieutenant Governor with a detailed statement of claim: "... and that the statement be accompanied by a reference to the agreements with the commissioners or engineers on which the charges are severally founded."[7] The next day McCully told Tupper his client could not comply with such a request because Cameron, who lived in New Glasgow, did not have any copies of the documents. Before leaving Halifax, Cameron had told McCully the railway commission retained any copies of those agreements: "Mr. Cameron, therefore, can furnish nothing of what is required, except as first furnished by the railway department, and that only, as I understand, after they obtain leave from the executive government."[8] Tupper directed the commission to provide McCully with copies of the necessary paperwork, which arrived with a letter from McNab (February 2nd 1859) showing that Laurie was the cause of the contention: "This statement would show a balance of £1356 17s. 5d. in Mr. Cameron's favor, but it is subject to certain questions which have been raised by Mr. Laurie, the Chief Engineer, and which, in fact, are the chief points at issue."[9]

McNab provided a copy of Laurie's report, which provoked a February 5th retort from McCully:

"Having furnished his reasons for not being able to comply with the request of His Excellency the Lieutenant Governor, to furnish detailed statements and agreements already in government custody, I had hoped that a long and wearisome correspondence would have been brought to a close, by leave to sue being given, or the offer to arbitrate being accepted.

I am sure that if contractors were aware that no means of redress under the laws of the land existed by which they could enforce these claims when thousands of pounds are withheld by the government, after being fairly earned, no sane man would ever again contract for such a government."[10]

This rather self-serving piece of rhetoric overlooks the fact that McCully was one of those who set up the machinery by which contracts were originally let. The fault for any lack of a mediation process appears, at least in part, to lie with him. Howe – now back on the benches as a member of the Legislature, and chairman of the House's committee empanelled to examine the matter – fired back a shot in support of Forman:

"Donald Cameron petitions to be paid £1356 17s. 5d., assumed to be due under his Contract No. 4, Windsor branch, and has some other claims for work done under agreement with, or instructions received from, the late engineer. Mr. Laurie takes exception to those claims which, in the absence of Mr. Forman, the committee regret that they have not been able to investigate to their entire satisfaction."[11]

Clearly Howe intended to push the point that Forman had been dismissed too hastily, but he added more support for Forman's performance:

"Mr. Cameron appears to have completed, or nearly completed, his work without any disputes with the board of commissioners or with Mr. Forman, and his year of upholdence terminated in October last. There is every reason to believe that, had the late engineer continued in charge, the claims arising out of this contract would have been amicably adjusted. As, however, points have been raised by Mr. Laurie, involving considerable sums of public money, about which, in the absence of the late Chief Engineer, a majority of the committee have not been able to come to any satisfactory conclusion, they recommend that Mr. Cameron be offered either of two alternatives – to accept a measurement of his whole work, subject to deductions as in the cases of the other contractors; or, if he prefers to press his claims against the government in a court of law, that permission should be given him to do so."[12]

This latter alternative was exactly what McCully had wanted. It was not what he got, and his frustration was made evident in a letter he sent to Laurie dated July 4th 1859. As a result of the opposition of the attorney general and other key government figures, Cameron did not get his day in court, but rather an appointment was made by Howe's railway committee, with Laurie, to re-measure the disputed works. Writing directly to Laurie, McCully noted:

"Your letter 27th June to D. Cameron, informing him of 'arrangements to commence measuring works on No. 4 W.B. [Windsor Branch], with a view to settlement under reports of railway committee,' has been received by Mr. D. Cameron, and handed to me with instructions to reply.

Mr. Cameron knows of no 'reports of railway committee,' under which contract No. 4 Windsor Branch requires re-measurement. This contract he completed in the terms of specification, except where slightly altered by mutual consent, and yet payment of a balance settled and adjusted has been most dishonestly refused – and arbitration has been refused – leave to sue the government has been refused; and if Mr. Cameron is not under a misapprehension, this has been done either at your express recommendation, or with your sanction."[13]

The final paragraph was intended to wound:

"The conduct of the Board and the present Government towards Mr. Cameron, throughout, has been so unjust, so shamefully dishonest and oppressive, and your own partiality and want of fairness, as well before the committee last winter as in your report, were so palpable, Mr. Cameron has no confidence in the Government you serve, nor in you as their Engineer. Any measurements taken by you, or under your direction, or subject to your control, would probably be as perverted as your report and your testimony; and he therefore respectively declines to commit himself to any proceedings you as their servant, or the Government undisguisedly hostile to his interests, and which has forfeited all public confidence, may see proper to adopt."[14]

Laurie must have bitten his tongue. His reply dated July 5th was terse:

"Your communication of the 4th inst., as counsel for Mr. Donald Cameron, relative to measuring work done on contract No. 4 Windsor Branch has been received.

Left: William Baillie Smellie – A Notman photograph from 1875 offers evidence that despite the assault on his reputation in Nova Scotia, Smellie was enjoying some professional success.
(National Gallery of Canada, no. 34992.45)

The want of truth and the base and blackguard spirit in which your letter is penned, prevent me from taking further notice of it to inform you that the measurements will be made at the time specified."[15]

The tenor of McCully's letter gives weight to Howe's assertion that, had Forman still been in charge, the matter could have been settled amicably. As it was, Forman, who was not present for the measuring or the report, was vindicated *in absentia* by Laurie.

By examining the correspondence between Cameron and Forman, the notes of Forman's lieutenant James R. Mosse, and by examining the state of the cuttings on the three contracts undertaken by Cameron, Laurie came to the conclusion that the contractor was entitled to some minor compensation for claims made on contracts 1, and 3, but No. 4 was an entirely different matter. The re-measurement uncovered events that tend to exonerate Forman even further. The procedure was conducted by William Baillie Smellie, an assistant to Forman since August of 1854, who had done the original survey (with Wightman). Richard Uniacke and George McHeffy, who had joined the project in 1856 and 1857 respectively, as students, checked his work.

After all three men certified their work, the measurements were inspected by C.E. Hewitt, another of Forman's assistants (hired in 1855), and Laurie, who discovered no fewer than eighty errors that would have given Cameron more than £2,000 to which he was not entitled. There followed some claims and counter-claims between Smellie, McHeffy, and Hewitt, but Laurie had no qualms about denouncing the affair as "fraudulent." The railway committee, headed by J.W. Johnston, and including Tupper and the railway commissioners, was inclined to agree:

"The following explanations were also now given by Mr. Smellie: Mr. Laurie was absent in Boston while the work was going on, and when he returned, all the calculations of quantities had been completed and checked by Mr. McHeffy, and Mr. Smellie had entered in ink in the ruled columns the greater part of the quantities as they were subsequently returned by him to Mr. Laurie, and soon after Mr. Laurie's return the whole quantities had been inked in. Mr. Hewitt was not employed in the office – his engagements kept him in the country, and he visited Halifax only occasionally or about once a month."[16]

Tupper's reaction was immediate. On January 7th 1860, he sent a letter to the chairman of the railway commission, James McNab, with an abrupt order:

"I have it in command from His Excellency the Lieutenant Governor to inform you that the Executive Government, having carefully investigated the evidence connected with the recent falsification of the returns of the measurement of Mr. Cameron's work on contract No. 4, are fully convinced of the culpability of Mr. Smellie; and I am further commanded to direct you to remove Mr. Smellie without delay from all connection with the railway department."[17]

It appears the real culprit behind Forman's disgrace was discovered, albeit too late to restore the Chief Engineer to his position. Smellie stood trial for the embezzlement of money from the treasury, being accused of a conspiracy with contractor Cameron and his solicitor, McCully. Smellie was acquitted, and by 1862 he was listed on McCully's railway board as Acting Engineer. He resurfaced in 1873 as one of the thirteen engineers left in charge of the construction of the Intercolonial Railway in Nova Scotia by Sandford Fleming. On February 14th 1860, McCully ended his association with Cameron, in order to resume his place on the railway board, this time as its chairman. His tone was markedly less vitriolic than the language he had used on Laurie:

> "I think the dispute is one that should be submitted, either to a court of law or to an arbitration, the latter probably would be the least expensive and most satisfactory mode of adjustment; but in any case I respectfully submit that the whole matter should be withdrawn from my consideration." [18]

In other words, McCully washed his hands of the affair, for as Cameron's former counsel he could take no part in any arbitration as the chairman of the railway commission.

Laurie had also made it clear that once the claims had been settled, his services would no longer be needed, and Tupper prevailed upon him to write a report suggesting ways to improve the operation of the commission. On October 3rd 1859, he replied in terms that again tended to exonerate Forman:

> "The right claimed and used, on the part of the Commissioners, to give directions to inferior officers, contractors, and employees, independent of those over them, is fatal to all systems of management, and at once leads to confusion and antagonism. The instant an intermediate officer is passed over, and directions given to those under him, he ceases to have control or responsibility.
>
> Aware that many of the difficulties existing at the date of my appointment as Engineer, had their origin in the want of system, the contractors running from one department to another, and making arrangements with and getting orders and instructions from each, I stipulated that the engineer staff and the contractors should be subject entirely to my order, and be under my control, as Chief Engineer, which is the common and usual course in railway construction. This, I understood, was assented by the Government; but it was soon apparent that the Commissioners entertained very different ideas, and adhered to what they considered their rights as Commissioners.
>
> My predecessor, in writing to the board, June 30th 1858, says – 'You are aware that latterly most of the communications with the contractors have been carried on directly by the Board.' The result was, a mass of conflicting agreements, counter-demands, and allowances but neither energy in the management nor progress in the construction of the works." [19]

Laurie clearly placed blame in the hands of the political appointees on the board:

> "Under the particular circumstances of my appointment, the object being to get the road in operation in a few months, I was willing to forego what, under other circumstances, I would have insisted upon, or resigned; as it was, the interference of the Board in matters which they did not understand came nigh defeating the completion of the road that season. There is no occasion for the services of an engineer, if the Board are qualified to conduct and direct the operations of construction.
>
> That it is the duty of commissioners, as it is that of every officer, to be vigilant guardians of the interests and properly entrusted to their care, no one will deny; but when

they undertake, in their board room, to manage in detail the operations and business of a railway, either in its construction or working department, it is attempting what can never be accomplished satisfactorily."[20]

He went on to outline how railways were then being managed in the United States, but noted Nova Scotia had taken a peculiarly local approach:

"Intimately connected with any efficient system of management is the manner of making contracts and payments.
On the Nova Scotia Railway, many agreements are made without proper specifications of the work to be performed, by a system of correspondence which, although common in commercial transactions, where the parties are supposed to be thoroughly conversant with the subject matter, is ill suited for railway purposes, and affords but imperfect information to the person superintending the works. This appears to have been the system largely in practice from the commencement. The only proper way is by specification and contract, or memorandum of agreement, which speak for themselves, and do not admit of that latitude of construction which letter correspondence allows.
The evils of the system are strongly illustrated by the correspondence, and the claims for extras, in connection with No. 4, Windsor Branch, and other contracts."[21]

Ideally, one can suppose the Nova Scotia Railway was based upon the model of the Belgian state railways, rather than those of England or the United States, in that the work was undertaken by the national government, but executed by private enterprise. This is borne out by the description given by Dionysius Lardner:

"The extraordinary expedition with which the Belgian railroads were completed, has been mainly caused by the circumstance of their having been executed by the state, and the execution being conducted under the superintendence of a special railway committee, invested with adequate powers. By this expedient, innumerable official formalities were avoided."[22]

Where the two projects differed is apparent in Lardner's explanation of the role of the engineers:

"The two engineers, MM Simons and Deridder, who had proposed the project, were invested with the general direction of the works; full powers were given them to form contracts, purchase land, and make other definitive arrangements necessary for carrying on the works, without reference to higher official powers."[23]

This clearly was not the case in Nova Scotia, where the board of railway commissioners, as Laurie noted, insisted on exercising total control over the distribution of contracts. It appears the commissioners also were unaware of Lardner's earlier admonishment on the proper organization of a functioning railway, whether it be in England, Europe or the United States:

"The organization of the administrative machinery necessary for the conduct of the practical business of a railway, or a system of railways brought under a common direction and management, includes the following four principal departments or services, more or less distinct from, and independent of each other. These are:–

    1st. The service of the way and works.
    2d. The service of the draft.
    3d. The service of the carriage.
    4th. The service of the stations.

Each of these departments has its separate staff, machinery, and stock."[24]

Forman did not enjoy such luxury, for the railway was opening for business immediately behind the navvy gangs just as soon as rail was laid, and he was expected to oversee the operation of the functioning part of the line in addition to the development of the extended right of way.

McCully deserves the credit for placing the railway on a sound economic footing. As chairman of the commission (by 1860 he was the lone commissioner) he instituted most of the reforms recommended by Laurie, even reducing the salaries of some highly placed employees in order to reduce costs. He rescheduled trains to make more stops at smaller stations, reduced the number of mixed trains, making passenger travel a little more convenient (passengers frequently had to wait for freight to be loaded before the train moved on), and concentrated the decision-making process in the hands of a superintendent and himself. He ran the department with an iron hand, leading a pundit of the day to pen a song in his honour:

> "I am the king of all I survey,
> My will there is none to dispute,
> The trains will run when I tell 'em to run,
> And toot, when I tell 'em to toot!"[25]

It may have been McCully's zeal for reform of the railway department, however, that led him to uncover the real cause of the faulty accounting that proved to be the Chief Engineer's undoing. His report of 1861 came too late to save James Richardson Forman.

"When I assumed office I found that the practice had been, for Mr. Morrow, the accountant, to receive from the superintendent of Traffic the entire amount of earnings of the road, and from this fund to pay working expenses. This was a very inconvenient practice. The tables of the office, for two or three days every week, were necessarily strewn with money, requiring to be counted in and counted out, and I therefore decided to abolish the practice altogether and instead, to require that the earnings of the road [be] counted, and labelled by the Traffic superintendent at Richmond, and be paid directly to the credit of the road, into the Bank of Nova Scotia.

This having been done ... it was superadded the recommendation of the committee of public accounts, that these deposits be transferred to the credit of the Receiver General; and that the necessary amounts for payment of working expenses be from time to time obtained from him, by requisition, and deposited in the bank to the credit of the Railway Department. Payments for all services are therefore now made by checks drawn upon this latter fund, until it is exhausted, when by further deposits it is again renewed. By this simple arrangement no money is now required to be counted in or out of the office, except what trifling sums are necessary for office disbursements, under a 'small cash' account – and a thorough system of checks is established." [26]

Morrow, who had been largely responsible for the state of the books of the construction accounts, retired in 1862 "due to infirmity and age" and had been relieved of much of his duties in 1860. George Taylor had replaced Mosse as superintendent of traffic that same year.

It is clear that Forman had taken on a formidable – perhaps even impossible – task, one that even Laurie admitted involved something of an "experiment." There is no apparent written record of Forman's character. He appears to have shied away from publicity and the public expression of his views, except for his letter of 1858. He was probably a very private man. We can suppose, however, that he more or less fit the mould of the man described, albeit romantically at times, in the August 1874 edition of *Harper's New Monthly* magazine:

"The first duty of a railroad surveyor, then, is to trace in a general way the course of the projected railroad upon an ordinary map by means of a careful study of its mountain ranges and its water-courses. The more detailed and elaborate the map, the more perfect can he make his preliminary and office survey. This being done, the real work of the survey begins. For this purpose the Chief Engineer makes a general reconnaissance of the whole ground, generally on horseback. He provides himself with the best map or maps he can obtain. He picks up as best he can more definite and precise local information. To succeed in his work he must have qualities which are rare, qualities which no mere school of engineering can impart. In his profession, as in every other, there is a certain something indefinable in native genius, something which may perish unused for want of development and training, but which no mere development or training can supply. The engineer must be a man of ready parts. He must have himself always well in hand. He must understand human nature, and know how to deal with it. He must be equally at home in the log-hut among the mountains and in the velvet carpeted and mahogany furnished office in the great city. He must be a man of quick eye and abundant resources, able to meet an exigency, or to vary in detail and on the moment a carefully matured plan for the purpose of avoiding an unexpected obstacle, and reaching the general result with the least expenditure of time and money. The engineer has tunneled the Alps, and an expert assures us that with money enough it would be possible to construct a permanent floating bridge across the Atlantic. But there are a great many things which it does not pay to accomplish, and the successful engineer must be able to subordinate professional pride to practical results; to avoid obstacles that can be avoided, and to overcome only those that he cannot escape; to make the fewest possible rock cuttings, tunnels, culverts, and bridges; and to be known and honored less for what he has done than for what he has avoided doing." [27]

The article goes on to describe in some detail the process of the survey, but makes note of a step that Nova Scotia Railway commissioners overlooked:

"At length the facts are all before the engineer-in-chief, and he is prepared to make his report. It goes before the board of directors. Its conclusions are scanned, its methods examined, its results subjected to the severest scrutiny. The counsel of other and often rival engineers is called in. A thousand questions must be raised, debated, determined, before anything can be considered settled." [28]

It seems the quest for economy was invoked by the commissioners in Nova Scotia, who were the *de facto* directors that any private line would have employed, for no one was called to give Forman's survey another examination – except Wightman. The commission appears to have been satisfied with taking an option decried in *Harper's New Monthly*:

"If the engineer could only be permitted to run his projected road where it would be easiest built, his problem would be a simple one, but he must consider what will be the cost of carriage, what will be expensive to maintain as well as to construct, where he will get custom, and how he may avoid local opposition." [29]

Unhampered by any competition, these factors were not given much consideration by a board that admittedly had little experience in such matters; indeed, no one in the British Empire had experience in organizing, building, and managing a government-owned railway. The *NovaScotian* pointed out, however, that when local experts were challenged to verify or discredit Forman's findings, none stepped forward. Similarly silent was Benjamin Smith, the farmer, government surveyor, and Justice of the Peace throughout his tenure as Conservative MLA for Hants County from 1851 to 1855. Running for re-election in 1858, amid accusations that he was allowing non-resident railway navvies to vote in the community of Rawdon, Smith belatedly began taking up Tupper's and Johnston's call against the overspending on the line. In a June 1858 comment, the newspaper noted:

"We have been applied to several times of late, by parties more immediately interested in the matter, if possible, to obtain and publish a copy of a letter written by the Railway Board, the first season of their operations, to Benjamin Smith, Esquire, on the subject of the site of the Windsor and Halifax Railway.
We are glad to be able to comply with the request – and we now furnish a correct copy of the letter in question.
Mr. Smith and his friends, we learn, have been trying to make political capital wherever it was thought it could safely be done, out of the fact that the short westerly line ought not to have been adopted.
In December, 1854, Mr. Smith was one of the County members for Hants. The Special Session, to settle the Reciprocity Act, had just been held. The Board took the opportunity to submit to the House at the extra session, the plan of the line then just discovered by the Railway Engineer, as the road is now located, and the matter was fully and freely canvassed in and out of the House.
To this, the letter in question refers – and we give it in full. It is as follows: –
'Nova Scotia Railway Office
18th Dec. 1854.
Dear Sir:-
Doubts having been expressed in the Legislature as to the accuracy and value of the Surveys conducted with a view to determine the best route for a Railway to Windsor, I have been instructed by the Board to request that you will confer with the Members for

Hants, and proceed to examine any tracts of country which you and they think favorable and which may have been overlooked, and to make such surveys as you consider will be useful in the ultimate determination of a question so important.

The Board will be happy to have reports from you from time to time. It will be prepared to pay you at the rate of 20s. per day, and also will cover your necessary expenses.

I am, your ob'dt Ser'vt.

J.R. Forman

To B. Smith, Esq.'" [30]

The special session for the Reciprocity Act, referred to in the opening of the editorial, was called so that Nova Scotia's members of the Legislature could decided upon their protest against fishing rights in Nova Scotia waters being given to US fishing fleets by the government of Canada in order to obtain greater advantages under the treaty for the interior colony. The newspaper then went to the meat of its objection, Smith's reluctance to get involved:

"This letter was forwarded to Mr. Smith forthwith. But no answer was ever written or received. Mr. Smith has said he was away from home when it reached his place of abode. But a few days were neither here nor there. Why did he not reply to it when he got home? Why did he not call attention to the probable locality where he thought the better site existed? He did nothing. He put the letter in his pocket and kept silence, till the spring of 1855, when the General Election was about to come off, and then he began to raise a hue-and-cry about the road being in the wrong place. This letter was then published in our columns, and he was as mute as a mouse. Now, however, he hopes it has been forgotten. But it hasn't – and here it is again staring him in the face, and again it will put him to silence." [31]

The newspaper suggested that Smith, "of all men in Hants," had a responsibility as a surveyor, to give credible answers to the questions he was raising at a time when he was seeking votes by courting the Roman Catholics he had denounced during the Gourley Shanty riots:

"As the publication of this letter in 1855 silenced Mr. Smith breasting up against and denouncing Roman Catholics, so in 1858 it will be found not to have lost its virtue, we trust, though he is now found fawning upon and courting these same people." [32]

Smith's ploy was unsuccessful. The Protestant Alliance waged a formidable lobby against him, allowing millionaire shipbuilder Bennett Smith of Windsor to take the seat for the Reform party.

Even after he left Nova Scotia, Forman's supporters, notably Howe and his newspaper the *NovaScotian*, refused to desert him. It took a royal occasion to bring out the final comment on Forman's work. On August 2nd 1860, the Prince of Wales undertook a visit to the province, en route to Canada. His trip from Halifax to Windsor, thence from Windsor to Truro, and on to Pictou (by coach), was seen as a royal seal of approval for the railway. It was not without its critics. Tupper and the opposition papers attempted to make a scandal out of the necessity of transporting the troops accompanying the Royal Train in second-class carriages, but the *NovaScotian* would have none of it, quickly refuting such claims. Indeed, the newspaper went even further, speaking in complimentary terms about the chairman of the board of railway commissioners, Jonathan McCully:

"Now, as to the Railway and its management. During the last ten days, we suspect we are not far astray in assuming that ten thousand people have traveled by rail in Nova Scotia. Extra trains, and special trains, by night and by day, have been thundering over the line in every direction – at all imaginable hours. On the very night preceding the Prince's departure from Windsor to Truro, Parodi and her troupe of players, with almost no notice, were expressed, through from Halifax to meet the [steamship] *Emperor* – leaving Richmond at half-past twelve at night; and not a scratch or a bruise has occurred, not a hair of the head of man, woman or child has been injured during this whole operation. That the efficiency of the management of the Nova Scotia lines of Railway have now been clearly and satisfactorily established, it were vain to deny. All the scandal written spoken or published, either as affecting the road or its management, the Chairman or the subordinates, have at length been thoroughly wiped out. The responsibility which had devolved upon the Chairman in conducting these operations, which have terminated so happily, so successfully, must have been immense. Few men would have envied him his situation, and fewer still could have sustained the fatigue and anxiety incident to it. And while the public have looked to him and while he would have been held responsible for any untoward event occurring from any cause, not beyond human control, yet amid the congratulations of friends, the Chairman uniformly declares, that it is to the skill, the precaution, the zeal, and ability of the subordinate officers, that so much success is attributable and owing. Where all have acquitted themselves so creditably, it were invidious to particularize, but to the Superintendent of the Locomotive department, Mr. Moir, the Road Inspector, Mr. Marshall, to the Road Masters, the Engine Drivers, the Conductors and the Station Masters, to all much credit is deservedly due."[33]

Having paid tribute to McCully, the newspaper went back to a familiar theme:

"But we have a word to say of another individual, who is no longer among us to witness the triumph. We refer to J.R. Forman, Esq., who is now, and deservedly, at the head of his profession in Scotland – who has spent the whole of the season nearly in London before Parliamentary Committees, and whose efforts there, we are glad to learn, have been crowned with entire success in every single engineering case in which his services have been secured. It had been industriously rumored – the enemies of Railways had assiduously labored, and but too successfully in many instances we fear, to impress the public with the belief that our Railroads had been laid down on such curves and grades that they could not be traveled over with any safety at a rate beyond twenty or twenty-five miles per hour. That slander, too, has been effectually refuted."[34]

Pressing home the point, the newspaper went on to make another claim in favour of Forman, that he actually saved the province money:

"We shall, therefore, hear no more after this, about insuperable grades and impassable curves. They, with the 'unfathomable lakes,' are destined to be among the myths of the past. With all these facts, incontrovertible, before us, witnessed by thousands upon thousands of all classes and creeds, with these accomplishments now on imperishable record, it is for the public, not for us, to say whether, in reference to the Railway Department, the right man is, or is not, in the right place – whether it would not have been more discreet, more politic, more just, on the part of Mr. Johnston, Dr. Tupper, Mr. Killam and others, to have waited a little before they attempted to condemn a public officer, whose only offence was the saving of about five thousand pounds a year in the management of one department of the public service."[35]

By early October of 1858, still reeling from his dismissal, and now seething with anger at the continuing barrage of abuse from members of Johnston's government, Forman had appealed directly to the Lieutenant Governor, the Earl of Mulgrave for some relief. His October 8th letter appears to have gone unanswered, but Forman repeated his assertions of previous letters, and made new points that have been overlooked in later examinations of the affair. For one thing, Forman queried why the board had been left without any legal adviser, a state he did not blame entirely upon Johnston's administration:

"Does he [Mulgrave] know that it was absolutely necessary for the Board to have a legal adviser upon whom they could depend, and who would take the responsibility of advising and keeping them right in carrying out the contracts, and direct the proper cure to be adopted for the purpose of urging forward the works and securing compliance with the Engineer's Reports."[36]

It appears that McCully, the only lawyer appointed to the board, was sorely missed after he left the board to take up the cause of the contractors, for as Forman goes on to point out:

"This absence of legal advice and want of hearty co-operation on the part of the Government, was the origin of many of the difficulties the Board had to contend with, and emboldened the Contractors to assume in the first instance that position which rendered subsequent exertion on the part of the Board unavailing."[37]

He did, however, find fault with Johnston for weakening the Board's authority by reducing its membership:

"But on the supposition that the Government did intend to carry out the views of their predecessors, how is it that they began by altering the constitution of the Board, and reducing it from six members to three? This was short-sighted and materially affected the efficiency of the management. So effective was the management under the first Board, that there is not one of its members who will not state that previous to the advent of the present Government, there was no difficulty getting the works pushed forward, and though the Railway was commenced under the most unfavorable circumstances, as regards both the labor and appliances found in the country, the Engineering skill was always sufficient, and the public cannot account for the subsequent difficulties and delays otherwise than by admitting a change of policy on the part of the Administration."[38]

Forman also blamed Johnston for placing him in an untenable position, one that was never intended by the enabling legislation of 1854:

"Mr. Johnston made the Engineer the leader and director of the Board, instead of which the Board, and not the Engineer, is the constituted manager. My duties, under the contract, were to direct the works, superintend the construction, and report to the Board verbally or by written communication, which was done almost daily; the power of enforcing the Contracts remained with the Board."[39]

After restating his position by quoting extensively from previously published correspondence, Forman's complaint then takes an interesting and personal twist, aiming directly at Johnston:

"The Attorney General seems to think it very bold and unworthy for me to have ventured an opinion that my removal was occasioned by the influence I alluded to, and that Mr. Laurie was brought to supercede me.
  I ask him if this was not the case, and if he felt interested in the success of the road under my supervision, why did he not come forward and render me the assistance I required – why he did not instruct the Board last year about the return [of the] books required by the Contractor's Counsel, in place of assailing them on the floor of the House? If he thought my opinion of the contracts was wrong, why did he not instruct the Board accordingly? Why was the interests [sic] of the Province not protected during the Railway investigation last winter, and the Board left to fight the Contractors and counsel without legal advice? So strong and uncalled for was the language used by the Contractor's Counsel, and so marked the indifference shown by the Attorney General, that the Board regretted that they had not retained special counsel independent of the law officers of the Crown for my protection. It was patent to all the world that I had no advocate to defend me before the Railway Committee, and that the assaults made on me from day to day, which a lawyer of any talent or zeal could easily have repelled, rather gave pleasure to Attorney General, whose business it was to protect, but who abandoned and betrayed me, to the opposite counsel. The course pursued by the Attorney General on that enquiry, both as it affected the public interest and myself, was without example in colonial history."[40]

Forman stops short of noting the relationship between Johnston and Mosse, the Attorney General's nephew, but one could easily draw the conclusion that Forman's dismissal could have been an attempt to place Johnston's nephew Mosse in charge of the works, at least in time to oversee the triumphant completion of the railway to Truro, and perhaps a ceremony in which Johnston, and not the hated Howe, could participate. He made his position clear, however:

"I abstain, my Lord, from going into a multitude of minor points suggested by the Attorney General's letter, which could be refuted with equal ease. The substantial issue before the country is this – were the delays in the completion of the Railway, first to Windsor, and then to Truro, attributable to the Board, [to] the Engineer, or to the Contractors; and if, the latter, does the responsibility extend to the Government as aiding and abetting them?
  Now I distinctly assert that the blame belongs altogether to the Contractors, and to the Government who upheld them, and that a more iniquitous attempt was never made than to fasten that blame upon me."[41]

He closed the letter with a Parthian shot, for by this time he had made up his mind to leave Nova Scotia and return to Scotland, as much to resume a career in a place where he felt comfortable, as it was to escape the ignominy heaped upon him in his homeland:

"It is enough to say that my professional competency Mr. Johnston and his colleagues are incapable of judging, while the charge of remissness and neglect they know to be untrue. My best vindication on both grounds may be drawn from the official correspondence open to all the world, and I am confident that every man who studies it will arrive at the conclusion, in which I cannot but think that Your Lordship will participate, that my dismissal from the work I had so long and so successfully conducted was one of the most tyrannical and indefensible acts ever perpetrated by a Government, and that the pretences by which they are endeavoring to sustain it are worse than the act itself."[42]

CHAPTER 7

Scottish Success

As the *NovaScotian* noted, James Richardson Forman's career did not end with his dismissal from the provincial railway. His obituary in the Minutes of Proceedings of the Institution of Civil Engineers, echoed in the *Engineer* and *Engineering* newspapers of July 13th 1900, indicate he achieved his greatest success in his second home. The success was not without a hint of scandal. Ten years after Forman's departure from Nova Scotia, his father, James Forman Senior – who had been implicated with him in the Protestant Alliance controversy – was embroiled in a new scandal involving his tenure as chief cashier of the Bank of Nova Scotia. Through his friend, president Mather Byles Almon, the bank had been a shareholder in the Nova Scotia Railway and a supporter of Joseph Howe. It would also become a backer of Samuel Cunard's ambitious plan to save his North Atlantic fleet of steamers (which carried mail between England and the North American colonies) from bankruptcy. According to Schull and Gibson, by 1870 these ventures had now obliged the bank to change its stature or character greatly. While Almon was still president, a number of directors had come and gone, but James Forman Senior was still chief cashier:

> "In the hierarchy of the Bank, slightly below the Directors and much above the clerks, was the Cashier, James Forman, who had now been the chief operating officer for thirty-eight years. The Directors had grown accustomed to relying on him to carry out their decisions; they respected his social position and his skill with columns of figures. He prepared the necessary reports and statements and kept the books."[1]

As part of his routine, Forman Senior took the books home with him every night and was entrusted with president Almon's keys to the vault, a practice never apparently questioned by any of the directors. According to the senior Forman's detractors in the city press, this allowed him unfettered access to the bank's assets, and led to a charge that he had embezzled $315,000 over a twenty-five year period, altering the books to cover his crime. The alterations in the books were first noticed in March of 1870 by a junior clerk, who looked upon it as an error for more than a month, and did not advise any of the directors for two months. When he did notify the bank's accountant, James C. Mackintosh, it confirmed a suspicion the accountant had harboured for a long time.

> "It fell to Almon to break the news to the board of directors at a meeting on July 28th 1870. Forman, he said, had been relieved of his duties. Since the cashier's figures could not be trusted, several directors began counting the gold, silver, and banknotes in the vault to find out how much the bank really had on hand."[2]

The matter could not be kept from the public:

127

"The next step was facing the shareholders. Brief notice inserted in Halifax newspapers called a special meeting during the second week of August. Newsmen were locked out but there was no shortage of disgruntled shareholders willing to spill the beans once the meeting adjourned.

The directors sheepishly reported that Forman had helped himself to an astounding $320,000 over the previous quarter-century. The cashier had already signed over virtually all his property – houses, building lots, carriages, the family home, even his silverware. Added to money put up by Forman's bondholders, an estimated $195,000 could be recovered.

One shareholder called for Forman's arrest, but a doctor told the meeting the cashier was so seriously ill that his life might be endangered by such a course. The decision on whether to pursue criminal charges was left to a committee of directors and shareholders set up to sift through the books.

The bank directors took their share of knocks in the Halifax press. The *Morning Chronicle* demanded they 'resigned [sic] or be removed from office. It was well known that [Forman] was engaged in heavy speculations, and that his expenditures were far too great for one of his means,' the paper observed in a pointed editorial. 'Yet the suspicions of those drowsy collectors were not aroused.'"[3]

The bank would survive the scandal, but the strain proved too great for the senior Forman:

"As the debate raged over whether to call in the police, Forman made himself scarce. For a man too sick to be arrested, he was well enough to travel. He left Halifax in mid-August on the pretext of visiting relatives, and eventually moved to England to escape the furor."[4]

He died in London, while his wife remained in Halifax, but with the matter never having gone to court, and no charge ever having been laid, it is not possible to decide the matter of his guilt. "A rumour at the time said that Forman had taken the money to help his son who was in financial difficulty, and this supposedly brought public opinion to Forman's side."[5] James Forman Senior, although obliged to specify how much money was taken, was never compelled to divulge how it was dispensed, leaving it unclear as to which son, or indeed if any son, was the recipient. This lack of clarity means it was possible that some of the funds might have been used to finance James Richardson Forman's career in Scotland, perhaps even purchasing for him a partnership with his old employer. It is also possible some portion of the money might have paid for the formal education of Charles DeNeuville Forman, James Forman Senior's grandson. While pointing out that it is not a definitive work, Patricia Lotz examines the details of James Forman Senior's life. Although the rumours failed to name the son, it most likely have would have been James Forman Senior's youngest son Robert, who went on from his temporary position as an employee on the Windsor branch railway survey, to become a wealthy merchant in the Nova Scotia iron foundry town of Acadian Mines near Londonderry, Nova Scotia.

The second phase of Howe's grand plan for the Nova Scotia Railway was to continue the line from Truro to the New Brunswick border, and connect with the line being built in New Brunswick toward Quebec, thereby completing the inter-colonial link which had been sought in 1846. (Had the negotiations for colonial union not gone well, Howe had planned to instead extend the line to Pictou, a task that was left to Laurie to initiate.) Although not recommended by Major William Robinson, the British officer of Royal Engineers who surveyed the route in 1846, the route would inevitably take the line past the rich iron deposits of Londonderry, an industry that, at the time, only Sandford Fleming seemed unwilling to acknowledge was of prime importance to both Nova Scotia and the British Empire. Fleming would later wage a lengthy battle with John Livesey – the British promoter of the mine – in order to secure a more direct access to the Springhill coalfields. It was a battle he would lose, and which resulted in the construction of the "Grecian Bend," a sweeping curve of railway that put Londonderry on the map, and still exists today.

According to Brian Forman, a great-great grandson of James Richardson Forman, the family was well aware of the profitable potential of the iron mines, and Robert Forman was one of the first to buy land in the region based on such speculation. Where Robert obtained the money – apparently having no previous professional or business credentials to his name – has never been determined, leaving the obvious conclusion that it was provided by his father from the accounts of the bank. Robert's success in land speculation (several engineers in the employ of the Intercolonial Railway survey also made money this way) appears to have been predicated on the understanding that his brother James Richardson Forman would ensure the railway passed through the township, despite its location in the difficult Cobequid Hills, on a route that would necessarily involve heavy grades and sharp curves. As the result of James Livesey's victory, Fleming was forced to keep James Richardson Forman's promise, and Robert Forman became a wealthy man, realizing a huge return on his investment in land.

Some of Robert's good fortune could also have come from having married well. His first wife was Louisa Tremaine, of the wealthy family that operated a brick works in Elmsdale, alongside the railway line built by his older brother. It is difficult to determine when Louisa died, but she left Robert at least four sons: James, Robert, Harry, and William. James would move to Vancouver and become a prominent insurance broker; his father later followed him to the Pacific coast; Robert, Harry and William remained at Acadian Mines, finding work in the iron foundry. Robert's second wife, Marion Steele, bore him a son and four daughters: Margaret, Marion, Walter, and Esther. This group, like their father, had left Londonderry by 1890.

In the meantime, James Richardson Forman found vindication in Scotland. Returning to Glasgow – and his former mentor Neil Robson – in 1860, Forman was welcomed with open arms; he was made a partner in the firm incorporated as Robson, Forman & McCall. (The other partner was David McCall.) This firm then became Forman & McCall on the death of Robson in 1868, then later Formans & McCall, when James' son Charles de Neuville Forman joined the business in 1875. The careers of father and son became intertwined, with both being credited for work on the same railways, although it appears from the obituaries posted in the Proceedings of the Institution of Civil Engineers that Charles had the greater impact. James Richardson Forman was immediately put to work on railway projects. His obituary briefly details his work:

"Among the undertakings with which he was connected were the Greenock & Ayrshire and Wemyss Bay Railways, the Blane Valley line, the Busby & East Kilbride, Stobcross, Kelvin Valley, Milngavie and Aberfoyle railways...."[6]

MAP

The Forman Lines in Scotland

Below: Map courtesy Ewan Crawford.
For more information, see www.railscot.co.uk
Graphics enhancement by Eric Clegg.

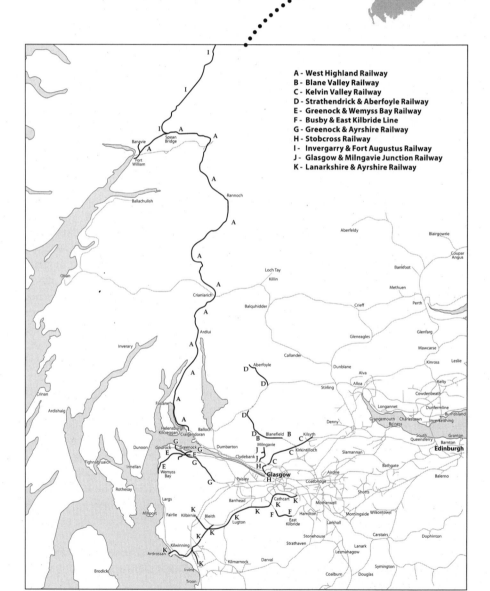

A - West Highland Railway
B - Blane Valley Railway
C - Kelvin Valley Railway
D - Strathendrick & Aberfoyle Railway
E - Greenock & Wemyss Bay Railway
F - Busby & East Kilbride Line
G - Greenock & Ayrshire Railway
H - Stobcross Railway
I - Invergarry & Fort Augustus Railway
J - Glasgow & Milngavie Junction Railway
K - Lanarkshire & Ayrshire Railway

This account does not do justice to James Richardson Forman's achievements, for each railway presented its own set of challenges, which one may suppose he resolved by drawing upon his experience in Nova Scotia. The Milngavie line was the first to be completed, opened in 1863, as a branch of the Glasgow, Dumbarton & Helensburgh Railway. Almost simultaneously, Forman was back on familiar ground, opening a railway to connect with the General Terminus and the Glasgow Harbour Railway, on which he had worked prior to returning to Nova Scotia in 1854. This line opened on May 15th 1865. The Wemyss Bay line diverged from the Caledonian Railway's Paisley-Greenock line to pass behind Greenock. The bay itself was a popular tourist resort, and with Scotland's growing middle class eager to spend time at the beach, traffic was not a problem.

Neither would traffic be a problem for the Greenock & Ayrshire line, which in effect gave the Glasgow & Southwestern Railway direct access to Greenock.

Above: Busby Viaduct – built to allow railway traffic by-pass Glasgow, this structure was typical of the Formans' work in metropolitan Scotland.
(Courtesy East Renfrewshire Council)

Below: Busby ruins – the viaduct as it appears today, long abandoned, stands in silent testimony to the skill of the Formans and their bridges.
(Courtesy East Renfrewshire Council)

This removed the need to use the Barhead and Paisley routes jointly with the Caledonian Railway. (The Busby viaduct on the Caledonian line to East Kilbride is a Forman work worthy of note, for it showed how father and son could build viaducts far more grand in scope than that at Bedford, Nova Scotia.) The Stobcross railway was originally conceived to provide rail access (freight) to the new Queen's Dock and the expanding west end of Glasgow, and the Blane Valley and Busby & Kilbride (opened 1868). The East Kilbride line climbed into the hills to the south of Glasgow, and a topography more testing than anything the Nova Scotia Railway had offered. The Kelvin Valley line runs across gentle country on the south side of the Campsie Hills, parallel to the Glasgow-Falkirk-Edinburgh main line and the Forth & Clyde Canal.

"The final railway route to be opened in East Dunbartonshire was the Kelvin Valley line in 1878-79, with stations at Bardowie, Balmore, Torrance and Twecher. This route was closed to passengers in 1951, as was the Kirkintilloch-Aberfoyle section of the Campsie line."[7]

The line opened June 1st 1878 via Lenzie for passengers and freight from Glasgow. By June 4th 1879, a further section had opened to Maryhill from Kelvin Valley East Junction for freight. This was followed in rapid succession by a line to Maryhill (October 1st 1879) then to Torrance, and on October 29th 1880 from Maryhill to Kilsyth for passenger service. On August 1st 1885, the line was absorbed by the North British Railway. In *The History of Stirlingshire*, William Nimmo reflected upon the full impact of Forman's achievement on the local canals:

"'Prodigious!' will no doubt be the vehement exclamation of many an heir to the present flying locomotive age, when the same distance can be done in about thirty minutes. But with one or other of those jolly and courteous captains – Napier, Risk, and Hay – at the helm, the passage from beginning to end was replete with interest of the most stirring sort. Veterans who remember when six passenger boats plied daily on the Union and the Forth and Clyde Canals, and when horses, with their red-coated and cocked-hat riders, did the duty of steam, must heave a sigh for the 'good old days,' on seeing what remains of the water passenger traffic between the two great Scottish cities. The tiny screw vessel which, in the summer season, still plies between Port Dundas and Castelcary, is the last link in the history of the swifts; and there can be no doubt that Kelvin Valley Railway, lately opened, will completely annihilate the old system."[8]

This outcome mirrored that of James Richardson Forman's line between Halifax and Truro, which put the Shubenacadie Canal out of business in short order.

The history of the Blane Valley line has been paraphrased in *The North British Railway. Vol. 2*, by John Thomas:

"The Blane Valley Railway was opened in 1866, left the Lennoxtown branch of the NB (North British) at that town, and ran for eight miles through the valley serving the hamlets of Campsie Glen, Strathblane, and the small village of Blanefield. The original promoters had a grand scheme for taking it on to the Trossachs but they ran out of money when the railway reached the turnpike road a mile or two beyond Blanefield. They planted a station at their involuntary terminus and called it Killearn although the village of that name was nowhere in sight. There the railway stuck for 15 years.

James Keyden, a lawyer and promoter of small railways, was the man behind the Blane Valley. It was in his office on 16 September 1879 that the Strathendrick & Loch Lomond Railway was first mooted. It was to be a continuation of the Blane Valley westward to Aberfoyle and on to Inversnaid on the east shore of Loch Lomond. It was grandly described as 'the new route to Loch Lomond.' The Duke of Montrose did not like the idea, so 'it was resolved that the meeting should be adjourned and that a future meeting should be called when His Grace is satisfied as to the Line.'

The parties met again in a month to consider a revised version of the project. The railway now was to be constructed in two parts. The first part was to run from its end-on junction with the Blane Valley to join the existing Forth & Clyde Junction Railway (Stirling-Balloch) near Gartness. The second part was to leave the F&CJ at Buchlyvie and cross Flanders Moss to Aberfoyle where it would terminate. The extension to Inversnaid was abandoned, but the company hoped to operate a coach service on the road to Loch Lomond. The new line would therefore, with the NB and Blane Valley and the Forth & Clyde, provide a direct rail link between Glasgow and Aberfoyle. A key part of the plan was for the railway company to build a private road across the mountains to Loch Katrine in the heart of the Trossachs. His Grace approved of the new railway, now renamed the Strathendrick & Aberfoyle Railway, and the NB and BV offered support. Present at the meeting were John Forman, engineer of Glasgow, and Provost Hugh Kennedy of Partick, a contractor by profession. Forman was invited to be engineer of the line and Kennedy the contractor."[9]

Thomas' reference to a "John Forman" is erroneous, and must have meant James Richardson Forman.

"Forman's estimate of the cost of the line was £51,947. Nine months after the first meeting Keyden had collected £7,534, but that did not deter him from putting out tenders. Kennedy undertook to build the line for £29,682 3s 9d. The meeting held to allocate the contract was actually in progress when Kennedy learned that a rival contractor had put in a bid for £28,521 0s 7d. He burst into Keyden's office and told the board that he had left the preparation of the contract to his son and that he had made a mistake in his calculations. The correct price, it appeared was £28,435 6s 9d. 'If you have any difficulty in getting the stock taken up I might take a little more,' Kennedy told the board. He got the contract, but not before he had parted with £1,000 in payment for a block of S&AR stock."[10]

James Keyden was a principal partner in the firm Keydens, Strang & Girvan, and became involved with Forman in successive attempts to establish a direct line to Oban. In this regard they found favour with the North British Railway, which was looking for a short line to compete against the Caledonian Railway route via Callandar. Scottish railway historian, Dr. John McGregor, Associate Lecturer, Open University in Scotland, notes that James Forman had opposed the Callander & Oban in 1865-66; he wanted the Oban promoters to choose the "direct" route to Glasgow via Loch Lomond. It was in this highly competitive environment that Forman began to thrive. The process required diplomacy and guile, and dealing with a parliament that was far more familiar with railway issues – both technical and financial – than Nova Scotia's elected body had been.

The association with Keydens, Strang & Girvan was a key in the Formans' later involvement in the Invergarry & Fort August (I&FA) line of the western highlands; the Keydens firm became the line's agent. Charles Forman was the force behind the I&FA, and the line from Spean Bridge to Fort Augustus was seen as a way of keeping the North British Railway out of Inverness. This was a small part of the complex theatre in which the Formans operated at the time.

The Strathendrick & Aberfoyle railway, opened for passengers and freight on August 1st 1882 was one of the last of James Richardson Forman's projects. It was significant for him in that it offered him a business opportunity removed from railway construction. At the time of his death Forman was chairman of the Aberfoyle Slate Quarry Company, established in 1858 with quarries on the south side of Craig Mhor and at various sites between Aberfoyle and Brig of Turk to the north. The *Stirling Journal* of April 8th 1883 offers more detail on the physical character of the railway:

"A new private line of railway connecting Aberfoyle Railway Station with the works of the Aberfoyle Slate Quarry Company, and having possibly the steepest gradient of any line in the country, was tested with the most satisfactory results on Saturday. The quarries are situated about two miles from the station, and almost 1000 feet above its level. When the present company got possession of the quarries, the access was by means of a road with a gradient in many places of one in five, and even steeper, and much loss was experienced through the breakage of slates in transit. Messrs Formans & McCall, civil engineers, Glasgow, who were consulted, recommended a narrow gauge railway with a self-acting incline to overcome the gradient. The railway line has now been completed and was tested on Saturday. On the steeper parts of the line the gradients vary from 1 in 2 to 1 in 6. The incline is worked by means of a steel wire-rope passing round a pulley, which is controlled by a screw brake of such a nature that one man is able to control the load at any point of the incline. On Saturday sixteen wagons – eight full and eight empty – were placed on the line at intervals of about 100 yards. It was found that this load, which was about 50% in excess of the usual working load, was completely under the control of one man. It was also further proved that one loaded wagon could set the machinery in motion. The experiments were entirely successful." [11]

It would appear that James Richardson Forman's time spent teaching in Nova Scotia served both him and his son well. Charles Forman's obituary in the February 15th 1901 edition of *Engineering* notes:

"He had splendid training. Born on August 10, 1852, he began engineering when fifteen years of age. His father, who died in July last, although belonging to an old Scotch family, was a Canadian by birth; he came to Glasgow in 1841, but for six years subsequently he filled a Government appointment in his native province of Nova Scotia. In 1860 the present firm of Messrs. Formans & M'Call [sic] was established, and Mr. M'Call still survives. It was with this firm that young Forman was articled for the five years from 1867 to 1872." [12]

It may seem a trifling technicality, but it is not true to say James Richardson Forman was "Canadian" by birth. Prior to Confederation in 1867, "Canadians" were those people born in what are now the provinces of Ontario and Quebec (then Upper Canada and

Lower Canada). Be that as it may, Charles Forman's career is described in some detail in the *Minutes of Proceedings of the Institution of Civil Engineers*:

"... in 1873 he was employed under the late Mr. James Deas, Engineer of the Clyde Trust, who was at the time engaged on the construction of the Queen's Dock. Returning to the office of Messrs. Forman & McCall in 1874, he was admitted as a partner in the following year, the style [name] of the firm becoming Formans & McCall.

Mr. Forman early developed strong commercial instincts and a clear insight into the principles which regulate trade, and with the aid of the opportunities afforded by the associations of the firm, he soon obtained prominence as a leader in railway enterprises. He carried with him a strong power of conviction, was naturally resourceful, and possessed an unusual command of details, coupled with which qualities he had a keen perception of character, with great determination and energy of mind. The firm has been continuously associated with the development of the railway system of the west of Scotland, and through Mr. Forman's energy and ability this undoubtedly received a decided impulse; in various instances long talked of enterprises were formulated, successfully conducted through Parliament, and eventually carried out under his guidance."[13]

Below: West Highland Railway. Lord Abinger turns the first sod on the West Highland Railway outside Fort William. Although Abinger is the only person positively identified in the photograph, it is believed Charles Forman (x) is standing to the right, behind the gentleman with the flowing white beard, top hat, and cape. (Courtesy West Highland Museum, Fort William)

At this point, the careers of the father and son became almost inseparable:

> "His first charge was the Kelvin Valley Railway, opened for traffic in 1878. This was followed in 1880 by the Strathendrick & Aberfoyle Railway, opened in 1884, to which were due the development of Aberfoyle as a summer residence and the formation of a company for the working of the slate on the Montrose Estate, which has since continued a thriving industry. About that time the North Monkland Railway, the Yoker Railway, and the Kilsyth & Bonnybridge line were also being carried through.
>
> Mr. Forman's first Parliamentary contest of importance was the promotion of the Clyde, Ardrishaig & Crinan Railway in 1887, which he successfully carried in face of a strong opposition – the powers were, however, subsequently allowed to lapse. The extension of the Strathendrick & Aberfoyle Line northwards by Loch Lomond to form a through line to Fort William had hitherto been kept in view, but this scheme was superseded by the Helensburgh route under the name of the West Highland Railway, extending from Craigendoran, near Helensburgh, to Fort William, a distance of 100 miles. The bill for this undertaking he was instrumental in carrying through Parliament in 1889, and the line was successfully completed and opened for traffic in 1894." [14]

McGregor of the Open University in Scotland has noted that the Clyde, Ardrishaig & Crinan railway firmly cemented the relationship between the Formans and the North British Railway; the terminus at Crinan could become the "Oban" in the North British

Below: Mallaig, the terminus of the West Highland Railway. This picturesque port was intended to become a major link to North America. (Courtesy VisitScotland, Scottish Viewpoint Picture Library, 7439)

plans, until the West Highland Railway was seen as a better prospect. Two other railways, the Kilsyth & Bonnybridge and the Stirling & Western direct line, along with the Kelvin Valley line, together would have given the North British a route through Stirling independent of the Caledonian Railway.

As a principal of Formans & McCall, James Richardson Forman found himself involved in his son Charles's adventures as engineer of the West Highland Railway, a line that ran through rugged country and exists today as one of Scotland's most popular tourist attractions. The line was to connect Craigendoran, on the Firth of Clyde, with Fort William on Loch Linnhe, passing by Loch Lomond and Ben Nevis, Scotland's highest peak. The West Highland Railway was authorized in 1889, and was successful largely because, as McGregor notes, the time was ripe for such a project, and a great many pieces of the complicated regulatory and financial jigsaw fell into place. Unlike so many other railway schemes, however, it appears that the political process was far easier than the survey. On January 29th 1889:

> "...seven gentlemen gathered at the hotel at Spean Bridge. On the following day they were to set out on a walk that was to take them across the Moor of Rannoch to Inverary, nearly 40 miles to the south. It was a walk that was to become a West Highland legend."[15]

The party consisted of Charles Forman, his Chief Engineer James Bulloch, assistant engineer J.E. Harrison, Robert McAlpine (head of the famous construction company), John Bett (factor of the Breadalbane Estates), Major Martin (factor of the Poltalloch estates), and N.B. MacKenzie, a solicitor and local agent for the railway company. The next day, they were taken by coach from Spean Bridge to Inverlair Lodge, and from there they set out to walk to the north end of Loch Treig. From that point they were rowed across the loch to stay overnight at Lord Abinger's Craig-uaine-ach Lodge. On the following day, the men set out to walk to Rannoch Lodge, but changed their minds and decide to continue on to Inveroran.

The wild highland weather then took hold and split the group as the day darkened. McAlpine decided to go on to Inveroran; Bulloch headed to Gorton cottage. Charles Forman's group, including McKenzie, Martin, Harrison and Bett, wandered on, nearly lost on the moor, until shepherds from Gorton guided them to a hut where they sheltered until the weather cleared. In the meantime, Bulloch reached Gorton, and on the following day McAlpine found shelter in a cottage by Loch Tulla. On February 2nd Charles Forman, McKenzie, Martin, Harrison, and Bett were taken to Gorton to join Bulloch, then made for Inveroran, via Loch Tulla, to pick up McAlpine.

The weather continued to worsen, and blizzard covered Rannoch Moor, forcing the party to work its way through deep drifts to reach Tyndrum station on the Callander & Oban Railway. McGregor warns, however, that Thomas's fascination with the romance of the Rannoch Moor expedition has been taken out of context. He postulates that the unseasonable weather was endured because:

> "...at some point between August and October of 1888, Forman substituted the Rannoch route for the Glen Coe route originally proposed. The deposited plans (November) show the line very much as later built, but no doubt there was fine-tuning

to be done. The promoters were already looking to a deviation between Rannoch and Corrour, sought by the landowners, for which powers would be sought in the next session of Parliament, 1889-90, after the West Highland Act passed in August of 1889. (The deviation was refused – one landowner had opposed it.)" [16]

The weather may well have been a harbinger. On October 12th 1889, Lord Abinger turned the first sod of the railway at Fort William, but construction soon ran into difficulty amid the mountain passes and ravines, and was abandoned in July of 1891, when the principal contractor, Lucas & Aird, sought revised terms. During the ensuing deadlock, construction was suspended for several months; the North British Railway mediated.

The company took the matter to court, and work resumed on October 14th 1891, when the West Highland Railway Company agreed to pay an extra £10,000, even though a court in Dunbarton had ruled in August of that year that Lucas & Aird must build the line for the amount specified in the contract. In order to avoid a further financial crisis in 1893, James H. Renton, a director of the company, donated part of his personal fortune to get the line completed. Renton was one of three of the North British Railway's directors – with Lord Tweeddale and Robert Wemyss – to consolidate that railway's control of the West Highland line. MacGregor notes that Renton was not exactly a benevolent donor. He was a speculative financier and gave what was in effect a bridging loan until the West Highland's capital powers could be enlarged retrospectively. His reward was to drive the last spike (September 5th 1893) on Rannoch Moor, one of the most difficult sections of the line. After the August 3rd 1894 official inspection by the Board of Trade, the line was opened with the customary ceremony eight days later.

Thomas goes into greater detail, although there appears to be an error in the history of the family company:

"The engineers of the West Highland were Formans & McCall of Glasgow, a firm founded in 1828 which had been responsible for some of the earliest Scottish railways. The title was adopted when Charles Forman, son of the Scots-Canadian founder, became a partner. The contractors were Lucas & Aird, a famous Westminster firm with strong Scottish connections. The dominant figure was John Aird, a Member of Parliament, whose crofter father had emigrated from the Highlands to London early in the nineteenth century to found and develop a contracting business with international ramifications. John Aird and Charles Forman were the key figures in the construction of the West Highland Railway." [17]

As has been noted, Formans & McCall was not established until 1859, when James Richardson Forman returned from Nova Scotia. Thomas gives Charles Forman great praise for his railway accomplishments:

"Charles deNeuville Forman deserves to be better remembered as a railway engineer.... During his 48 years he signed his name to the plans of many important railways and he put more railway mileage on the map of Western Scotland than any other railway engineer. Among his projects were the intricate Glasgow Central Railway built under the streets of the city, the Lanarkshire & Ayrshire Railway, the line from Glasgow to Clydebank via Yoker, and the Strathendrick & Aberfoyle Railway. He took time off from the West of Scotland to engineer the Foxdale Railway in the Isle of Man, and in a moment of aberration he built a coach road: it was the exciting one from Aberfoyle over the hills to the Trossachs. Among projects of his that did not come off were the Glasgow, Berwick, & Newcastle direct railway and the Fort Augustus to Inverness railway.

On 23rd October 1889 a party of railway and contractors' men went to a spot outside Fort William opposite the Glen Nevis distillery. There, in the presence of a least half the populace (all the shops had been closed at noon), John Aird handed Lord Abinger the silver spade with which he dug the first sod. That was the end of the ceremonial for the time being." [18]

This reference indicates the Formans were not above engaging in speculation. McGregor notes the Clyde-and-Tweed trunk line across the Anglo-Scottish border had been promoted several times since the 1830s. In the 1880s, the Formans hoped to exploit disputes within the companies proposing the line to promote their own Manchester, Newcastle & Glasgow Railway.

Below: The family of Charles Forman, taken at Davos, Switzerland in 1897. From left: son James, wife Anna (who died in Perthshire in 1906), son Arthur, an unnamed cousin, and son Charles. Three other children were at school at the time of this photograph.
(Courtesy Brian Forman)

"The North British was at odds with its English partners, the North Eastern and Great Northern – Forman saw the opportunity to offer the English companies a new route to Glasgow. At roughly the same time he tried to engage the Glasgow & South Western, the North British and the Midland (the N.B.'s other English partner) behind a cut-off route from the Clyde to Carlisle, which would reduce the advantage of the Caledonian route over Beattock." [19]

Despite its remote location, the West Highland line was built on a sound, if speculative premise, as Thomas notes:

"At that time the steamship route from Liverpool to Quebec was 2,625 miles and the time taken on the voyage was 6 days 12 hours. From Fort William to Quebec via Skerryvore and the Ross of Mull was 2,083 miles, and the estimated time of the voyage was exactly 5 days. From London to Liverpool was 5 hours by rail; London to Fort William was 14 hours by rail, so that the Fort William-Quebec route was 1 day 3 hours shorter than the existing Liverpool-Quebec route.

And Fort William had other claims. Loch Linnhe was a large natural harbour with a bottom of firm blue clay and no rocks. It was deep enough to take the largest liners at any state of the tide, and it was safe and perfectly sheltered by the surrounding mountains. Loch Eil nearby was available as an additional anchorage. Furthermore, there were 1,200 acres of flat ground by the lochside, and plenty of local stone for the building of wharves and warehouses. On paper Fort William looked a likely choice for a new Atlantic port. The big ships went to Southampton, but it is intriguing to picture the Queen Mary arriving at Fort William and her 2,000 passengers trying to make their way down the West Highland, perhaps in December with Rannoch Moor not on its best behaviour." [20]

The West Highland Railway sod turning sparked a great deal of excitement:

"A minor railway mania seized the West Highlands with the coming of the railway. Railways were projected hither and thither, and more often than not the indefatigable Charles Forman was behind them. He surveyed an extension of the West Highland down the east shore of Loch Linnhe from Fort William to Ballachulish, over the route that Waldron-Smith planned for the Glasgow & Northwestern Railway. At the same time he planned a Caledonian sponsored branch from the Callander & Oban at Connel Ferry up through Appin to Ballachulish." [21]

This project again served the North British ambitions. McGregor notes the railway regarded the proposed West Highland Ballaculish line as an insurance policy aimed at keeping the Caledonian Railway away from Fort William and Mallaig, without actually having to build it!

"Other Forman enterprises within a 30-mile radius of Ben Nevis included a line from the West Highland at Spean Bridge to Fort Augustus in the Great Glen, and a continuation up Loch Ness to Inverness. Of Forman's projected grand cross-country route from Oban to Inverness, all the links between Oban and Fort Augustus were authorized. The Spean Bridge to Fort Augustus line was built by an independent company.... The Callander

& Oban built the Connel Ferry-Ballachulish link, but the West Highland did not use its powers to take its branch from Fort William to Ballachulish.

Meanwhile, further south, two Forman schemes came into direct conflict with each other, which was not surprising considering that he simultaneously engineered a Caledonian and a North British scheme to reach the same objective. Inveraray, the county town of Argyll, lay isolated among mountains near the head of Loch Fyne, and attempts were made to get railways to it from two directions. On behalf of the Callander & Oban, Forman planned a line running south from a junction with the parent system at Dalmally, a distance of 14 miles; the cost of £142,568 was to include a pier at Inveraray, through which the railway hoped to benefit from the then intensive Loch Fyne herring-fishing trade." [22]

Of the Loch Fyne railway, McGregor notes:

"The Loch Fyne contest saw Forman's Dalmally-Inveraray line set against the Arrochar-St. Catherine's line. The latter was to be a light railway, under the 1896 Act, and it was surveyed by Benjamin Blyth. After the defeat of Forman's line, the North British sought and obtained the requisite Light Railway Order, but did not use it. It may well be that Forman surveyed a West Highland branch to Loch Fyne, but Thomas is wrong in attributing the St. Catherine's light railway to him – it was Blyth's work, at least so far as the Board of Trade was concerned." [23]

The Callander & Oban Railway project brought Charles Forman into an association with the railway's Chief Engineer, John Crouch, who in 1887 signed Charles Forman's application to join the Institution of Civil Engineers (ICE). Crouch was also a powerful supporter of the West Highland Railway scheme when the Formans took it before parliament for approval. Charles Forman's ICE nomination was proposed by his father. Thomas' history continues:

"At the same time, Forman surveyed a West Highland branch that was to leave the main line at Arrochar, pass round Loch Long, and cross to Loch Fyne by the Rest and be Thankful, so to reach St. Catherine's opposite Inveraray. From Glasgow to Inveraray by the West Highland route was 54 miles, by the Caledonian and Callander & Oban line. Inveraray was a feudal enclave dominated by the castle. The Duke of Argyll favoured the West Highland scheme if only because it decently kept out of his preserves. But the Dalmally line [would have] passed under the castle windows and the Duke had no difficulty in inducing Parliament to throw out the bill. The West Highland had enough on its plate in the north-west without adding the Inveraray branch. It was never built.

The wave of optimism that swept Lochaber when the railway came spawned two transport schemes, one basically sound, the other plausible but with more than a touch of fantasy. From time to time schemes had been proposed for building a railway to the summit of Ben Nevis. The Ben was the highest mountain in Britain and already very much a 'tourist' mountain. Moreover, since 1883 there had been a permanent observatory on the summit, inhabited all the year round and connected with the base by an easily negotiated pony track. Much more difficult peaks in Europe and elsewhere had been given rack railways that had paid their way and brought prosperity to their base towns. Everybody who climbed Ben Nevis wrote his or her name in the visitors' book at the observatory, and these books provided a ready-made census of potential traffic for a mountain railway."[24]

It was at this time that the younger Forman embarked upon his most ambitious project:

"In 1893 Charles Forman considered building a railway up Ben Nevis. When the West Highland was opened, a London company took up the challenge and planned to construct a line starting near the West Highland station and, following the pony track for the first 2,000 ft, reach the summit by striking east round the shoulder of the mountain. The line was to be 4 3/4 miles long and have a maximum gradient of 1 in 2:62 for 600 yards. The company expected to spend £30,000 on the venture (the price inclusive of a large hotel on the summit), and estimated that the revenue from 15,000 passengers a year at fares of 1s 6d return and 1s single would enable 6 per cent to be paid on the capital. The scheme was revived several times between 1894 and 1913, but nothing came of it. If ever a mountain was ready for a railway it was Ben Nevis. It was a pity both for the future prosperity of the West Highland Railway and Fort William that the line was not built."[25]

Thomas notes that Formans & McCall were also the engineers of the Invergarry & Fort Augustus Railway (James Young of Glasgow was the contractor) which did not open (1903) until after Charles Forman's death in 1901. This line faced geographical problems that doomed it to failure, not the least of which were the steep grades that added to its operating cost. One local history notes:

" The problem was always the terrain. A train cannot climb a steep incline and curves had to be very gentle indeed. Few of today's roads in the area are very straight, so imagine the task that was before the engineers who built the line. But in the engineering tradition that seems to have found a home in the area, they made it happen. But not without extensive cost. An example of this is the fact that the section between the canal and the Fort Augustus pier, a distance of less than two miles, cost as much as the rest of the track to Spean Bridge. No expense was spared however; all the bridges bore elegant castellations, and there is even a tunnel in one section. This is not to mention the millions of pounds spent on lawyers in London where the railway companies fought the battle to get to Inverness in the courts as well as across the Scottish highlands."[26]

McGregor offers more specific detail:

"Invergarry & Fort Augustus runs through relatively easy country, by the general standards of the Highlands, and reaches no great height, but bridges and culverts had to be generously provided, to cope with side streams prone to sudden torrents. The Fort Augustus pier extension needed a swing bridge and a large viaduct; there were two other sizeable viaducts (Spean and Gloy); the heavy cost ultimately lay in Forman's shaping the line, ... keeping the gradients within bounds, with an eye to eventual through traffic to Inverness. The line climbed out of the valley of the Spean to a mountainside terrace above Loch Lochy, whence it dropped steadily to Invergarry.

As a light railway, the I&FA might have had a future."[27]

Charles Forman's achievements did not stop there, as his obituary in the *Minutes of the ICE* notes:

"The most important of Mr. Forman's undertakings was the Glasgow Central Railway, which brought the Lanarkshire coal-fields of the Caledonian system into direct communication with the Queen's Dock, formed an underground city and suburban line for Glasgow, and opened the way for the extension of the Company's lines into the county of Dumbarton. Powers were applied for and obtained in 1888 after a prolonged struggle, the Caledonian Railway Company having in the interval become possessed of the undertaking. Work was commenced in 1890, and the line opened in 1896. The railway traversed in covered way the busiest thoroughfares of the city, and at such a depth as to necessitate an extensive scheme of intercepting sewers. The execution of the work was much hampered by restrictions for preserving the traffic of the streets from interruption, and what with these and the difficult nature of the subsoil, the many drains, water-, gas-, electric, and other pipes to be dealt with, and important structures to be underpinned, the work may well be classed among the most important engineering undertakings of the day."[28]

Engineering goes into greater detail on this aspect of Forman's life:

"This line has proved of immense advantage to the citizens, and in connection with it reference may be made to Forman's insight into character, for he succeeded in surrounding himself with young men imbued with the same energy and grasp of details, and thus we find one of his assistants on the Central Railway now master of works of the city of Glasgow; another is Chief Engineer to the Caledonian Railway, a third is at the head of an Edinburgh firm carrying out the waterworks there and other undertakings, while more of them are still with Messrs. Formans & McCall."[29]

McGregor notes that this involvement underlines the totality of the Formans' understanding of railway politics:

"The Glasgow Central line and Lanarkshire & Dumbartonshire line, taken together, broke the North British monopoly north of Clyde. Forman's projects often exploited Caledonian-North British rivalry – and the West Highland is just another case in point."[30]

It is easy to believe that the lessons learned by James Richardson Forman when working with his students in Nova Scotia, were brought to benefit the public works of Scotland. The Institution's obituary goes on to note:

"Consequent on the commencement of the Glasgow Central Railway, Mr. Forman was engaged in 1890 in the promotion of the Lanarkshire & Dumbartonshire Railway, and after being defeated in that Session, powers were obtained the following year for the line. This railway forms a natural extension of the Glasgow Central line and traverses the north bank of the Clyde between Glasgow and Dumbarton, connecting the Caledonian Railway with the riverside lands, and bringing the coalfields and steel works of Lanarkshire on that Company's system into direct communication with the shipbuilding and other industries below Glasgow. Forming as it did a direct invasion of the North British Railway

Company's territory, the enterprise demanded unusual skill in its promotion. The extraordinary development of the lands for public works along the route of the line since its opening has fully justified the evidence laid before Parliament. The construction of these lines involved a considerable extent of intricate tunnel and city work.

Besides having carried out various minor lines, Mr. Forman had in hand at the time of his death the construction of extensions of the Lanarkshire and Ayrshire Railways, which afford that Company an independent access between the Lanarkshire coal-fields and the port of Ardrossan, the Paisley and Barrhead district railways connecting the last-named line with Paisley and its environs to the south and west. Also the Invergarry and Fort Augustus Railway – this last being the outcome of repeated efforts to obtain the extension of the West Highland line to Inverness." [31]

The Lanarkshire & Ayrshire line of the Caledonian Railway invaded the Glasgow & Southwestern Railway's territory, another indication that the Formans had mastered the art of exploiting rivalries. The Paisley and Barrhead railways were an indication that they were not always successful; both schemes failed, although McGregor attaches some success to the Lanarkshire line:

"The Lanarkshire & Ayrshire was successful in that in brought the Caledonian deep into Ayrshire, tapping Irvine, Ardrossan and Arran traffic. Extension to Ayr itself was not achieved. The Caledonian sought to subdue the Glasgow & South Western – or, at least, to establish a claim for joint ownership if the G.& S.W. fell to the North British. There was a vastly expensive parliamentary battle in 1889-91." [32]

Charles Forman's early training on dock construction came full circle in his final endeavour, as the *ICE* obituary explains:

"Mr. Forman's last efforts were directed against the monopoly claimed by the Clyde Trustees, as custodians of the River, to control the power to construct docks thereon, and the prolonged contest extending over three Sessions, and the ultimate passing of the Renfrew Dock and Harbour Extension Bill, to which he devoted the greatest energy, are characteristic of his great determination and ability in this particular sphere." [33]

There is no need to speculate on the character of Charles Forman; the *ICE* obituary is effusive in its praise:

"By his constitutional activity of mind, which permitted no rest, and his devotion to work, Mr. Forman was led to disregard his bodily requirements, and though naturally of a strong and sound constitution, the strain and lack of recreation began to take effect in 1898. With the accumulation of his personal responsibilities at this time, however, he did not allow himself opportunity to sufficiently recruit his strength, and the prolonged Parliamentary contest with the Clyde Trustees, carried on concurrently with his other work, was a severe tax on his health.

In the summer of 1900 he was seized, while in Spain, with an attack of paralysis, notwithstanding which he still pursued his work. This attack being soon followed by other warning in October of that year, he was forced to suspend work and seek rest abroad.

His health, however, continued to fail, resulting in his death at Davos Platz, Switzerland, on the 8th February 1901, at the early age of forty-eight.

Mr. Forman had a wide circle of friends, and was well known and highly respected in Scotland, and at the Parliamentary Bar as an engineer unusually powerful in the promotion of commercial enterprises. He was ever ready to give advice to all who might make him their confidant in matters of business or otherwise, and his quick perception and farsight, coupled with self-forgetfulness and a generous disposition, caused him to be burdened with many responsibilities regarding others. Mr. Forman's loss is much felt by many in Glasgow and the West of Scotland, and his short career is a remarkable instance of personal influence in stimulating both industrial and professional activity within his sphere of action.

In much of his work since 1888 Mr. Forman was more or less intimately associated with Sir John Wolfe Barry, K.C.B., Past-President, and at the date of his death was carrying out jointly with Sir John the Ballachulish extension of the Callander & Oban Railway.

Mr. Forman was elected a Member of the Institution on the 6th December, 1887."[34]

These glowing tributes, however, belie a political savvy in Charles Forman that was perhaps wanting in his father. McGregor suggests that Charles Forman was very much in tune with the political tactics of railway building in Great Britain. The strategies were similar to those used by American railroad speculators, playing communities and competing companies off against each other to promote lines that were not always economically sound:

"That he had an eye for the opportunities created by the rivalries of the Scottish companies seems to me beyond doubt. But Charles Forman was also too much his own man for the liking of those companies, whose mutual suspicions he exploited....

The Highlands offered opportunities for this sort of speculation, the more so when, in the 1880s and '90s, there was the possibility of government assistance in response to agitation and distress."[35]

McGregor believes the promotion of the West Highland line cannot be fully appreciated without attempting to understand the machinations of Formans & McCall, the contractors Lucas & Aird, and the North British Railway:

"The Invergarry & Fort Augustus is much more a speculative venture than popular accounts have recognized. As the West Highland progressed, Forman actively pursued further schemes which might be grafted to the new route – especially the Great Glen and Laggan projects, but also lesser projects like the little funicular which he proposed to link Whistlefield and Portincaple. The North British, wary of Forman's restless activity, were not unhappy to see the West Highland Mallaig Extension entrusted to Simpson & Wilson; for Simpson was a 'safe' North British client and subsequently a North British director."[36]

The Foxdale railway was one project that Charles Forman appears to have undertaken independently of his father's firm. Now a part of the world-renowned Isle of Man tourist railway, this 2 mile, three-foot gauge (914 mm) line was built specifically to transport the lead and zinc ore of the Isle of Man Mining Company and was no bagatelle:

"The Foxdale Line was built in 1886 by the Foxdale Railway Company, an offshoot of the Manx Northern Railway, as an opportunist venture to win lucrative mineral traffic from the Isle of Man Railway.

Prior to the building of the railway to Foxdale, all the ore was taken by horse and cart to St. Johns for onward transmission by the Isle of Man Railway to Douglas Station. It then had to be loaded again into horse drawn carts and taken to the harbour at Douglas. The contract for the carriage of the ore came up for renewal and the Manx Northern bid was successful." [37]

The railway had an immediate effect upon the development of the community:

"It is hard to imagine now what this area was like at the height of the mining boom with lead and silver being produced to an annual value of £50,000 at the time that the railway was built. There were 350 people employed in the mines. The three main shafts in Foxdale were Pott's, Beckwith's, and Bawden's. The deepest was Beckwith's, which reached a depth of 320 fathoms (1920 feet) by 1902, and yet by 1911 the industry had declined and the Isle of Man Mining Company had ceased working." [38]

The company was founded cheaply enough. Porter's Directory for the Isle of Man of 1889 lists the company's capital as £18,000. Its only station was at Ramsey, and its chairman was Robert Cowley, chairman of the Ramsay board of town commissioners. It presented Forman with an engineering challenge far greater than the West Highland Railway, a work of vastly greater scale. The entire length of the Manx line had a continuous gradient of 1 in 49, much of the route being cut out of the side of the South Barrule Mountain. It was this connection with mineral traffic that led Forman to write

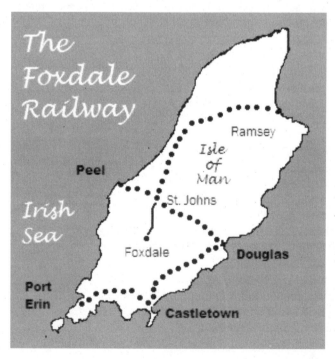

a treatise entitled *Economy in Handling and Transport of Minerals,* presented to the Engineering Conference of 1899. Only the roadbed of the Foxdale line remains today, used by tourists as a walking trail.

The publication *Engineering* gives Charles Forman credit for other innovations in railway construction:

"Here it may not be inappropriate to mention that Forman was a strong advocate for concrete work for arches, abutments, piers etc., and on the West Highland Railway he made large use of the timber which abounded along the route for footbridges and sheep-crossings. He also introduced in most of his lines the island platform, and broke through convention with his buildings, giving a wayside station an aesthetic picturesqueness foreign to the prevailing dinginess of most of our country railway buildings." [39]

The use of concrete is a contentious issue, for many histories credit the contractor, Robert "Concrete Bob" McAlpine with that innovation. McGregor suggests it is proper to recognize that McAlpine's fame lay in the scale in which he worked with concrete, for he was wasn't an innovator, and concrete was already in use across Great Britain at the time. Robert McAlpine was probably a man after James Richardson Forman's heart. He was the only contractor to engage in the trek across Rannoch Moor, and his company endured all of the hardships attendant with such a project, including some setbacks with which Forman was very familiar. Iain F. Russell has noted:

"On the Mallaig Railway contract, McAlpine were unable to attract sufficient numbers of men to the works to push on with the job at the greatest speed. As on the Talla pipeline

Opposite Left: Isle of Man/Foxdale Railway.

Right: Robert McAlpine, the Scottish contractor who became famous for his use of concrete, was a risk-taker who approached business with a no-nonsense attitude that could only have pleased the Formans. (Courtesy Sir William McAlpine)

and Leadhills & Wanlockhead Railway contracts, shortages of labour were due in part to the remoteness of the sites. There were other reasons for these labour shortages. The outbreak of the Boer War, which lasted from 1899 until 1902, prompted many navvies to enlist in the army."[40]

Unlike forty years earlier, the Formans did not have to deal with sabre-rattling provincial politicians, but did have to deal with unrelenting weather:

"Bad weather also led to labour shortages on more remote contracts, as well as hindering building operations. There were severe storms and heavy rainfall in the Talla Valley during the early period of the construction of the pipeline. The engineers Formans & McCall reported to the directors of the Lanarkshire & Ayrshire that work on their railway had been disrupted by 'the exceptionally wet autumn and winter' of 1900-01."[41]

The two situations often converged to compound the problems of contractor and engineers alike. Russell notes labour shortages were more acute when inclement weather struck the remote sites: labourers forced to sit out the storms in cold, wet, draughty

Below: Glenfinnan Viaduct, the massive bridge on Scotland's West Highland Railway line, is notable for the scale in which concrete was used by contractor Robert MacAlpine (known as "Concrete Bob"). It was one of the largest structures built by the Formans.
(Courtesy VisitScotland, Scottish Viewpoint Picture Library, 1543)

huts more often than not chose to leave the works and seek employment in any of the myriad other projects underway in Scotland at the time.

Allowing for the possibility that business practices had matured somewhat over the forty years since Forman left Nova Scotia, it may be unfair to compare McAlpine's attitudes with those of the inexperienced contractors of the colony when the Nova Scotia Railway was being built. The difference may have been that McAlpine was accustomed to accepting risk, and meeting a crisis face-to-face:

> "McAlpine paid for materials by issuing their suppliers with bills which were usually discounted within six months. Wages were paid weekly in cash. McAlpine received monthly payments from the client according to the engineer's estimation of how much of the work detailed and priced in the schedule had been completed, but the expense of carrying out extra works was not usually recouped until the *completion* [italics added for emphasis] of these unscheduled jobs. Clients sometimes refused to consider claims for extras until the contract was completed. The Mallaig Railway opened in May of 1901, and the firm made a good profit of over £50,000 after claims were settled at the end of that year."[42]

Such determined patience on the part of a contractor must have made the Formans' work all the more bearable, and may have resulted in some forbearance on their part when disaster struck:

> "The most serious delays in completing contracts during the period, and the subject of most of McAlpine's claims, were serious unforeseen engineering problems which developed on the sites. On 21 April 1899 three arches of a concrete viaduct being built at Lugton for the Lanarkshire & Ayrshire's extension line collapsed into the valley below. Although the railway company's engineer, Charles Forman, could offer no certain explanation for this failure, he assumed 'that the accident must be due either to a certain defect in the material or to some outside force.'"[43]

The immediate impact concrete had upon the cost of railway construction and maintenance lay in its ease of use, which freed the contractor from employing masons and a massive workforce (although the craftsmen needed to construct the forms into which the concrete was poured were an expensive and scarce commodity). The durability of concrete reduced the necessity for frequent re-pointing of the stone. The Glenfinnan viaduct is the prime example of the utility and artistry that concrete offered railway builders. The bridge is a curved viaduct, one hundred feet high and 1248 feet long, consisting of 21 fifty-foot wide arches. Local folklore tells that during construction a horse and cart fell into one of the piers of the viaduct and was entombed by the concrete being poured on top. Dr. McGregor notes that the horse was subsequently discovered through Dr. Jim Shipway's investigation – but in Lochnanuamh viaduct, not Glenfinnan.

It is clear that James Forman's experience with bottomless bogs in Nova Scotia provided a lesson well learned by the engineers, as the Flanders Moss section of the Aberfoyle line indicates, since it was impossible to find a rocky bottom. This was determined by a summer survey of the soft subsoil, although not even a Scottish winter would have rendered the subsoil as hard as that of a Nova Scotia winter. Therefore, the Formans turned to George Stephenson's process used to cross Chat Moss on the

Manchester & Liverpool railway: filling the bogs with turf and brushwood before laying the ballast.

The stations, however, were not a trait of the father's work in Nova Scotia, where "The Station houses are built, however, with a special view to economy."[44] The stations on the West Highland Railway were given a different architectural feature, designed in the style of a Swiss chalet, with over-hanging roof and walls clad with shingle imported from Switzerland. While this undoubtedly reflects Charles Forman's love of the alpine country where he and his family frequently spent holidays, he did not design the buildings in detail, specifying only the island platforms and chalet style that became the standard on the line. The frugal principles of the railway commissioners that guided James Richardson Forman's misfortune in Nova Scotia would have no place in the land where Scots thrift was invented.

James Richardson Forman was also active in American business ventures, including the Edinburgh American Land Mortgage Company, which financed the immigration of Scottish nationals to the United States. He held the post as chairman of the company for more than twenty years. According to listings in the 1890-91 and 1900-1901 editions of the Edinburgh and Leith Post Office directories, the company had been registered in 1878 with capital of £500,000 through the sale of one hundred thousand £5 shares.

Below: Rannoch station. Ornate in a Swiss chalet style, the buildings on the West Highland Railway were in complete contrast to those James Richardson Forman erected in Nova Scotia. They may have reflected Charles Forman's love of Switzerland, where he spent his holidays. (Courtesy Scottish Screen)

The board of directors in 1890 was composed of several prominent Edinburgh men, including city magistrate James A. Russell, and M.T. Stormont Darling, the MP for the city and Solicitor General for Scotland. The listing states:

> "The securities upon which the Company's Funds are invested have been carefully selected, and are mostly First Mortgages over improved farm lands in certain parts of the United States, in respect of advances not exceeding about 40 per cent of the appraisers' valuations." [45]

The firm reported £360,000 of subscribed capital, £72,385 worth of paid up capital and a reserve fund of £23,000. By 1901, with Forman no longer chairman but still on the much-reduced board of directors, the reserve fund, which was invested in "readily realizable securities," had grown to £37,000. This represented modest success for a company involved in American land speculation at the time.

Forman's most lucrative venture, however, was the Edinburgh-based Arizona Copper Company, which became a major player in the development of that American state's mineral resources. The firm's history is described in the history published by the Phelps Dodge Mining Company, which eventually became the largest copper producer in the United States:

> "The Morenci operations of Phelps Dodge Mining Company traces its origins back to 1865 when a U.S. Army patrol, in pursuit of Indians who had stolen some horses, noted strong copper mineralization on the surface. Five years later, a group of ranchers from Silver City, New Mexico came to the area and claimed areas over the copper mineralization, hoping to find gold. These areas were later to give rise to the towns of Metcalf and Morenci. (Metcalf was named for brothers James and Robert, two of the ranchers; Morenci took its name after the Michigan hometown of a financier, William Church.) Church raised fifty thousand dollars from the Phelps Dodge Corporation in New York and formed the Detroit Mining Company, with he and Phelps Dodge as joint owners of the Morenci property. In 1886, Church sold his half of the company to Phelps Dodge, which built the first copper concentrator in Arizona. In 1882, the Metcalf brothers sold their interests in the Metcalf property to the Arizona Copper Company of Edinburgh, Scotland, which built a concentrator, leach plant and smelter at Clifton, Arizona." [46]

This company quickly proved itself to be a leader in the industry:

> "A depression in the price of copper in 1892 threatened both the Morenci and Metcalf operations. The Detroit Mining Company shut down operations, but the Arizona Copper Company was able to continue because, in 1885, they developed a unique leaching operation that could economically treat tailings from the Clifton concentrator. The leaching operation was further extended to mined oxide-type copper ores. These ores consisted of copper oxide, carbonate, silicate and sulfates from the Metcalf mine. Ten tons of sulfuric acid per day was provided from an acid plant at the Clifton smelter. Copper was separated from the leach solution using a process known as cementation, whereby the solution is contacted with scrap iron, causing the copper in solution to be exchanged for iron while the copper plates onto the scrap. Copper was recovered from the resulting cement copper by feeding it into the smelter together with the sulfide concentrates. By

using this combination of smelting and leaching, the company was able to survive the economic depression."[47]

This innovation was the creation of James Colquhoun, a Glasgow resident who left Scotland at the age of twenty-five with the title of general manager of the struggling Arizona Copper Company and a mandate from Forman and his colleagues to make money from the site. In doing so, Colquhoun earned himself a place in the American Mining Hall of Fame.

Forman's railway expertise may have proved useful to the company, which built its own railway to transport the raw ore and finished metal to and from the mine, on a mixed-gauge line that combined a 20-inch "baby" gauge track with a narrow gauge (30-inch) track. These ventures made James Richardson Forman a wealthy man, so much so that at the time of his death, he was resident of Craigpark, a large estate at Ratho near Edinburgh, and a pillar of his local church. His obituary notes: "Since 1880 he resided at Ratho, and took a lively interest in all connected with that village, having been Chairman of the local School Board and parish Council."[48]

He had purchased Craigpark in 1876, and the advertisement of its availability for sale in the Scotsman of September 13th 1876 made it sound very attractive:

Below: Craigpark House, James Richardson Forman's estate near Edinburgh. The property was purchased in 1876, cost a fortune, and came to symbolize the extent of his success in his profession.
(Courtesy Ron Day)

"To be Sold by Public Roup, within Dowell's Rooms, 18 George Street, Edinburgh, on Tuesday, 24th October, at 2 o'clock afternoon unless disposed of by Private Bargain, the MANSION HOUSE and LANDS of CRAIGPARK, in the Parish of Ratho about 10 miles west of Edinburgh. The lands extend to about 80 Acres Imperial of which about 70 are Arable Pasture, and 10 occupied by the Mansion House and Offices and Garden.

The house stands above the village of Ratho and has a commanding and extensive view of Edinburgh and the surrounding country to the north, east, and west. The house contains 4 Public Rooms, and Servants and other accommodation, and is lighted with Gas and Heated with Hot Air.

The Offices are large, and contain Double Coach Houses with stabling for 6 Horses. The Policies are tastefully laid out and there is a good walled Garden and Flower Gardens with Vinery. Two greenhouses, and a Conservatory attached to the Drawing Room.

There is a large supply of pure Spring Water on the property.

The property is 1½ miles from Ratho Station, and contains good sites for Villas or for a Hydropathic Establishment. Rental, Including Assessed Rental of Mansion House and Policies £405. 7s. 7d. which could be considerably increased by laying the Land down in Grass. Public Burdens, £13 13s 11d. The Feu Duty is nominal. The Teinds are valued and nearly exhausted. The property may be seen on Wednesdays and Fridays from 12 to 4 afternoon. Upset price £14,500." [49]

That Forman could afford the price speaks volumes about his wealth. The £14,500 he paid in 1876 would be the equivalent of £1.3 million today.

James Richardson Forman was accepted as a member of the prestigious Institution Civil Engineers on May 1st 1866, joining a pantheon of geniuses – men who had distinguished themselves in a variety of fields and countries. He lived out his days in unassuming success and obvious wealth, as indicated by the education he provided his children. Charles Forman's obituary lists his schools: "The subject of this notice was educated at Glasgow High School, at private schools in St. Andrews, London, and Edinburgh, and at Glasgow University." [50] By the census of 1891, James Richardson Forman was listed as being both a civil engineer and a farmer. It is left to his daughter, Blanche, to describe the comfortable life the expatriate Nova Scotian created for himself in old Scotland. Writing for the Ratho local history group in 1997, Anne Thomson notes:

"Of Craigpark House, she [Blanche] speaks of the gardens and the splendid gardener, who with the help of a boy, a garden woman, and an orraman (who also helped with the field work) kept everything in shape. She also mentions the trees her father had planted along the canal banks. Stirling, a north country man who had a strong dialect, looked after the fields. Her father had difficulty understanding his accent, but Blanche remembers that on most occasions she could translate for her father. There was, however, a request made by Stirling for a rig-waddy, which puzzled her. This turned out to be the balance chair across the cart horse's saddle." [51]

This idyllic life is further described by Blanche:

"Sunday School picnics by canal barge were a highlight of her early days. The canal also featured in her memories of winters at Ratho. During the winter of either 1880 or

1881, the ice was so thick that a group of young people skated all the way to Edinburgh. On another occasion, she remembers that the ice at the canal basin suddenly cracked and gave way with quite a number of people thrown into the water. They were lucky; no one drowned. One of a party of lads, who one Sunday borrowed the raft which the quarrymen used to get between the north and south quarries, was not so lucky. When the raft capsized, he was drowned." [52]

It is ironic that the canal bordering Forman's Ratho estate was one which had its business siphoned off by the railways the Formans built – just as the Nova Scotia Railway had effectively killed off the Shubenacadie Canal. In turn, Dr. McGregor of the Open University of Scotland has provided perhaps the most fitting epitaph for James Richardson Forman's career:

"Formans & McCall proposed an outer suburban route (to encourage speculative house building) on the west side of Edinburgh, making a sweep from Barnton to Balerno, via Ratho and linking existing Caledonian and North British lines. If this scheme had succeeded it might today be serving Edinburgh airport, where a rail link is much needed." [53]

It becomes obvious that James Richardson Forman went on to enjoy a career resurrected from circumstances in Nova Scotia that might have ruined any other man. In addition to his engineering career, he was also a justice of the peace. However, his death was not unexpected. The death certificate signed by Dr. H.A. Leebody on July 8th 1900, listed the causes as "senile heart failure / acute gout (six days) / Cerebral Congestion (one and a half days)." His death was registered by his son, Charles Forman of Struan Bearsden, a suburb of Glasgow. James Richardson Forman's body was transported by

Left: James Richardson Forman's grave in New Glasgow's labyrinthine Necropolis, is as much a monument to his professional success as the railways he left behind in his adopted land.
(Ronnie Scott)

train from Edinburgh to its resting place at Glasgow's Necropolis. The firm survived the death of both men, as A.J.C. Clark notes:

> "Formans & McCall were associated with Crouch & Hogg from the mid 1930s, being absorbed into the latter company in 1949. Crouch & Hogg was established in 1863 and now practices as Crouch Hogg Waterman, a major civil and structural engineering consultancy." [54]

Railways have long since passed from the firm's area of practice. Crouch Hogg Waterman was active in the biological treatment of wastes, biotechnology, and chemistry consultancy, and aspects of environmental waste management. In 1997, it merged with Sir William Halcrow & Partners, to provide services in structural, civil, geotechnical and environmental engineering. The company has offices in London, Swindon, Leeds, Manchester, Newcastle, Edinburgh, Falkirk, and Glasgow.

EPILOGUE

THE significance of James Richardson Forman's story is three-fold. Firstly, the impact his railway had on travel in Nova Scotia cannot be overstated. For all the money the colony spent on maintaining its few major highways and bridges – an expense some politicians condemned as ruinous – the roads were horrendous, as witnessed by English traveller Isabella Bishop in her journal of 1856:

"With the finest harbour in North America, with a country abounding in minerals, and coasts swarming with fish, the Nova-Scotians appear to have expunged the word progress from their dictionary – they still live in shingle houses, in streets without side walks, rear long-legged ponies, and talk largely about railroads, which they seem as if they would never complete, because they trust more to the House of Assembly than to their own energies. Consequently their astute and enterprising neighbours the Yankees, the acute speculators of Massachusetts and Connecticut, have seized the traffic which they have allowed to escape them, and have diverted it to the thriving town of Portland in Maine."[1]

This disparaging statement seems to have been crafted from intelligence gleaned from the anti-Howe element in Halifax, and offers oblique criticism of the development of what would become British North America's first crown corporation, the Nova Scotia Railway. With the line unfinished upon Bishop's arrival, she and her party took the road to Pictou by way of Hiram Hyde's stage coach line:

"Ready equipped for the tedious journey before us, from Halifax to Pictou in the north of the colony, I was at our inn-door at six, watching the fruitless attempts of the men to pile our mountain of luggage on the coach.
   Do not let the word coach conjure up a vision of 'the good old times,' a dashing mail with a well-groomed team of active bays, harness all 'spick and span,' a gentlemanly-looking coachman, and a guard in military scarlet, the whole affair rattling along the road at a pace of ten miles an hour.
   The vehicle in which we performed a journey of 120 miles in 20 hours deserves a description. It consisted of a huge coach-body, slung upon two thick leather straps; the sides were open, and the places where windows ought to have been were screened by heavy curtains of tarnished moose-deer hide. Inside were four cross-seats, intended to accommodate twelve persons, who were very imperfectly sheltered from the weather. Behind was a large rack for luggage, and at the back of the driving-seat was a bench which held three persons. The stage was painted scarlet, but looked as if it had not been washed for a year. The team of six strong white horses was driven by a Yankee, remarkable only for his silence. About a ton of luggage was packed on and behind the stage, and two open portmanteaus were left behind without the slightest risk to their contents.

Twelve people and a baby were with some difficulty stowed in the stage, and the few interstices were filled up with baskets, bundles, and packages. The coachman whipped his horses, and we rattled down the uneven streets of Halifax to a steam ferry-boat, which conveyed the stage across to Dartmouth, and was so well-arranged that the six horses had not to alter their positions.

Our road lay for many miles over a barren, rocky, undulating country, covered with var and spruce trees, with an undergrowth of raspberry, wild rhododendron, and alder. We passed a chain of lakes extending for sixteen miles, their length varying from one to three miles, and their shores covered with forests of gloomy pines….

… A dreary stage of 18 miles brought us to Shultze's, a road-side inn by a very pretty lake, where we were told the 'coach breakfasted.' Whether Transatlantic coaches can perform this, to us, unknown feat, I cannot pretend to say, but we breakfasted. A very coarse repast was prepared for us, consisting of stewed salt veal, country cheese, rancid salt butter, fried eggs, and barley bread: but we were too hungry to find fault either with it, or with the charge made for it, which equalled that at a London hotel. Our Yankee coachman, a man of monosyllables, sat next to me, and I was pleased to see that he regaled himself on tea instead of spirits.

We packed ourselves into the stage again with great difficulty, and how the forty-eight limbs fared was shown by the painful sensations experienced for several succeeding days. All the passengers, however, were in perfectly good humour, and amused each other during the eleven hours spent in this painful way. At an average speed of six miles an hour we traveled over roads of various descriptions, plank corduroy, and sand, up long heavy hills, and through swamps swarming with mosquitoes.

Every one has heard of corduroy roads, but how few have experienced their miseries! They are generally used for traversing swampy ground, and are formed of small pine-trees deprived of their branches, which are laid across the track alongside each other. The wear and tear of travelling soon separates these, leaving gaps between, and when, added to this, one trunk rots away, and another sinks down into the swamp, and another tilts up, you may imagine such jolting as only leather springs could bear. On the very worst roads, filled with deep holes, or covered with small granite boulders, the stage only swings on the straps. Ordinary springs, besides dislocating the joints of the passengers, would be wrenched and broken after a few miles travelling.

Even as we were, faces sometimes came into rather close proximity to each other and to the side railings, and heads sustained very unpleasant collisions. The amiable man who was so disappointed with the American climate suffered very much from the journey. He said he had thought a French diligence the climax of discomfort, but a 'stage was misery, oh torture!' Each time that we had rather a worse jolt than usual the poor man groaned, which always drew forth a chorus of laughter, to which he submitted most good-humouredly. Occasionally he would ask the time, when some one would point maliciously to his watch, remarking, 'Twelve hours more,' or 'Fifteen hours more,' when he would look up with an expression of despair. The bridges wore a very un-English feature. Over the small streams or brooks they consisted of three pines covered with planks, without any parapet – with sometimes a plank out, and sometimes a hole in the middle. Over large streams they were wooden erections of a most peculiar kind, with high parapets; their insecurity being evidenced by the notice, 'Walk your horses, according to law,' – a notice generally disregarded by our coachman, as he trotted his over the shaking and rattling fabric."[2]

EPILOGUE

The trip did not improve beyond the valley of the Shubenacadie:

"Eleven hours passed by not at all wearisomely to me, though my cousins and their children suffered much from cramp and fatigue, and at five, after an ascent of three hours, we began to descend towards a large tract of cultivated undulating country, in the centre of which is situated a large settlement called Truro."[3]

Prior to the opening of the railway, this trip could not be undertaken twice in a day, leaving the commercial traveller to stay overnight in either Halifax or Truro before facing the bone-rattling ride homeward. Contrast Bishop's account with that of Elizabeth Frame, who traveled with ease and comfort by rail from Halifax to Truro in 1864:

"... We enter the railway carriage, and are whirled round Bedford Basin, past Sackville – lose sight of the city – over bridges – now past lakes and ice stores. 'Windsor Junction,' says the conductor, as the train stops for a moment, and we see the diverging line of rails laid over rocks. 'All on board.' And we move on – on through hemlock forests and rocky barrens. Past lakes, sparkling in the sunbeams, and reflecting the huge granite cliffs which rise from their margin, sometimes grey, cold, and bare, sometimes clothed with hanging wood, a duck or a loon winging its solitary way to the distant beyond. How silent the forest! You might travel for miles and hear only the sound of your own footfalls, the lapping of the water on the shingle of the lake sides, or the sound of the wind through the trees. Only for the rails and the cars you would think that here man had forgotten his prerogative to be a fellow-worker with his Maker in the rearing and adorning the fitting and the beautiful.

Now we pass Elmsdale and the down train from Truro. Here the Nine Mile River delivers its tribute waters to the Shubenacadie. In passing, the eye catches sight of a narrow vale, elm trees, brick kilns, potteries, and two small churches.

'To our left,' remarked Mr. Urban, 'extends the Settlement of Nine Mile River, which is an excellent farming district. That river,' he added, 'is the Shubenacadie,' pointing to a lazy stream between two clover banks."[4]

This revolution in travel has been overlooked in the conventional histories of the railway, along with the program James Richardson Forman initiated of building a railway to higher standards than elsewhere in North America, along the British model in which he had been trained. The typical North American practice had been to lay down ties and rail as quickly as possible, improving the road at a later date when it began to demonstrate an ability to make money. Even James Laurie had noted that Forman's construction had been substantial from the outset, yet history prefers to credit Sandford Fleming with this practice when he built the Pictou Branch eastward from Truro, prior to embarking upon construction of the Intercolonial Railway.

Secondly, it could be said that Forman's political misadventure in Nova Scotia cost him an opportunity to be the engineer – or at least one of the engineers – who built the Intercolonial Railway, and help create a nation out of a fractious cluster of colonies. Had he remained with the Nova Scotia Railway, Forman would have been present during the June 1860 visit of the Prince of Wales. Joseph Howe, as premier of the colony during the Royal occasion, would undoubtedly have put Forman in the limelight as the home-grown genius who had made the railway a reality. As it was,

Howe and Jonathon McCully, the lone commissioner of the railway, would share that glory – McCully would open the door to the Prince's carriage as he left Halifax for Windsor.

It was not Albert Edward, the Prince of Wales (later King Edward VII), who would have exerted any influence on Forman's future, but Henry Pelham-Clinton, the Fifth Duke of Newcastle, who travelled with the Prince as he rode the railways of Nova Scotia, New Brunswick, and Canada. It was when he attended the ceremonies of the Prince's trip along the Northern Railway from Toronto, that the Duke first met Sandford Fleming, the expatriate Scot who was engineer-in-chief of the line, and an ardent imperialist brimming with ideas of an "All-Red line" of railways, steamships, and telegraph lines across British North America, to link the Mother country with its Asian possessions. Newcastle would later become the colonial secretary to whom the colonials would pitch their plan for union, and as Confederation gained impetus and the Intercolonial Railway became an integral part of the compact, conventional history suggests Newcastle would willingly accept Fleming as the unanimous choice of all four parties to head the design of the railway.

The only flaw in that history is that Fleming was not a unanimous choice. The original agreement had called for a three-man committee of engineers, representing the colonies' and the Imperial government's interests, and Fleming was certainly not New Brunswick's choice. New Brunswick and Nova Scotia were to be represented jointly by one engineer, Canada by another (Fleming), and the Imperial administration by the third. Alexander Luders Light was among the choices of New Brunswick Lieutenant Governor Arthur Hamilton Gordon, but the nomination came long after Forman had returned to Scotland. Upon learning that Fleming was not the unanimous choice of all three provinces, as he had been led to believe, the Duke rescinded his approval of Fleming as the joint engineer, and awaited nominations from Nova Scotia and New Brunswick. In the meantime a considerable argument developed over the sharing of the cost of the survey. It reached such a point that, in 1863, the Canadian government announced that, to prevent further delay, Fleming would begin the survey, and the bill would be considered later. A case could be made that had Forman been allowed to complete his railway unimpeded by political intrigue, he would have been Nova Scotia's candidate for the proposed triumvirate.

The other obstacle in Forman's way might well have been Howe's election loss in 1863, and Charles Tupper's accession to the leadership of the colonial government. With Forman dismissed from the railway, and the government previously having accepted Laurie's premise that a chief engineer was no longer necessary after the first phase of the project had been completed, Tupper would turn to Fleming as the engineer to continue the line from Truro to Pictou, when it appeared a line from Truro to Amherst and the New Brunswick border was not imminent. There could be no way for Tupper to consider Forman's involvement, even if he had not been dismissed in 1856. Had Howe not lost the election of 1863, Confederation might have become much less likely, for he would have continued his resistance to a plan that would ultimately subjugate his beloved colony's role in the Empire. Howe sought equal footing for Nova Scotia within the Empire itself; he wasn't satisfied that it be merely an equal partner in a nation that took an inferior position to Imperial possessions like India, the "Jewel in the Crown."

Given his experience at the hands of Nova Scotia politicians, it is unlikely Forman would have accepted any position on the Intercolonial Railway: Why would he give up the certain security and prestige he enjoyed in his adopted home in Scotland for a repeat experience of the venality and pettiness he could feel sure would await him on his return to British North America? Indeed, it seems Forman would have been the wrong man for the job, and Fleming entirely the right man. Fleming was a political animal who knew how to play the game, and appeared to enjoy it; he played politicians off against each other as adroitly as any Tupper or McCully.

The political battles that swirled around the ten years of construction of the Intercolonial would make the few years of machinations in Nova Scotia pale by comparison. This marks the third significant aspect of Forman's story. It is not difficult to determine how his experience in Nova Scotia became a benefit to Forman; there was a marked change in how he dealt with politicians when he returned to Scotland, and how his career advanced as a result.

What impact the encounter had on Tupper is more difficult to discern, except that it almost certainly dictated how he approached railway construction when he entered federal politics, and that it inevitably played a role in the history of the Canadian Pacific Railway. Tupper surely learned that railway policy was a powerful tool in politics, one he mastered quickly. Longley notes, for example, that Tupper favoured building the Pictou extension of the Nova Scotia Railway as a private enterprise, but allowed himself to be overruled when faced with opposition from within his own caucus. That does not mean he failed to profit personally; the rumours of his personal stake in the line were so persistent that ten years after his death, Longley was issuing faint denials, noting that Tupper:

"… had formerly been intimately associated with him [Fleming] in connection with the construction of the Pictou Railway when Tupper was Premier of Nova Scotia. It was alleged that Fleming had condemned the work done and some of the material used by the contractors, that they had refused to go on with their undertaking, and that construction had come to a standstill. At this stage Mr. Fleming had offered to finish the work himself at the rates agreed to by the contractors; Tupper had accepted his offer, , and Mr. Fleming had proceeded with the work and completed it. It was known that Mr. Fleming had made a large sum of money in this venture, and his opponents often made the insinuation that Dr. Tupper had shared in these profits. But although not the slightest evidence was ever produced in support of this, the recollection of these transactions no doubt served to engender suspicions as to their honesty."[5]

In its June 8th 1867 edition, *The Eastern Chronicle & Pictou County Advocate*, the leading critic of the deal forged by Tupper and Fleming, noted some of the differences between how Forman worked as chief engineer, and how Fleming was given a free hand:

"We strongly denounced the policy of the Government in virtually allowing Mr. Fleming to drive the original contractors off the works. It is urged in excuse that the necessities of the case demanded that such an extreme course should be pursued. Perhaps so. But the necessities of the case did not demand that the whole line should be handed over to Mr. Fleming by private bargain, without furnishing security of any kind for the faithful performance thereof. We opposed such a proceeding because it was unfair to our local contractors, because it was a flagrant violation of the Railway Act, and because it established a precedent which may be dangerously acted upon in the future."[6]

The newspaper also noted Fleming had wrung a special concession out of Tupper, negating a requirement from which Forman would not allow his contractors to escape:

"On the existing lines of railway, we believe, the contractors were compelled, at their own cost and charges, to uphold their respective sections for one year. Mr. Fleming's contract does not bind him to do this, and on this point we claim that the Government have not faithfully looked to the interests of the country. Let Mr. Fleming now carefully finish up what remains to be done on the line, and then voluntarily assume the upholding of the line for one year. By the expiration of that time the embankments will be pretty well settled, the general character of the line will have been fairly tested, and where there are obvious defects they can be remedied."[7]

The force of Tupper's personality, the reverence in which he was held as a Father of Confederation, and the subsequent reluctance among historians to delve deeper into the affair, spared Tupper's reputation until Lorne Green noted in his 1993 work on Fleming:

"The opposition were not in the slightest convinced; they impugned Fleming's honesty, pointing out that Fleming allowed an estimated $140,000 for iron girders, when in fact there were only two main bridges on the entire Pictou line, costing $14,500. The government easily turned aside the censure motion, but the opposition had done its damage. Tupper and Fleming were left with a legacy of mistrust that would shadow them for years to come. However, Tupper did get his Pictou Railway on time and within estimate, and Fleming had grown suddenly very wealthy – whether from the proceeds of his private business deals with Tupper or otherwise is a matter of conjecture. His private papers for the period record large transfers of spare cash: $15,000 to his father-in-law to invest for him, $40,000 to his bank account in Montreal, £16,000 to a Kirkcaldy bank account, and the purchase of $40,000 of Northern Railway bonds. Fleming bought property in Montreal and paid £17,000 for a new collier ship which he ran between Pictou harbour and Montreal with coal shipments. He urged his brother, David, to open a coal yard in Montreal to stock coal that was not sold immediately from dock side. Fleming paid $4,000 to Tupper for the balance due on a coal mining venture in Cumberland County; he bought David's farm in Weston in 1869 and gave it to his sister, Jane, and the following year he bought several lots of prime land on the Northwest Arm of Halifax, amassing nearly 41 hectares. It bears recalling that Fleming's annual salary on the Intercolonial was $4,800."[8]

So intimate was the connection between the engineer and cabinet minister that in his essay on their relationship in *Character and circumstance: essays in honour of Donald Grant Creighton*, (ed. J. S. Moir, Toronto, 1970), Alan Wilson called Fleming and Tupper "Siamese twins." Green emphasized the more personal aspect by paraphrasing Wilson's work:

"Tupper and Fleming became fast friends; the premier was also a medical doctor and became family physician to the Fleming family. The two men schemed to develop resources in Tupper's part of the province, and became business partners in Springhill coal and Cumberland salt ventures. Sandford and [wife] Jeanie thus found themselves at the pinnacle of Halifax society. They were always invited to parties at Government House."[9]

Howe and Forman never appeared to have had a similarly analogous relationship, but their circumstances never offered an opportunity for personal profit through shares or contracting. (In his analysis of the downfall of Tupper and Fleming, Wilson paints Tupper as being an innocent victim of the cabal that included Montreal bankers, Conservative politicians, jealous engineers, and finally Sir John A. Macdonald himself. But to suggest Tupper was honestly overcome by "shock and disgust" when presented with the ultimatum to dismiss Fleming from the Canadian Pacific Railway survey overlooks or ignores the similarity of the events that had occurred twenty years earlier when Forman was dismissed, and the part Tupper played in that event.)

Despite his own family's apparent later involvement in profiteering from railroad speculation, it is doubtful that Forman would have entertained any opportunity for the provincial secretary to earn personal fortune from the construction of the Pictou line which, as a coal-carrying line with Halifax as its principal market, offered much greater financial returns than the line from Halifax to Truro.

The Windsor-Annapolis line was similarly supposed to have been an extension of the provincially owned line, however, Tupper was adamant that railway would be a private venture. In the event, it was a venture in which he would become a shareholder, albeit it in a clandestine manner. Such investments, while not illegal in those times, were clearly recognized as being construed as politically unacceptable, hence Tupper's shares were controlled by William Black, a prominent Cumberland County merchant. Likewise, Tupper never opposed the creation of the Intercolonial Railway as a government-owned line, openly placing his confidence in Sandford Fleming, and he participated in the organization of the Canadian Pacific Railway as a federal project. Yet, when Fleming's administration of the Pacific railway threatened to become fatal to the completion of the line, Tupper did not hesitate to replace him and back private capitalists as the saviours of the project.

Quite aside from being railway engineers, Forman and Fleming shared at least this one deleterious common denominator in their careers, for inasmuch as Tupper engineered Forman's removal, Tupper was unable to counter a similar strategy employed by his political opponents who appeared determined to unseat him, or at least his political proxy Fleming – who was to Tupper what Forman had been to Howe. The opportunity came in 1880, when Conservatives – anxious to thwart Tupper's ambition to replace Sir John A. Macdonald – seized upon the cost overruns of the Canadian Pacific Railway, on Tupper's long association with Fleming, and on rumoured profit-taking in connection with the Pictou railway. It has been recorded that the ringleader of these Conservatives was Dalton McCarthy, who led the clamour against Tupper in connection with the contracts awarded and the cost overruns associated with them.

The charges levelled against Fleming in the House of Commons mirrored those Tupper had made against Forman; indeed in many respects, Fleming's defense of his professional integrity shared a remarkable similarity to that of Forman almost thirty years earlier. In his memorandum to Tupper, then Minister of Railways and Canals, in March of 1880, Fleming noted:

"An engineer is in no way answerable for the policy adopted by the Government in making contracts; but once a contract is entered into and placed in his hands, he is responsible to the Government, through the Minister of the Department, that it be honestly fulfilled. It is his duty to carry out and enforce its conditions, to see that the work is properly performed and full value given for the money paid. It is equally his duty to do justice to the contractor, as to the public; indeed, to act as a judge between parties whose views of right are not always identical. It is moreover, his duty to submit to the Minister any changes, in construction or otherwise, he may hold to be desirable, and, on obtaining the Minister's authority, to have them carried out." [10]

Where the cost overruns were concerned, Fleming first pleaded innocence by virtue of his being on leave of absence when the excess were discovered, but he noted, as Forman had done:

"The original bills of quantities were made up without the exact data necessary for forming estimates with accuracy. They were prepared, from the best information, by engineers who had charge of each particular survey. As there was great pressure to have the work placed under contract, and definite quantities were indispensable, the results were, to a certain extent, assumed." [11]

Indeed, Fleming's defence pointed to a lesson that engineers had not learned three decades after Forman's subordinates had made the same error at Gaspereau Lake in the depths of winter:

"Much of the line passes through muskegs and marshes. The surveys were mostly made in the winter when the ground was frozen. This circumstance doubtless, in some cases, deceived the surveyors as to its character, and led them to mistake marsh and muskeg for firm earth." [12]

Whereas Forman found himself being judged by a single professional colleague, however, in 1882 Fleming found himself left to the tender mercy of a partisan three-man tribunal which Tupper could not control. Fleming there found himself exposed to the same threat that Forman suffered at the hands of Tupper in 1856. Complaining of his treatment, this time to Secretary of State J.A. Mousseau, Fleming noted:

"I feel it due, not simply to myself, but to each of the several administrations which I served as Engineer-in-Chief of the Pacific Railway, that I should point out that the criticisms of the Commission are not sustained by the facts of the case, and are even at variance with the evidence submitted." [13]

Where Forman benefitted, however, was that his judge was a professional and not a political animal. As Fleming noted:

"It seems to me that the Commission have, in their examination of witnesses, displayed a decided one-sidedness, and they have evinced an unmistakable animus throughout their report. They have suppressed evidence of importance which I submitted, and they have brought against me grave charges on the testimony of hostile witnesses, without asking me a single question on the points raised against me, without affording me an opportunity of giving any explanation, and without the least knowledge on my part that such charges were made until I read them after the report was laid before Parliament." [14]

But where he won in 1856, Tupper did not necessarily lose in 1882. In order to keep the peace within his party, Sir John successfully had Fleming resign rather than be dismissed; he ushered Tupper into "retirement," giving him the job as Canada's High Commissioner in London, a position into which he comfortably grew from his son-in-law's residence at Bexleyheath.

It is certain Tupper had become a shareholder in the Canadian Pacific Railway at this point in his life, and even Longley's attempt to dispel that rumour could not wipe away the taint of scandal:

"He was Minister of Railways during the construction of the Canadian Pacific Railway and also while contracts were entered into with Onderdonk and others for the construction, as a government work, of a portion of the line to the Pacific coast. It is reasonably certain that Onderdonk made handsome profits on his contracts. It is equally true that many persons made fortunes in contracting for the Canadian Pacific Railway Company. It was a common belief, industriously propagated by his opponents, that the Minister of Railways received substantial advantages from these large transactions. But again there is an entire absence of proof." [15]

Longley falls short of an outright denial of any personal profit accruing to Tupper:

"He had a right, in common with every citizen, to acquire Canadian Pacific Railway stock or any other stock in the market, and if his faith was rewarded by a rise in value, this cannot be imputed to him as a reproach. The millionaire fiction lasted only a few years and then it became known that the story was untrue." [16]

Despite biographer Longley's assertions as to his subject's honesty, there is sufficient evidence to show that, with both Forman and Laurie out of office (and McCully or Pictou County Nova Scotia lawyer James MacDonald as the sole commissioner of the Nova Scotia Railway), opportunity existed for many politicians to enrich themselves, and that Tupper would later indulge in dispensing political patronage – through the provincial railway (as Green has documented) and later through the Intercolonial Railway when he was in the federal arena. This aspect has not been fully documented previously, but Fleming provides some clues in his 1876 history of the construction of the federal line. His appended list of names of the more than ninety engineers and surveyors who worked on the survey for the line in 1864 to its completion in 1876 includes Fleming's own brother, John Arnot Fleming (1835-1876), and Edward and Walter Lawson, members of the influential Halifax family of Jessie Grant, wife of Fleming's close friend, Rev. George Munro Grant. Jessie Lawson Grant was a daughter of William Lawson Jr. of Halifax, merchant trader and a founder, along with his namesake father, of the Bank of Nova Scotia.

Tupper also had a family connection through his wife, which is outlined by Cyrus Black:

"Amos Botsford resided at Westcock, Sackville. He was empowered by the British Government to get this country settled, and exerted himself in arranging the settlement of Sackville. His son, William, was the only lawyer in Westmorland for many years and was subsequently appointed Judge of the Supreme Court of New Brunswick.

Colonel Joseph Morse, one of the grantees of land at Cumberland, had a son named Alpheus who settled at Cumberland and had five sons and three daughters. The eldest two sons – Alpheus and John – settled at River Philip. James Shannon, when young, left home to go to the United States. Calling at lawyer Botsford's, Mr. Botsford persuaded him to remain, and offered to take him as a student-at-law. Mr. Morse complied, and at an early age got his profession, and, for many years, was the only lawyer in Cumberland. He was elected several times to represent the township of Amherst in the Assembly, generally by acclamation. He was also a member of the Legislative and Executive Councils of the province. Of his sons, one is a physician, and three were lawyers, one of whom is Judge of the County Court. Joseph Morse, son of Alpheus 2nd, removed to the United States. Silas had two daughters. One was married to Dr. (now Sir Charles) Tupper, and the other to W. M. Fullerton, Queen's Counsel." [17]

Frances Amelia Morse, later Lady Tupper, was kin to Charles and J.E. Morse, who both found work on the Intercolonial Railway, with Charles Morse going on to survey for the Canadian Pacific Railway in the Algoma region of Ontario.

The intriguing but never-to-be-answered question then arises: How would the Intercolonial or the Canadian Pacific projects have fared had Forman gone on to become chief engineer of one or the other, and had Tupper continued in his meteoric rise to political stardom?

There is one final aspect of James Richardson Forman's story that deserves to be investigated, if for no other reason than it involves the politically intriguing mix of sex and money! Both men had attended Horton academy, Tupper entering the year before Forman, in August of 1837. While they were not necessarily in the same class, they must surely have been aware of each other, and it could not have been entirely pleasing for Tupper. In circumstances, they could not have been more dissimilar. James Richardson Forman, son of a wealthy banking executive, almost certainly never had to concern himself about his financial situation. Charles Tupper, son of an Evangelist minister from Amherst, had to work his way to get his education, as biographer Longley records:

"Young Charles, equally desirous of obtaining a higher education, had qualified himself for a school teacher, and with what assistance his father could give him and a small sum obtained by teaching, began his studies at Horton Academy, Wolfville. Here according to tradition he eked out his scanty means by work at a shoemaker's bench." [18]

Had the two young men known each other at the school – and it is unlikely in such close-knit surroundings that they could have avoided each other – surely Tupper must have found reason to envy the younger student who enjoyed the benefits of wealth?

Coincidentally both of them went to Scotland to further their educations, Forman to Glasgow, Tupper to Edinburgh, where he entered university and procured his doctor's degree. This seems like a great leap forward in the fortunes of a student who worked at a cobbler's shop to get his primary education, and Longley notes rumours swirled about Tupper long afterward:

> "Much gossip prevailed at this time as to the manner of his obtaining the means for this Edinburgh course. It was hinted that he had engaged the affections of a young lady in Amherst and, under promise of marriage, received from her the money necessary to pursue his medical studies in Edinburgh, but that after his return to Nova Scotia he declined to fulfil his engagement." [19]

This gossip would lead to a political scandal in Halifax when Joe Howe pointedly raised the matter in the House shortly after Tupper took his seat in 1855. The failed engagement would not be the lone incident in Tupper's love life (although when he married Frances Morse in Amherst on October 8th 1846, it would mark the beginning of a life-long relationship). In his biography of Tupper, Philip Buckner makes note of another unsuccessful engagement: "After returning to Nova Scotia he broke off an engagement he had entered into at age 17, briefly became engaged to the daughter of a prominent Halifax merchant...." [20] Who this young lady was is not recorded, but it is certain she would have been known to James Richardson Forman's bride. Isabella Hill was from a prominent family in that small circle that was Halifax's social elite. She and her sister Elizabeth were legendary for their beauty. Social gossip would surely have made her privy to the details of this aspect of Tupper's life – and a man who cherished his dignity so dearly as Longley has claimed, must surely have resented that knowledge.

It is entirely possible the young lady in question could have been the future Isobel Forman, or one of her sisters. Charles John Hill had ten daughters among his thirteen children, five of whom could have been courted by young Doctor Tupper in his search for a wife on his return to the colony. Anne, the oldest daughter, was born on August 4th 1819 in Halifax, and married James J. Grieve on June 13th 1846 in Halifax. Grieve was born in Green Oaks, Nova Scotia, a village on the banks of the Shubenacadie River at the Bay of Fundy, where in 1846, he had become a merchant in a community that shared in the wealth of the province's world-wide shipping and ship-building industry. Elizabeth was born on February 18th 1821 in Halifax, and was married twice, the first time (May 19th 1840) to George Fergusson in Nova Scotia. Fergusson died, and Elizabeth married a second time (October 25th 1854 in Southampton, Hampshire) to Arthur James Herbert. Isabella, the third daughter, married James Richardson Forman. She died on July 3rd 1896 in Halifax, an indication that the Formans retained their family connections in Nova Scotia long after being ushered unceremoniously out of the province.

Jessie Hill was born on August 11th 1826 in Halifax and married well, in the same way Forman's sister Louise had. She married a young Royal Navy officer, Edmund Heathcote, in Halifax on March 19th 1852. Heathcote died as an admiral in October of 1881, and Jessie lived on "on her own means" until she died December 19th 1915 at Fritham House, Fritham, New Forest, Hampshire. Mary, the last daughter that Tupper might have married, was born on August 11th 1829 in Hursley Park, Hampshire. She was also twice married, the first time to Hector J. Macaulay (June 21st 1845) in Nova Scotia, and the second time to George Washington Sprott (September 19th 1857) in Greenock, Renfrew, Scotland. Sprott was born about 1829 in Nova Scotia, and died on October 26th 1911 in Musquodoboit, Nova Scotia. The other daughters, Amelia (born in March 1833), Grace (August 1839), and Georgina (April 1841) were all too young to be married at the time of Tupper's engagement. Two daughters died at an early age; Adelaide was six years old when she died in 1838, and Florence was little more than a year old when she died in the same year.

Could jealousy over family fortunes, or the knowledge of his past romantic failures, be reasons for Tupper's apparently passionate personal and political animosity toward Forman? If one considers history to be something of a matter of fate, then a confrontation between the engineer and the doctor was inevitable, and with the unity of an emerging nation hanging in the balance, it is perhaps just as well that the battleground was the relative backwater of Halifax, rather than Ottawa, and that neither man ultimately had to forfeit his career.

AFTERWORD

James Robert Mosse almost certainly escaped any recrimination from his involvement in the Nova Scotia Railway's problems by virtue of his family connections. In addition to being a nephew of premier James W. Johnston, his wife Harriet was a sister of Phillip Carteret Hill, who would also become the mayor of Halifax from 1861-1864, and premier of Nova Scotia from 1875-1878. With a namesake in the heroic captain of HMS Monarch, who died at the Battle of Copenhagen serving under Admiral Lord Nelson, Mosse was born on May 31st 1823 and wed Harriet Hill (no apparent relation to the Hill family into which James Richardson Foman had married) on June 20th 1855. His wife died after childbirth on February 8th 1857. That tragic event may also have spared him from the public opprobrium or press scrutiny for any role he might have played in the railway controversy.

His mother-in-law was a member of the Binney family, which counted among its number the Right Reverend Hibbert Binney, the fourth bishop of the Church of England in Halifax. Mosse was the son of Charles Mosse, a captain of the Royal Artillery, who had married Sarah Ann Almon at St. Luke's parish in Chelsea, London on May 8th 1817. His mother came from the ranks of one of Halifax's leading families. She was a daughter of William James Almon, and sister to Mather Byles Almon – the banker from whom James Richardson Forman's father had allegedly embezzled a substantial amount of money – and Dr. William Bruce Almon, whose daughter Amelia had married James W. Johnston in 1821. Captain Charles Mosse was a hero in his own right, having earned a silver medal as a member of Count Von Alten's light division at the battle of Nive during the Peninsular War, December 10th to 14th 1813. It was this battle that heralded Wellington's advance into France. (James Mosse shared a patriarchal connection with Nova Scotia's Lieutenant Governor at the time. Sir John Gaspard LeMarchant's father – also John Gaspard LeMarchant – died at Salamanca during the Peninsular War in 1812.)

All of James Mosse's relatives – with the exception of William James Almon – were alive at the time of the railway controversy, and must have shuddered at the release of the correspondence surrounding his dismissal by Jonathan McCully. In a letter to Joseph Howe dated March 19th 1860, McCully made his disdain for Mosse quite evident:

"Having shown that Mr. Mosse's fidelity is not of that kind which is considered one of the first qualifications for a government employee, I am frank to admit that I have not much confidence in his judgement or capacity for the office of chief engineer, or that of superintendent of traffic. His engineering mistakes in one single instance – I refer to the case at Grand Lake – upon which the Messrs. Sutherland successfully based their application for extras – cost Nova Scotia, as is well known, a large amount of money, and not only so but it paved the way successfully for other and similar claims."[1]

McCully pointed to other examples of Mosse's "unskilful [sic] management" of the traffic accounts as sufficient reason to dismiss him from office. Mosse would recover from the ignominy. His obituary published in the *Proceedings of the Institution of Civil Engineers* in 1904 (he became a member in 1862) portrays him as a veteran of the art, having begun his studies in 1838 with Captain W.S. Moorsom, one of the first to investigate the possibility of a trans-continental railway across British North America. He was hired by Peto, Jackson, Brassey and Betts of Birkenhead, England to assist in the survey of the inter-colonial railway route from Halifax to New Brunswick, and may have been with James Beatty, Peto's surveyor who discovered the route through the Cobequid Hills later chosen by James Richardson Forman, reluctantly used by Fleming, and exploited to personal advantage by Robert Forman.

When Laurie left the Nova Scotia Railway, Mosse became manager and chief engineer until, in 1862, he came to the attention of Sir George Hawkshaw, who was building the government railways on Mauritius, a British possession in the Indian Ocean. By 1868 Mosse had become general manager of the Mauritius system, and then went on to build railways in Ceylon (now Sri Lanka), and became a prominent member of the institution. The obituary notes: "Mr. Mosse possessed a wide and varied knowledge of railway engineering and management, was of scrupulous rectitude, extremely courteous and charitable, and was much respected by his staff and among his colleagues in his profession."[2] The obituary does not explain the association with Hawkshaw, but Mauritius was an intensely industrialized island, despite its small size, and among its chief exports were sugar, cinnamon, and other spices. These were commodities that just happened to be among the major imports at the port of Halifax (most coming from the Caribbean) and held great interest for the likes of Mather Byles Almon, Mosse's uncle.

Left: Hiram Blanchard. His defense of William Smellie prevented the engineer from becoming another of Tupper's victims and uncovered a conspiracy led by James W. Johnston. (Nova Scotia Archives and Records Management Service, 52962 n-9485)

William Baillie Smellie had no such connections to protect him when he was dismissed from his post on the engineering staff, and it seemed as though his career might end ignominiously. While there was blame aplenty to go around for the cost overruns, Smellie was the only member of the engineering staff to stand trial for fraud, accused of having conspired with others to award contractor Donald Cameron £2,000 more than he was due under the terms of his contract. The trial took place in Nova Scotia in 1860, two years after his chief engineer had returned to Scotland and was unable to testify on his behalf, but Smellie was ably defended by Hiram Blanchard, a colleague of Howe's and destined to become premier of Nova Scotia in his own right – albeit briefly – from July to November of 1867.

The charges were laid as a result of the re-measurement of Cameron's contract on section No. 3 of the Windsor branch of the railway. It was alleged that the figures transcribed on the schedules of work had somehow been altered, and suspicion fell upon Smellie. There was a similar suspicion that Laurie had made the alterations, but this was never proven. With James Richardson Forman gone, Tupper seemed determined to have a sacrificial lamb he could place before the Nova Scotia public. William Smellie was the next available victim. As Blanchard noted in the debate that took place in the Nova Scotia Legislature on March 12th 1861, a full three years after Forman had been exiled, and a year after Smellie had been acquitted:

"The hon. member for Cumberland [Tupper] has seen fit to revive and bring here the case of Mr. Smellie. Intimately acquainted with all the circumstances of the case I should have allowed his vituperation to pass just at its worth; but I do feel it my duty – not as that gentleman's advocate – for our connection in a business point of view has long since terminated – to wipe out the impression the member for Cumberland sought to create that Mr. Smellie's acquittal was owing to his having 'the benefit of a doubt.' Sir, if any man was ever followed with an inveterate and determined malignity – with deep and deadly vindictiveness – that man was Smellie. Long ago it was evident to me that a secret plot was concocted to effect that man's utter, irretrievable, irremediable ruin; and that the most persevering determination existed to make him out a guilty man. Was it not patent to all the world – does not every man who hears me – know that months before the trial – before that innocent man had an opportunity of vindicating his character from the reproach his dismissal had cast upon it – through the pages of the *Colonist* newspaper it was heralded to all the world that a gross fraud upon the public had been attempted, and that Smellie and none other than he was the guilty party?"[3]

Blanchard made it clear he considered Tupper responsible for the "secret plot," and Tupper's connection with the *Colonist* – and his role in the ousting of Forman – was undoubted:

"Week after week was the public mind impregnated with this idea – and advantage taken of the power of the press which was a disgrace to those who made use of it; prostituting a noble public institution to the vile purpose of perpetrating a flagrant individual wrong. The member for Cumberland says that Smellie was ingenuously defended. Sir, I take no credit for ingenuity in that defence. I established a plain, simple, straightforward case – nor did I make a single appeal to passion or to prejudice.

On the jury were men of all classes, and of nearly all creeds – certainly of all shades of politics – and after patiently investigating the whole case they went out and in fifteen minutes returned a verdict of acquittal."[4]

Blanchard had amassed a phalanx of character witnesses to testify on Smellie's behalf, so many that the magistrate formally acknowledged the defendant's reputation in order to shorten the proceedings. Tupper had claimed that Smellie, although acquitted, had left the trial without a shred of his reputation left, for which Blanchard publicly admonished the good doctor:

"Let the member for Cumberland, then, refrain hereafter from indulging in such license of speech respecting a man whose honour, probity, and honesty his [Dr. Tupper's] own political friends universally respect and esteem. It would be well for any gentleman around these benches if, in time of need, he could command such testimony; and the day may come when even the hon. member for Cumberland may find it no easy task to get so many respectable political opponents to say as much for him."[5]

In the same debate, responding to Tupper's repeated defamation of Smellie, Howe exposed the perfidy of the Tory leaders, and specifically accused Johnston, the attorney general, of a conspiracy to railroad Smellie, a conspiracy that went unnoticed in the press:

"Then Smellie must come in for his share of vituperation. That villain Smellie – the conspirator – who we were told last year with Donald Cameron and McCully entered into a conspiracy to mutilate public documents and to take two thousand pounds out of the treasury. What did I say when this matter was here last year? I could say noting but this: may the almighty protect the young man if he be innocent; if he be not, may his guilt be proved. I never pledged myself to anything else, pro or con. Sir, I left the matter to be settled by the judicial tribunals of the country. But, I prayed in my inmost soul that if innocent, he might be extricated from the danger that encompassed him. For a more dammed [sic] plot, a more vile scheme, to destroy the very life and soul of a human being was never concocted in any country. You may take up any noval [sic] or romance, you may pry into the secret history of men in city or country, and you will hardly find the story of a man placed in greater peril than was Smellie last year. His defence fell on my learned friend beside me (Mr. Blanchard). I could not attend that trail throughout, but I heard enough of it. In the most moderate and proper style was he defended; there was no appeal to the passions – nothing but common sense. And then, when I heard the Judge's charge, my hair almost stood on end. The hon. member read passages of it in my hearing today. Did he read it all? No; there was one fact brought out in that trial which drew the marked comment of the Judge. When this poor young man, Smellie, was first accused, when this plot first developed itself, what was done with him? He was bought into one of the public departments, and there he met the Executive Council and others. With an impartiality and a gravity exceedingly edifying, a document was drawn up by the Atty. General, and that document was produced in court, and upon it an attempt was made to convict Smellie. It not only made him admit the undoubted facts, which nobody disputed, but also that he was guilty of the fraud. Judge Bliss, with his impartial and discriminating mind, said, surely

Mr. Smellie never signed that, knowing what he signed. A juryman asked, did he read it himself, or did you read it to him? What turned out to be the fact? That the hon'ble member for Annapolis, the Atty. General, had put into that document, signed by Mr. Smellie, what was a damming [sic] confession of guilt – what Mr. McNab said could not be true, because Smellie never admitted anything of the kind. That transaction did amuse me. I will not say it was intentional; and I hope it was not. The jurymen in ten minutes brought in a unanimous verdict of "Not Guilty." Does it become the Hon. member for Cumberland, after that, in this Legislature, in distant counties, or in any part of this Christian country, to try Smellie over again, and retail these scraps from the Judge's charge?"[6]

Howe then gave his most certain indication that he would have re-hired James Richardson Forman, as he did Smellie, when the storm clouds of a manufactured scandal had passed over the affair:

"The moment that verdict was recorded I said to my colleagues, this young man has been blackened and maligned for ten months, his salary stopped, his prospects blasted; he must be employed again, and I never did an act that afforded me more satisfaction than when I put him back into the public service, in atonement for what he had suffered. Let me suppose he had been guilty, and that he had served out his time in the penitentiary; well, sir, the great God above would drop a tear on his past life, and would not shut him out from all human sympathy and human employment. And, sir, just what the Creator would not do, human legislators and governments ought not to do – drive the guilty to despair. Shall the innocent be shunned because they have been falsely accused?"[7]

True to form, Howe could not restrain himself from launching another personal salvo at Tupper, lecturing him in self-righteous oratory, dutifully transcribed for the public record:

"I will say to the hon. member that I think he will never in this country make that use of his abilities which he ought to make – never cultivate that wide circle of friends that he should cultivate – never command that influence which he wishes to attain, until he has more of the milk of human kindness permeating through his mental system – more of Christian charity in dealing with his fellow-men."[8]

Clearly Smellie bore the brunt of an attack Tupper had prepared for James Richardson Forman, had the chief engineer not made his retreat to Scotland. Smellie was not long in forging his own connections, perhaps to shield himself from anything further that Tupper may have planned after his exoneration in court.

Born about 1820 in Glasgow, Scotland, Smellie had worked for a short time on the Grand Trunk Railway in Upper Canada for the British firm of Peto, Jackson, Brassey & Betts. In Nova Scotia he married Maria Chipman Lovett of Annapolis January 2nd 1866. Her father, James Russell Lovett had been the member of the legislature for Annapolis from 1826-1830. *The Directory of the Members of the Legislative Assembly of Nova Scotia: 1758-1958* indicates Lovett died at his son-in-law's home in

Halifax in 1864. Hutchinson's *Directory of Nova Scotia* for 1864-65 shows William B. Smellie as boarding at 68 Hollis Street at the time, and more interestingly, that he was First Principal in the Royal Union Chapter No. 137 of the order of the Freemasons. This is evidence that he had re-acquired much of his respectability and was still practicing his profession, while Tupper was still active in Nova Scotia politics. Some of this was due to McCully, who appointed Smellie acting engineer of the Nova Scotia Railway when he became sole commissioner in 1861. It was a significant move, as McCully's report to the Legislature in 1862 indicates:

> "Immediately after the prorogation of the Assembly, in accordance with suggestions contained in a report of a committee of the House of Assembly, I took action on the subject of the unfinished engine house at Richmond, which resulted in a decision to erect a new building on a new site, upon a new principle. The able report of W.B. Smellie Esq., C.E., (Appendix E) under whose direction the completion of this work, as well as the erection of a new wharf at Richmond, and other extensive operations there, have been conducted, leaving me scarcely anything to add. Mr. Smellie, having finished the design of the new wharf, and prepared the specification for the new engine house, I decided to place him in charge, and authorized him to oversee the erection of the work. He has discharged this duty to my entire satisfaction, and I have reason to believe that under his inspection the several contracts referred to in his report, have been thoroughly executed. His engagements with the department would have closed

Left: James Forman Smellie, the son of William Smellie, bore his father's colleague's name with dignity as a lawyer and registrar of the Supreme Court of Canada. (Courtesy James Smellie)

with the year, but for an application on the part of Major-General Doyle, commander of the forces, for the use of the large building situate upon the old wharf, and the stone building formerly used as an engine house, for the purpose of fitting them up as barracks. This request having been complied with, I engaged Mr. Smellie's services until the war department shall have completed an undertaking entered into on their part to alter and fit up the buildings in question, and to build for the department a new store as a substitute for that occupied as barracks, and which is in course of erection. The understanding being that the war department shall bear the expense of Mr. Smellie's salary for superintending until the completion of their engagements."[9]

This new military installation was the direct result of the British mobilization of the army in the aftermath of the Trent Affair of 1861, when the seizure of a British ship by the Union navy threatened to turn the US Civil War into an Anglo-American conflict. The barracks housed many of the troops hastily sent by Westminster and then dispatched by Doyle through New Brunswick to defend Upper Canada from a suspected American attack.

William and Maria Smellie had at least one son, and it may be his life that provides the most fitting epitaph to James Richardson Forman's career in North America. James Forman Smellie was born on September 16th 1869, in Glasgow, Scotland – an indication that his father also spent some time back in the "auld" country, perhaps to recover from the political fallout he endured in Nova Scotia. That his father survived the ordeal meted out to him by Tupper is evidenced by the fact James Forman Smellie was educated at Lincoln College and sent to Queen's University in Kingston, Ontario. This required both intelligence and money. It may also have required a family connection. After serving briefly under McCully (who had been named as a co-conspirator in the Cameron case, but as commissioner he was never indicted) on the Nova Scotia Railway, William Smellie worked for Sandford Fleming on the Intercolonial Railway from 1870-71 and again in 1874. Fleming was also a Freemason, of the Scottish rite, but on arriving in Halifax in 1864 to begin the survey for the Intercolonial Railway, Smellie would have been one of the first civil engineers with whom he made an acquaintance. Fleming – a close personal friend of Rev. George Munroe Grant, the principal of the university – was named Chancellor of Queen's in 1880. Oddly, Fleming was also a political ally and personal friend to Tupper.

James Forman Smellie was something of a sportsman in his youth, depicted in the Queen's yearbook as a member of the university's 1886 championship hockey team, after an historic game between Queen's and the Royal Military College. His teammates included Sydney Davis, Walter Fleming (it is not known if this was Walter Arthur Fleming, sixth child of Sandford Fleming), Hendry Leggett, Clem Burns (later Librarian of the Supreme Court of Canada), A.B. Cunningham (later a barrister and King's Counsel), and H.A. Parkyn.

Graduating from Osgoode Hall with his law degree (and where he also played varsity hockey), James Forman Smellie was called to the bar of Ontario in 1893, and went into private practice. It is evident he did very well, being named King's Counsel in 1928. The title King's (or today Queen's) Counsel was at that time not one given lightly, although its use has been diminished over the years (federal appointments ceased in 1993). An honourary title given for life, the accolade was placed in jeopardy by none other than Tupper (by then Sir Charles), who attempted in 1896 to appoint 173 of his political cronies – many of them undeserving of the honour as Queen's Counsel – as his short-lived government prepared to hand over power to Laurier's Liberals.

This politically crass act, opposed by many lawyers who had yet to achieve the title, and many more who had received it, actually helped set a new official standard for men like Smellie who could obtain the honour only after having at least ten years' standing at the bar anywhere in the British Empire, a law degree from a university in the Empire, must have acted as leading counsel in no fewer than twenty-five contested trials in the Supreme Court of their province, or the then-Exchequer Court of Canada, have contested applications before Royal Commissions or committees of the Parliament or legislature, or have acted as leading counsel in at least fifteen appeals to the highest appellate court in their province.

The new attorney general Oliver Mowatt was successful in having the Governor General – the Earl of Aberdeen – refuse to accept the nominations on the grounds that:

"An examination of the list shows that the selection of the names was not made on the basis of professional or personal merit. On the contrary these are names in the list of gentlemen in regard to whom there could be no pretence or supposition of their having any claims on these grounds, and on the other hand many gentlemen have been omitted from the list whose professional merits exceed that of many of those named." [10]

In the meantime James Forman Smellie developed family connections of his own, having married Amy Maud Vernon Ritchie on October 12th 1904. She was the daughter of Sir William Ritchie, Chief Justice of the Supreme Court of Canada. It may be a stroke of delicious irony that Justice Ritchie was a nephew of James W. Johnston. Smellie's career was capped in 1930 when he was appointed registrar of the Supreme Court of Canada. He served in that position until 1940, and died in 1948. In an era when the naming of a child after a family friend, or an acquaintance held in high regard, was considered to be the greatest tribute one could pay to that person, there can be no doubt of William Smellie's admiration for his former chief engineer. There's also no doubt that James Forman Smellie bore that acknowledgement with dignity.

☙

END NOTES

Introduction

[1] James Shipway. *ICE Newsletter,* Institution Civil Engineers, London, (March 1999).
[2] G.R. Stevens, *Canadian National Railways, Vol. I: Sixty Years of Trial and Error* (Toronto: Clarke, Irwin & Co., 1960), 176.
[3] Jay Underwood. "Alexander Luders Light: The Forgotten Man," *Canadian Rail* 494 (May-June 2003): 97.

Chapter One

[1] Henry J. Morgan, *Bibliotheca Canadensis, or A manual of Canadian Literature* (Ottawa: G.E. Desbarats, 1867), 391.
[2] Joseph Schull and Douglas Gibson, *The Scotiabank Story* (Toronto: MacMillan, 1982), 20.
[3] J. Murray Beck, *Politics of Nova Scotia: Vol. 1: 1710-1896* (Tantallon: Four East Publications, 1986), 107.
[4] Phyllis Blakely & Diane Barker, *Dictionary of Canadian Biography, Vol. 10* (Toronto: University of Toronto and the Université Laval, 2003).
See also http://www.biographi.ca/EN/index.html
[5] C. Bruce Fergusson, *Directory of MLAs of Nova Scotia* (Halifax: Public Archives of Nova Scotia, 1958), 123.
[6] http://www.chapter-one.com/vc/award.asp?vc=500
[7] Marguerite Woodworth, *The Dominion Atlantic Railway* (Kentville: Kentville Publishing, 1936), 27.
[8] *Glasgow Herald,* 2 February 1818, cited by Moore *q.v.*
[9] John Moore. *Glasgow Surveyors, 1719-1854: an index.* Occasional Paper, Department of Geography and Topographic Science, University of Glasgow, No. 32.
[10] Ibid.
[11] Institution of Civil Engineers, *Minutes of Proceedings* Vol. 142 (1899-1900): 356.
[12] *The NovaScotian,* 6 September 1858, Vol. 18, No. 35.
[13] Patricia Lotz, *Banker, Builder, Blockade Runner: A Victorian embezzler and his circle: A biography of James Forman* (Kentville: Gaspereau Press, 2002), 100.
[14] Ibid., 113.
[15] *Journal and proceedings of the House of Assembly of Nova Scotia 1854* (Halifax: R. Nugent, 1854), App. No. 1, 14.
[16] Ibid., 15.
[17] Ibid., 15.
[18] Ibid., 16.
[19] Ibid., 17.

²⁰ J. Murray Beck, *Joseph Howe: Voice of Nova Scotia* (Toronto: McCelland & Stewart, 1964), 5.
²¹ Ibid., 7.
²² Ibid., 124.
²³ Ibid.
²⁴ *Politics of Nova Scotia: Vol. 1*, 140.
²⁶ *Banker, Builder, Blockade Runner*, 124.
²⁷ Nova Scotia Railway Act, Public Statutes of Nova Scotia, 1854, Chapter 1.
²⁸ *Journal and proceedings of the House of Assembly of Nova Scotia 1853* (Halifax: R. Nugent, 1853), 363.
²⁹ *Joseph Howe: Voice of Nova Scotia*, 5.
³⁰ *Journal and proceedings of the House of Assembly of Nova Scotia 1852* (Halifax: R. Nugent, 1852), App. No. 1, 4.

Chapter Two

¹ *The NovaScotian*, 19 June 1854, p. 1.
² *Journal and proceedings of the House of Assembly of Nova Scotia 1855* (Halifax: R. Nugent, 1855), App. No. 17, 143.
³ Ibid.
⁴ Ibid.
⁵ Ibid.
⁶ Ibid., 144.
⁷ Ibid., App. 95, 449.
⁸ *The Dominion Atlantic Railway*, 39.
⁹ *Journal and proceedings of the House of Assembly of Nova Scotia 1856* (Halifax: R. Nugent, 1856), App. No. 4, 59.
¹⁰ *Joseph Howe: Voice of Nova Scotia*, 142.
¹¹ *Politics of Nova Scotia: Vol. 1*, 144.
¹² Paul Walsh, *Political Profiles: Premiers of Nova Scotia* (Halifax: Nimbus Publishing, 1986), 5.
¹³ *Railway Record*, London, 2 October 1847, 4.
¹⁴ *Papers Relative to Emigration to The British Provinces in North America* (British Parliamentary Papers, 1854), 1763. See also http://ist.uwaterloo.ca/~marj/genealogy/reports/report1853.html
¹⁵ *The NovaScotian*, 2 June 1856, p. 3.
¹⁶ *Morning Chronicle*, 17 June 1856, p. 2.
¹⁷ Ibid.
¹⁸ Ibid.
¹⁹ Ibid.
²⁰ Ibid.
²¹ Ibid.
²² *Politics of Nova Scotia: Vol. 1*, 145.
²³ G.R. Stevens, *Canadian National Railways, Vol. 1: Sixty Years of Trial and Error* (Toronto: Clarke, Irwin & Co., 1960), 161.
²⁴ James Wilberforce Longley, *Sir Charles Tupper* (Toronto: Morang Ltd., 1916), 255.
²⁵ Ibid., 253.

26 Ibid., 258.
27 *Politics of Nova Scotia: Vol. 1*, 146.
28 Ibid., 147.
29 *The New Statistical Account of Scotland* (Edinburgh: William Blackwood & Sons, 1845), 901.
30 Ibid., 902.
31 *The NovaScotian*, 7 June 1858, p. 5.
32 Cyrus Black, *Historical Record of the Posterity of William Black* (Amherst: Amherst Gazette Steam Printing House, 1885), 79.
33 Ibid., 80.

Chapter Three

1 David Allison, *History of Nova Scotia, Vol. 2* (Halifax: A.W. Bowen & Co., 1916), 734.
2 B.W. Milner, *Moncton Daily Times*, 27 November 1920, p. 3.
3 http://www.canals.com/shuben.htm
4 http://www.alts.net/ns1625/nshist08.html
5 Terry Coleman, *The Railway Navvies* (London: Pelican Books, 1965), 93.
6 "The Men Who Made The First Railways," *Orange Blossom Special Magazine* No. 32.
7 *The Railway Navvies*, 47.
8 *Papers Relative to Emigration to The British Provinces in North America*, XLVI, 1763, See also http://ist.uwaterloo.ca/~marj/genealogy/reports/report1853.html
9 Ibid.
10 Ibid.
11 *The Railway Navvies*, 213.
12 Ibid.
13 *The Illustrated London News,* March 1855, as found in *The Railway Navvies,* 214.
14 http://www.budgettechnologies.com/MollyMaguires. The lack of attribution does not detract from the validity of the information. The web site creator was contacted by the author, but could not recall which of the books he had consulted was the source of the information.
15 Ibid.
16 Ibid.
17 Leonard Seton. "The Intercolonial, 1832-1876," Chapter II, Provincial Railway Construction in British North America, *News Report,* Canadian Railroad Historical Association, (April 1958): 53.
18 *Morning Chronicle*, 3 June 1856, p. 1.
19 Barbara Grantmyre, *The River That Missed The Boat* (Hantsport: Lancelot Press, 1975), 85.
20 Ibid., 86.
21 *Morning Chronicle*, 19 June 1856, p. 2.
22 Ibid.
23 Charles Tuttle, *Popular History of the Dominion of Canada* (Montreal: Downie, 1877), 456.
24 J.M. & Edw. Trout, *The Railways of Canada* (Toronto: Monetary Times, 1871), 103 as found in *Coles Canadiana Collection,* 1970. Quoted by Seton.

[25] *Morning Chronicle*, 9 December 1856, p. 2. The errors in this report lead to a conclusion that the Chronicle's editor did not attach much importance to the proceedings to warrant sending a more capable reporter.
[26] Ibid.
[27] Ibid.
[28] Ibid.
[29] *Morning Chronicle*, 11 December 1856, p. 2.
[30] Ibid.
[31] *Morning Chronicle*, 23 December 1856, p. 2.
[32] *Morning Chronicle*, 27 December 1856, p. 2.
[33] http://www.budgettechnologies.com/MollyMaguires: Another unattributed reference, but the material was considered to be valid despite the lack of scholarship involved in its presentation.
[34] http://www.geocities.com/ri_aoh/mollies.htm
[35] http://www.geecoders.com/MollyMaguires/seamus.html Jim (Seamus) Haldeman is a member of a group claiming to be descendants of Molly Maguires of Pennsylvania.
[36] http://www.aohdiv1.com/articles/AOH_coal_miners.htm: Boyle's position an historian of this group allows some credibility to be attached to his information.
[37] http://www.history.ohio-state.edu/projects/coal/MollyMaguire/mollymaguires.htm
[38] *Politics of Nova Scotia: Vol. 1 1710-1896*, 144.
[39] Lyman Abbott. "The American Railroad," *Harper's New Monthly Magazine* (August 1874) as found in *The Builders' Compendium* (1975), 13.
[40] Ibid.
[41] *The Morning Chronicle*, 30 August 1856, p. 2.
[42] Ibid.
[43] *Journal and proceedings of the House of Assembly of Nova Scotia 1866* (Halifax: R. Nugent, 1866), App. No. 17, 2.
[44] Ibid., 5.
[45] Ibid.
[46] *The River That Missed The Boat*, 64.
[47] Ibid.

Chapter Four

[1] *Journal and proceedings of the House of Assembly of Nova Scotia 1851* (Halifax: R. Nugent, 1851), App. No. 7, 27.
[2] Ibid., 24.
[3] *Journal and proceedings of the House of Assembly of Nova Scotia 1858* (Halifax: R. Nugent, 1858), Railway Committee Evidence, 1.
[4] Ibid.
[5] Ibid.
[6] James Laurie, ref. *Journal and proceedings of the House of Assembly 1858*, App. No. 35, 278.
[7] *Politics of Nova Scotia: Vol. 1*, 139.
[8] James Laurie, ref. *Journal and proceedings of the House of Assembly 1858*, 278.
[9] Ibid., 279.

10 *The NovaScotian*, 29 March 1858, p. 1.
11 *Canadian National Railways, Vol. 1*, 161.
12 *Journal and proceedings of the House of Assembly 1858*, App. No. 31, 260.
13 Ibid., 261.
14 Ibid., 269.
15 http://www.asce.org/150/laurie.html
16 *Canadian National Railways, Vol. 1*, 162.
17 *Journal and proceedings of the House of Assembly 1858*, Railway Committee Evidence, xviii.
18 Ibid., xvii.
19 Ibid., xxi.
20 Ibid., xxviii.
21 Ibid., xliv.
22 Ibid.
23 Ibid., xlv.
24 George Wightman. "A treatise on roads in two parts: Part first. On surveying and engineering," *The Nova Scotian*, 1845: Preface.
25 *Journal and proceedings of the House of Assembly 1858*, Railway Committee Evidence, xxxvi.
26 Ibid.
27 Ibid., xxxviii.
28 Ibid.
29 Laurie, ref. *Journal and proceedings of the House of Assembly 1858*, 316.
30 Ibid., 317.
31 *Journal and proceedings of the House of Assembly 1856*, App. No. 4, 56.
32 Ibid.
33 Laurie, ref. *Journal and proceedings of the House of Assembly 1858*, 285.
34 *Journal and proceedings of the House of Assembly 1858*, xcvii.
35 Ibid.
36 Ibid.
37 Ibid.
38 Laurie, ref. *Journal and proceedings of the House of Assembly 1858*, 287.
39 *Journal and proceedings of the House of Assembly 1851*, 447.
40 *The NovaScotian*, 29 June 1858, p. 5.
41 *The NovaScotian*, 29 March 1858, p. 3.
42 Ibid.
43 Ibid.
44 Ibid.
45 *The Dominion Atlantic Railway*, 43.
46 Ibid.
47 *The NovaScotian*, 28 June 1858, p. 1.

Chapter Five

1 *The NovaScotian*, 2 February 1857, p. 1.
2 *The NovaScotian*, 18 August 1858, p. 2.
3 Ibid.

4 Ibid.
5 Ibid.
6 Ibid.
7 Ibid.
8 Ibid.
9 Ibid.
10 Ibid.
11 *Journal and proceedings of the House of Assembly 1860* (Halifax: R. Nugent, 1860), Appendix – Railway Correspondence, 120.
12 Reported in *The Nova Scotian,* 6 September 1858, p. 2.
13 http://www.heritage.nf.ca/govhouse/governors/g45.html
14 *The NovaScotian,* p. 2.
15 *The NovaScotian,* 30 August 1858, p. 1.
16 Ibid.
17 Ibid.
18 *The NovaScotian,* 6 September 1858, p. 1.
19 Ibid.
20 Ibid.
21 Ibid.
22 Ibid.
23 *The British Colonist,* 6 September 1858, p. 5.
24 Ibid.
25 John Beswarick Thompson. "The Development of Canadian Rail and Track," *Canadian Rail, (November 1973): 241.*
26 *The British Colonist,* 6 September 1858, p. 5.
27 *The British Colonist,* 31 August 1858, p. 3.
28 Ibid.
29 Ibid.
30 Ibid.
31 Ibid.
32 Ibid.
33 *The NovaScotian,* 6 September 1858, p. 2.
34 Ibid.
35 Ibid.
36 Ibid.
37 Ibid.
38 Ibid.
39 Ibid.
40 Ibid.
41 Ibid.
42 Ibid.
43 Ibid.
44 Ibid.
45 Ibid.
46 Ibid.
47 Ibid.
48 *The NovaScotian,* 6 September 1858, p. 2.

⁴⁹ Ibid.
⁵⁰ Ibid.

Chapter Six

¹ David E. Stephens, *Truro: A railway town* (Hantsport: Lancelot Press, 1981), 30.
² *The NovaScotian,* 28 March 1859, p. 1.
³ James Wilberforce Longley, *Sir Charles Tupper* (Toronto: Morang, 1916), 60.
⁴ Paul B. Waite, *Dictionary of Canadian Biography (*University of Toronto and Laval University). See: http://www.biographi.ca/EN/ShowBio.asp?BioId=39261&query=\
⁵ *Journal and proceedings of the House of Assembly of Nova Scotia 1859* (Halifax: R. Nugent, 1859), App. No. 61, 593.
⁶ Ibid.
⁷ Ibid., 594.
⁸ Ibid., 595.
⁹ Ibid.
¹⁰ Ibid., 598.
¹¹ Ibid., 599.
¹² Ibid.
¹³ *Journal and proceedings of the House of Assembly 1860,* 67.
¹⁴ Ibid., 68.
¹⁵ Ibid.
¹⁶ Ibid., 79.
¹⁷ Ibid.
¹⁸ *Journal and proceedings of the House of Assembly 1860,* Appendix, 97.
¹⁹ Ibid., 98.
²⁰ Ibid., 99.
²¹ Ibid.
²² Dionysius Lardner, *Railway Economy* (New York: Harper & Bros., 1850), 353.
²³ Ibid.
²⁴ Ibid., 52.
²⁵ Quoted by Ernest Coates in "Famous People of Cumberland County," (Cumberland Come Home, 1980), 1.
²⁶ *Journal and proceedings of the House of Assembly of the province of Nova Scotia 1861* (Halifax: R. Nugent, 1861), App. No. 4, 1.
²⁷ "The American Railroad," *Harper's New Monthly Magazine:* 8.
²⁸ Ibid., 10.
²⁹ Ibid.
³⁰ *The NovaScotian,* 30 June 1858, p. 3.
³¹ Ibid.
³² Ibid.
³³ *The NovaScotian,* 6 August 1860, p. 1.
³⁴ Ibid.
³⁵ Ibid.
³⁶ *The NovaScotian,* 18 October 1858, pp. 4-5.
³⁷ Ibid.
³⁸ Ibid.

39 Ibid.
40 Ibid.
41 Ibid.
42 Ibid.

Chapter Seven

1 *The Scotiabank Story*, 45.
2 Dean Jobb, *Bluenose Justice: True Tales of Mischief, Mayhem and Murder* (Lawrencetown: Pottersfield Press, 1993), 30.
3 Ibid.
4 Ibid., 32.
5 http://www.biographi.ca/EN/ShowBio.asp?BioId=39110&query=
6 *Proceedings of the Institution of Civil Engineers* Vol. 146 (1900-1901): 283.
7 http://www.eastdunbarton.gov.uk/Web+Site/Live/EDWebLive.nsf/LU-AllContent/MMAN-5F5HX4?OpenDocument
8 William Nimmo, *The History of Stirlingshire*, Third edition (London: Hamilton, Adams & Co., 1880).
See also http://www.electricscotland.com/history/stirlingshire/chap16.htm
9 John Thomas, *The North British Railway: Vol. 2* (Newton Abbot: David & Charles, 1975).
10 Ibid.
11 *Stirling Journal*, 8 April 1883, p. undetermined.
12 *Engineering*, 15 February 1901, 213.
13 *Institution Civil Engineers Minutes of Proceedings* Vol. 146 (1900-1901): 282.
14 Ibid, 283.
15 John Thomas, *The West Highland Railway*, (London: Pan Books, 1965), 39.
16 Dr. John MacGregor, private correspondence with the author.
17 *The West Highland Railway*, 59.
18 Ibid.
19 McGregor, op. cit.
20 *The West Highland Railway*, 83.
21 Ibid., 80.
22 Ibid., 80.
23 MacGregor, op. cit.
24 *The West Highland Railway*, 83.
25 Ibid., 81.
26 http://www.ipw.com/lochness/html/fort_augustus_railway.html
27 MacGregor, op. cit.
28 *Institution Civil Engineers Minutes*: 283.
29 *Engineering*, 15 February (1901): 213.
30 McGregor, op. cit.
31 *Institution Civil Engineers Minutes*: 283.
32 MacGregor, op. cit.
33 *Institution Civil Engineers Minutes*: 284.
34 MacGregor, op. cit.
36 MacGregor, op. cit.

[37] Stan Basnett, *Great Walks in the Isle of Man,* 19 July 2002: 2
[38] Ibid, 3.
[39] *Engineering,* 15 February 1901: 213.
[40] Iain F. Russell, *Sir Robert McAlpine & Sons: The Early Years Wiltshire, 1988:* 88.
[41] Ibid.
[42] Ibid., 90.
[43] Ibid.
[44] Henry Youle Hind, *The Dominion of Canada: containing a historical sketch of the preliminaries and organization of confederation: also, the vast improvements made in agriculture, commerce and trade, modes of travel and transportation, mining, and educational interests, etc., etc. for the past eighty years under the provincial names: with a large amount of statistical information, from the best and latest authorities* (Toronto: Stebbins, 1869), 696.
[45] *Edinburgh and Leith Post Office Directories* (1890-91): 30 and (1900-01): 23.
[47] http://www.copper.org/innovations/2001/08/phelpsdodge.html
[47] Ibid.
[48] *Institution Civil Engineers Minutes* Vol. 142 (1899-1900): 356.
[49] *The Scotsman,* 13 September 1876, p. undetermined.
[50] *Institution Civil Engineers Minutes:* 283.
[51] Anne Thompson, *The Ratho Reviewer* Vol. 1 (Fall/Winter 1997): 9.
[52] Ibid.
[53] MacGregor, op. cit.
[54] A.J.C. Clarke, *The Ratho Reviewer:* 9.

Epilogue

[1] Isabella Bishop, *The Englishwomen in America* (London: J. Murray, 1856), 17.
[2] Ibid., 23.
[3] Ibid., 29.
[4] Elizabeth Frame, *Descriptive Sketches of Nova Scotia in Prose and Verse* (Halifax: A. & W. MacKinlay, 1864, 67.
[5] *Sir Charles Tupper,* 178.
[6] *The Eastern Chronicle & Pictou County Advocate,* 8 June 1867, p. 1.
[7] Ibid.
[8] Lorne Green, *Chief Engineer: Life of a nation builder – Sandford Fleming* (Toronto: Dundurn Press, 1993), 43.
[9] Ibid., 24.
[10] Sandford Fleming, *Memorandum addressed to the Honourable the minister of railways and canals by the engineer-in-chief of the Canadian Pacific Railway* (Ottawa: MacLean, Roger & Co., 1880), 3.
[11] Ibid., 5.
[12] Ibid.
[13] Sandford Fleming, *Letter to the Secretary of State, Canada, in reference to the report of the Canadian Pacific Railway Royal Commission* (Ottawa: MacLean, Roger & Co., 1882), 1.
[14] Ibid.
[15] *Sir Charles Tupper,* 273.

[16] Ibid., 274.
[17] *Historical Record of the Posterity of William Black*, 190.
[18] *Sir Charles Tupper*, 6.
[19] Ibid.
[20] http://www.biographi.ca/EN/ShowBio.asp?BioId=41869&query=

Afterword

[1] *Journal and proceedings of the House of Assembly 1860*, Appendix – Railway Correspondence, 122.
[2] *Institution Civil Engineers Minutes*, (1904-1905): 395-96.
[3] *The debates and proceedings of the House of Assembly during the second session of the twenty-second Parliament of the province of Nova Scotia, 1861* (Halifax: Queen's Printers), 73-74.
[4] Ibid.
[5] Ibid.
[6] Ibid., 91-92.
[7] Ibid.
[8] Ibid.
[9] *Journal and proceedings of the House of Assembly of Nova Scotia 1862* (Halifax: R. Nugent, 1862), App. No. 20, 5.
[10] http://www.nsbs.ns.ca/qc/qc_historical.htm

INDEX

(Page numbers in **_bold italic_** font indicate illustrations.)

Aberfoyle Slate Quarry: 134.
Abinger, Lord: **_135_**, 138.
Albion, Ye sons of: 44.
Almon, Mather Byles: 8, 127, 170.
Anderson, Jonathan: 24;
   letter of support: 87.
Arizona Copper Company: 151.
Asylum, provincial: 62 *et seq.*

Bank of Nova Scotia: 8;
   banking scandal, 127 *et seq.*
Bedford, bridge over Sackville River: **_4,_** 79, **_80._**
Belgium, railway model: 117.
Benedict, Roswell, G: colleague of Smellie, 91.
Bidder, Samuel: example of railway management, 81.
Big Bog Brook: washout, **_70,_** 111.
Blanchard, Hiram: **_170;_**
   defends Smellie, 171.
Blane Valley Railway: 132.
Bliss, Judge William Blowers: presides over Gourley Shanty trial, 47.
Boggs, DeWolfe & Campbell (immigration agents): 54.
Brassey, engineering firm: 17, 39.
Busby Viaduct: **_131._**

Callander & Oban Railway: 134, 141.
Catholics: 26;
   bring down Young government: 30, 33, 53, 88.
Chesborough, Ellis Sylvester: 73.
Cody, Patrick (Gourley Shanty rioter): 49.
Condon, William: 28, 30, 46.
Craigpark: 152, **_152._**
Creelman, Eliakim: 64.
Crimean War: 26, 42 *et seq.*
Cunningham, P.M: 24, 117.

Easton, Robert (Gourley Shanty riot witness): 47.
Edinburgh American Land Mortgage Company: 150.
Ellershouse: 70, 111

Elmsdale: **40,** 45, 58, 129, 159
   grog shop 29, **40**
Enfield: 37, **40,** 46, 55, **56,** 58, 104
European & North American Railway: 17, 39, 43.

Fairbanks, Charles William: 7;
   reports on Shubenacadie canal, 55;
   disagrees with Wightman's route to Windsor, 57.
Faulkner, William: 57.
Fenerty Lake: 57.
Fleming, Sandford: 116, 129;
   not unanimous choice as Intercolonial Railway engineer, 160;
   similarities with Forman, 163.
Flodden Field: 7.
Forman, Blanche: memories of Ratho, 153.
Forman, Charles: 19, 128;
   education, 134, ***135;***
   career, 138; family, ***139;***
   railway schemes, 141;
   character, 144.
Forman, James Senior: cashier Bank of Nova Scotia, ***13,*** 33;
   supports Protestant Alliance, 34;
   banking scandal, 127 *et seq.;*
   dies in London, 128.
Forman, James Pringle: 7.
Forman, James Richardson: **6,** 7 *et seq.;*
   education, 9–10;
   marriage, 11;
   applies for position, 14;
   position as engineer, 19;
   first report 1856, 25;
   asked to investigate asylum contract, 62;
   praised by McCully, 65;
   praised by Laurie, 67;
   dismissed, 86;
   Tupper's letter, 86;
   first letter to newspapers, 91;
   refuses to hand over documents, 100;
   detailed letter to the press, 101;
   death of his son, 109;
   blames Johnston for weakened position, 124;
   returns to Scotland, 129;
   purchases Craigpark House, 153;
   final days, death, 154;
   possible engineer on Intercolonial Railway, 160;
   similarities with Sandford Fleming, 163;
   at school with Tupper, 166.

INDEX

Forman, John: 9.
Forman, Robert: 9, 58, 128;
    family at Londonderry, Nova Scotia, 129.
Foxdale Railway: 146;
    map, *146.*
Franklin Institute: report on best type of rail, 90.
Frier, John (contractor): testifies at riot trial, 49.

Gaston, Robert (Gourley Shanty riot witness): See Easton, Robert.
Gaspereaux Lake: 58.
Glenfinnan Viaduct: front cover, *148,* 149.
Gourley, Elisha: 34.
Gourley, James Forman: 35.
Gourley Shanty riot: 23 *et seq.,* 37 *et seq.;*
    trial of rioters, 47 *et seq.*
Gourley, Thomas: 47.
Grand Lake: 55, 58, 64, *70.*
Grand Trunk Railway: 59, 73, 81, 173.
Grassie, George: 7.
Great Western Railway: 91.
Greenock & Ayrshire Railway: 131.
Grogan, family connection: 9.

Haliburton, Thomas Chandler: 10.
Hall, Francis: 38.
Harper's New Monthly magazine: 53, 119.
Hill, family connections: 11, 167.
Hill, Henry G. (engineer): 62.
Horton Academy: 9, 166.
Howe, Joseph: 7, *12;*
    letters to Forman, 14 *et seq.;*
    railroads as government projects, 18;
    recruiting for Crimean War, 43;
    attacks Catholics, 50;
    out of office, 59;
    fires Mosse, 86;
    quoted in the *Colonist,* 95;
    questions Laurie's salary, 109;
    more support for Forman, 113;
    praises Smellie, 172.

Invergarry & Fort Augustus Railway: 142.
Irish labourers: Pemberton reports on suitability, 26, 43 *et seq;*
    wages, 45.
Isobel Hill Forman: 11.

Johnston, James William: 30, *31;*

defends shanty rioters, 48;
misses railway vote, 59, 83;
weakens railway commission, 123.

Keith, Alexander: 9.
Kelvin Valley railway: 132, 135.
King-Hall, William: 9, 14.

Lanarkshire & Dumbarton Railway: 143.
Lanarkshire & Ayrshire Railway: 139, 144, 148.
Lardner, Dionysius: railway study, 117 *et seq.*
Laurie, James: **60;**
    biography, 63;
    praises Forman, 67;
    under personal attack in the press, 74;
    branded "a spy", 82;
    insulted by McCully, 115;
    blames politicians, 116.
LeMarchant, Sir John Gaspard: **20,** 21, 23, 42, 87, 169.
Lyons, Patrick (riot witness): 49.

Mallaig: **136**
McAlpine, Robert: on Rannoch Moor, 137,
    uses concrete in construction 147, **147;**
    as a businessman, 149.
McCall, Thomas: 11.
McCully, Jonathan: 24, 27, 64 *et seq.*, 89, **110;**
    character, 111 *et seq.*; insults Laurie, 115;
    abandons contractor, 116;
    role as commissioner, 118.
McCully, William: 73.
McNab, James: 30;
    letter of support 87, 101 *et seq.*, 106.
Milngavnie Railway: 130.
Molly Maguires: 50 *et seq.*
Molson, John: describes Shubenacadie canal, 38.
Morningside Railway: 11.
Mosse, James: 59, 66;
    identified as culprit, 84–85;
    fired by Howe, 86;
    career after Nova Scotia 169.
Mulgrave, Earl of: 75, **76,** 87, 123.

Navvies: 26;
    assaults, 28–29;
    working for Brassey, 38 *et seq.*;
    competition for, 42.

Necropolis, Glasgow: *154.*
Nova Scotia Railway: act of 1854, 18;
   first sod turned, 23;
   opening to Sackville, 25; map, *68.*

Oakfield Park: 58, *70.*
O'Brien, James (Gourley Shanty rioter): 48.
O'Brien, Patrick (Gourley Shanty rioter): 48.

Peto, Jackson, Brassey & Betts: 17, 38 *et seq.*
Pictou branch: 92, 109.
Pineo, H.G. (immigration agent): 54.
Prince of Wales: rides line, 122, 159.
Protestant Association: 33, 88.
Pryor, William Junior: 24;
   letter of support to Forman, 87.

Rannoch Moor: railway survey, 137.
Rannoch Station: *150.*
Regiment, 76th Foot: arrest rioters, 45.
Robertson, Charles (riot witness): 49.
Robinson, Major William: 7, 129.
Robson, Neil: 10–11, 129.
Rowland, Thomas: 29.

Sackville: 79; river and bridge: *80*
Scott, Archibald: 97.
Scottish railways: *130 et seq.;*
   map, *130.*
Shannon, Samuel L.: 97.
Shubenacadie, bridge: *40*, 104.
Shubenacadie, canal: 38, 46;
   locks on Grand Lake, 55.
Smellie, James Forman: *174 et seq.*
Smellie, William Baillie: 65, *114*, 115;
   defended by Hiram Blanchard, 171 *et seq.*
Smith, Benjamin: 120–121.
Strathendrick & Aberfoyle Railway: 133.
Strike, on Windsor branch: 29.
Sutherland, Spencer: 58 *et seq.*, 64.
Sykes, James: bids on railway project, 17.

Third Lake: 57.
Thorne, Stephen: 63.
Tobin, Thomas (railway commissioner): 24.
Travel, in Nova Scotia: before railways, 157;
   by railway, 159.

T-rail: 89.
Truro: 11;
   line opened, 109.
Tupper, Charles: 30 *et seq.*, **32,** 59, 62, 83;
   dismisses Forman, 86;
   impact of his association with Forman, 161 *et seq.;*
   at school with Forman, 166;
   possible interest in the Hill sisters, 167.

Wemyss Bay Railway: 130.
West Highland Railway: 137 *et seq.*
Wightman, George: 7, 57, 65, 72, 93, 99, 120.

Windsor branch: 11, 67 *et seq.;*
   opening, 75;
   earnings, 85, 104, 110;
   Royal passenger, 122.

Young, William: 26, 30, **31;**
   prosecutes shanty rioters, 48.

MEMBER OF SCABRINI GROUP

Québec, Canada
2007